JIM CRAMER'S
REAL MONEY

SANE INVESTING

in an

INSANE WORLD

JAMES J. CRAMER

Simon & Schuster Paperbacks
New York   London   Toronto   Sydney

SIMON & SCHUSTER PAPERBACKS
A Division of Simon & Schuster, Inc.
1230 Avenue of the Americas
New York, NY 10020

First Simon & Schuster trade paperback edition January 2009

SIMON & SCHUSTER PAPERBACKS and colophon are registered trademarks
of Simon & Schuster, Inc.

For information about special discounts for bulk purchases,
please contact Simon & Schuster Special Sales:
1-800-456-6798 or business@simonandschuster.com

Designed by Elliott Beard

Manufactured in the United States of America

10   9   8   7   6   5   4   3   2   1

Library of Congress Control Number: 2005042499

ISBN-13: 978-0-7432-2489-5
ISBN-10:   0-7432-2489-2
ISBN-13: 978-0-7432-2490-1 (pbk)
ISBN-10:   0-7432-2490-6 (pbk)

ACKNOWLEDGMENTS

I want you to be rich. Really rich. That's my goal. I don't want you to just do better. And I don't want you to try to make ends meet. I know I can help you get there. I've made too many other people rich for me to think that I won't do it with you.

I got rich using commonsense principles, not elite precepts and training, and I know you can, too. The arithmetic you need to know to navigate the stock market is fifth-grade math. I know it because I help a fifth grader every night with her numbers.

When I wrote *Confessions of a Street Addict,* I used to go into Amazon to read the reviews until my wife decided they were driving me nuts. What I found were people who loved the story of my life but were disappointed that I didn't tell how I made my money.

That's what this book is for. I tell everything. In fact, I'm debating, as I write this, whether to go back to managing money using the same rules and principles I outline here, because I am so certain that they work.

But before you get to it, I want you to know who was instrumental in helping me explain how I really made those millions of dollars. First, my wife, Karen, who figured so prominently in *Confessions,* has to again take center stage here. She is a testament to the non–Ivy League nature of what I am about to write, as she spent more time breaking me of Harvard habits than celebrating them when we worked together at Cramer & Company.

My father, Ken, is instrumental in my analysis as he spent countless days when I was growing up and then long after explaining the power of the business and inventory cycles. He understood it intuitively. I had to learn it. I would be remiss in not thanking his late mother and father, two fabulous businesspeople, long since passed, who instilled an ethic that was both indelible and hardwired by the time it got to me. My late mom, Louise, never got to see me reemerge as a writer. Since she cared about the "soul" more than the money, she'd be happy how things turned out.

While I am celebrating family, I have learned a tremendous amount about business and winning in the markets from my brother-in-law, Todd Mason, who may be the smartest man on the planet, aside from his obvious intelligence in marrying my sister Nan.

In my work life, I have so many to thank, so many who have taught me the right way to do things, but let's start with Bill Gruver and Richard Menschel, two deacons who once ruled Goldman Sachs's equity side. I'll add Marty Peretz, who first gave me money to manage and then insisted that I make it grow at a pace that exceeded everybody else's. Thanks, Marty!

Of late, I want to send kudos to Will Gabrielski and David Peltier of TheStreet.com as well as David Morrow, the editor-in-chief of TheStreet.com, for helping along the manuscript, and, of course, the larger-than-life Tom Clarke, the CEO of TheStreet.com, who must next run money because he has the patience and the fortitude to do so.

I can't go without a thanks to my friends at CNBC, the fabulous Susan Krakower, Larry Kudlow, Matt Quayle, Linda Sittenfeld, Donna Vislocky, Andrew Conti, Christine Dooley, and, of course, Bob Fasbender, who helped turn me into an alleged TV star. My friends at WOR deserve equal gratz: Mike Figliola, my producer, and the great folks who work with Rick Buckley there, including Joe Billota, Bob Bruno, and Maurice Tunick. I want to thank Cheryl Winer, too, as I would never have discovered radio without her persistence that I belong in that great medium.

I want to thank all of those professionals who keep me out of trouble—my agents Suzanne Gluck and Henry Reisch and my lawyers Eric Seiler and Bruce Birenboim. The last guy deserves my undying love because I would have long since given up any public life without his counsel.

And of course to David Rosenthal and Bob Bender, my publisher and editor, who really get me and whom I love very much and would die before I'd disappoint.

Lastly, I want to thank Cece and Emma, who put up with countless weekends without me as I toiled over this book, and who remind me, constantly, of what really matters: family. No matter how rich you get, it can't come near the joys of fatherhood and a loving family.

To my fabulous daughters, Emma and Cece Cramer,
two little savers whom I love so much

CONTENTS

JIM CRAMER'S
REAL MONEY

If you're picking up this book, you know you need help. Unless you're incredibly lucky, your portfolio has probably come through 2008 with serious losses. You may feel like your retirement money is in danger, or maybe it's college tuition for your children, or just that extra bit of money you'd hoped to get from the stock market to supplement your paycheck. This book will help you stop the bleeding and start making money again. Right now, most of you are not trying to get rich, you are just trying to stay solvent. I wrote this book four years ago to help you get rich in the stock market using the same methods that worked so well for me at my old hedge fund. But the same tools and disciplines that I laid out in this book to help you get rich by investing in stocks are also the best way to stay afloat even in the worst of markets.

It's been nearly four years since this book was first published, and in that time we have seen a phenomenal global bull market turn into one of the worst bear markets since the Great Depression. We have seen oil prices skyrocket to $147 a barrel and then fall back to less than half that price. We have seen the values of our homes soar and then sink like the *Titanic*. We have seen obscure mortgage-backed derivatives that most people had never heard of take our financial system close to total ruin, with investment banks that were once titans—like Bear Stearns and Lehman Brothers—collapsing. And, most distressing for a stock guy like myself, we've seen the major indices return to levels they hadn't touched since the dot-bomb era. In October 2008, the Dow Jones Industrial Average was trading at October 1998 levels. The crash of 2008—and make no mistake, if the action we saw in September and October 2008 wasn't a crash, nothing is—wiped out an entire decade's worth of gains.

I don't blame you for feeling like stocks have failed us. This is the ugliest, most difficult market I have seen in my entire life. It's the kind of market that makes you want to throw up your hands, along with your lunch, and give up. It makes you want to stop opening your monthly statements from your 401(k) just so you don't have to look at your losses, or turn off the TV so you don't have to watch more of your wealth evaporate. It makes you want to panic and get out of stocks for good.

But every one of these moves is exactly what you should not be doing. You do not need to give up on the market; what you need is help investing during a difficult period. It may feel like everything has changed, and things certainly are different now than they were four years ago, but the fundamental insights in this book, the basic disciplines that allowed me to make millions at my hedge fund in good times and bad, are more relevant than ever. Hard as it may be to believe in this awful environment, stocks are still the best way for you to try to get rich, as long as you know what you're doing. But it has gotten harder.

We've been through financial crises before, in 1932 and more recently in 1990, and we came back. It took a couple decades after 1932, but thankfully it now looks like widespread bank failures have been avoided courtesy of the $700 billion Troubled Assets Relief Program, or TARP. We *will* get through this. You need to know how to manage through the crisis; *Real Money* will get you there.

When I wrote this book, I wanted to share with you the tools I used at my hedge fund to make millions for myself and my clients. What I didn't do was write a guide for making money only in bull markets. Any joker can turn a profit in the fat years; it's how you do in the lean years that really counts. If you follow the advice in this book you can survive and even thrive during the absolute worst of times. I know crashes and I know recessions. I was entirely in cash for the Great Crash of 1987, sidestepping a vicious decline, and I've made money in two previous recessions, 1980 to 1982 and 1990 to 1991, as well as in the minirecession of 2000 to 2003. In fact, I was up 36 percent at my hedge fund in 2000, a year when the S&P 500 was down 11 percent. It's possible to make money when the market is going down and the economy is in awful shape. I've done it, and in this book I will teach you how to do it.

What, if anything, have we learned from the financial crisis and the crash of 2008? First of all, the ideology of buy and hold, the strategy, if you can call it that, that says the best way to make money in the market is to buy "blue chip" stocks and hang on to them forever—a notion that I devote much of *Real Money* to debunking—is now more discredited than ever. No one should ever again take seriously the peddlers of this misguided philosophy, and they are many—often the same people who were declaring that the fundamentals of the economy were sound even as we slipped closer and closer to financial Armageddon, and I screamed my lungs out on television trying to warn you. When I wrote this book I talked about the foolish stigma associated with selling stocks, with "trading"—the idea that it's never right to sell. Once again, recent events have shown that those who sold made out okay, while those who mindlessly held on to their stocks, even as it was clear we were on the verge of disaster, got crushed.

My alternative to buy and hold, the idea of buy and homework that

I explain here, has never looked better. I am always emphasizing homework, one hour of research per week per stock, so that you know what's actually going on with your holdings. I teach you how to do the homework in this book, and I never shut up about it on my television show, *Mad Money,* where every day I explain what's happening in the market and why, which groups are working and which groups aren't, and generally try to continue the project of educating people about stocks, a project that this book is at the very core of. The financial crisis has shown us just how important homework is, as many figures in the highest echelons of the federal government, not to mention numerous hedge fund investors, failed to do their homework and so failed to see the crisis coming.

Those of us who did our homework on the banks and the brokers, who realized how much damage could be done by toxic mortgage-backed securities and derivatives—garbage packaged by financial alchemists on Wall Street that was treated like gold until the summer of 2007—avoided major losses in the financial sector. The banks, brokers, and insurance companies with the most opaque, hardest to understand financial statements, such as Fannie Mae, Washington Mutual, Bear Stearns, Lehman Brothers, and AIG, all went down in flames. If you followed the so-called wisdom of buy and hold, you would have been stuck in these broken companies all the way down. If you'd done your homework, you knew to get out.

With the financial crisis we saw a massive, collective failure to do the homework, from the hedge funds who bought this mortgage-backed junk to the ratings agencies that said it was just fine, right on up to Ben Bernanke, the chairman of the Federal Reserve, and Hank Paulson, the treasury secretary, both of whom refused to acknowledge the gravity and scale of the problem until way too late. These policy makers should have been working hard to understand what was going on; instead it often seemed like they were hardly working, with the Federal Reserve worried about inflation even as we headed into what may turn out to be the worst deflationary spiral since the Great Depression. If we've learned anything from the financial crisis, it's that you have to rely on your own homework, not the government's, not some rating agency's.

These last few years have also reinforced the importance of the kind of investing discipline I emphasize so strongly in this book. We saw tremendous multiyear runs in agriculture, minerals, natural gas, oil and oil service, and infrastructure, with many stocks in these groups up 200, 300, even 400 percent at their peaks. But starting in July 2008, and accelerating in September and October, with very little warning all these groups collapsed. Prices for everything from wheat to oil to fertilizer to copper fell dramatically. You name it: If it was a commodity, it was in trouble. And the commodity stocks, along with the infrastructure names, which relied on healthy commodity prices and the healthy global economy to keep prices high, tumbled right along with them.

I did not catch the commodity collapse before it happened. On my television show, *Mad Money,* I did warn my viewers to get out before much of the damage happened, but if you were invested in these stocks and you followed the rules I laid out in this book, specifically investment rule number one—bulls make money, bears make money, pigs get slaughtered—you would not have needed the warning. The rules and methods in this book would have had you taking profits in these winners when you had them, so that even if you still owned the commodity stocks as they collapsed, some of them erasing two years' worth of gains in a few months, you would already have booked plenty of gains. The commodity collapse is unassailable proof that discipline should always trump conviction, another rule I lay down in this book. You may have had the conviction that these stocks would keep working, but the discipline of taking something off the table when you have a winner would have helped you avoid tremendous losses.

We've also seen just how important it is to know your fellow shareholders. Not everyone sells because they want to; in a downturn many investors sell because they have to. One reason why the crash of 2008 was so severe is that many hedge funds, funds that had already lost quite a bit of money, were forced to sell. If you owned stocks that these hedge funds were concentrated in, mainly the same energy and commodity stocks that got crushed courtesy of the commodity collapse, you lost even more money as these hedge funds had to liquidate their positions. Some hedge funds had borrowed money, buying stock on margin—something I tell you in this book never, ever to do—and, after taking big losses, they were forced to sell when they had to come up with the money to pay back the brokers they had borrowed from. This didn't just happen to hedge funds. Even megarich moguls who'd bought shares of their own companies on margin and lost money were forced to sell, guys like Sumner Redstone, who had to liquidate large positions in Viacom and CBS, and Aubrey McClendon, the CEO of Chesapeake Energy, who also happens to be my friend.

If you knew your fellow shareholders, you could have seen the forced selling coming and avoided the declines. But this kind of forced selling isn't all bad; it also creates opportunities. A large institution liquidating a huge chunk of stock at once tends to push the price of the stock down to bargain-basement levels, as long as the stock itself is worth owning in the first place.

Since I wrote this book the rules of the game have also changed, and I mean that literally. On July 6, 2007, the Securities and Exchange Commission repealed the uptick rule, a regulation that dated back to the Great Depression. It required that short-sellers (investors who bet against stocks by borrowing shares, selling them, and then buying them back at a lower price—if all goes well—returning the shares to their original owner, and pocketing the difference between the price at which they sold the shares and the price at which they bought them back or "covered") sell at a price that was higher than the previous trade. The uptick rule prevented short-sellers from creating panic by pushing a stock down with their sales, something they have done with abandon, especially to financial stocks, since the uptick rule was repealed. The SEC did a study during the bull market in 2006 and 2007 and determined that the uptick rule didn't matter. Of course, the whole point of the rule is to prevent short-sellers from fomenting panic in a *bear* market, and its absence has allowed short-sellers to annihilate stocks that would otherwise have been protected.

Not only that, but the SEC under Christopher Cox has effectively failed to enforce rules against "naked short-selling," which is when you sell a stock short without first finding shares and borrowing them. This basically gives the shorts unlimited ammunition if they want to push a stock down, because they can effectively sell shares they don't have. When I was running my hedge fund, the rules against naked short-selling were enforced much more aggressively. Back then we had an even playing field. Now things are tilted toward the shorts and against the longs, the regular investors who own stock, the people I think of as the good guys. These two factors, the absence of the uptick rule and widespread naked short-selling, contributed in large part to the rapid declines of Bear Stearns, Lehman Brothers, AIG, Fannie Mae, and Freddie Mac. Across the entire market things have gotten easier for the shorts and harder for the longs than when I wrote *Real Money*.

One more point. This is something I discuss in the book but, given how difficult the market has been in 2008, it deserves more attention: cash. On October 6, 2008, I went on the *Today* show and told people that any money they need for big expenditures over the next five years should be in cash because the short-term outlook for stocks was too risky. That week turned out to be the worst week in the history of the market, with the Dow declining 18 percent, its largest one-week percentage decline ever. Telling people to sell before the open that Monday, a position I had been espousing for weeks on my own television show, was probably the best call of my career. Nevertheless, I was relentlessly criticized, not for being wrong, but for being "reckless" and "irresponsible." I tell this story because it shows the insane degree to which there is a bias against selling, and more importantly, against being in cash. When the market is doing badly, cash is king. A lot of nonprofessional investors think that they should be fully invested at all times, meaning there should be no cash in their portfolio, every penny should be in stocks. Now, I'm *the* stock guy, and I'm telling you:

always have cash in your portfolio, especially during a bear market. I still believe, passionately, that the stock market is the best place to make money over the long-term. I have continued to contribute to the stock portion of my retirement account because I do not need the money short-term. But having cash is no sin, and staying on the sidelines with a great deal of it makes a ton of sense while the economy is wallowing in a recession.

In addition to letting you sidestep declines, cash gives you the ability to buy stocks as they go lower. Cash is probably the most important ingredient in a portfolio that stresses capital preservation, and when the market is lousy, everyone's portfolio should stress capital preservation. How do we do that, other than making sure we have enough cash? Until we start to see some light at the end of the tunnel, the trick is to own the stocks of companies with high-dividend yields as long as you've done the homework and believe the company will be able to keep paying its dividend. What else works? Stocks that are trading at or near their cash per share and generate consistent cash flows—so for example, if a company has $10 of cash per share and its stock price is $12, that stock could be a good capital preservation candidate because the cash puts a floor under the stock's price. And finally, you want to buy the traditional recession stocks, any company that makes something you can eat, drink, smoke, wash with, or use as medicine.

I know that this market is incredibly challenging, that it's become harder to find stocks that can make money. But it's not impossible, far from it. I still believe that if you use the disciplines I describe in *Real Money*, follow the rules I give you, and devote enough time and energy to investing, you'll be able to make money even in the worst of markets.

JIM CRAMER'S
REAL MONEY

1

STAYING
in the
GAME

If you look through my wallet, you will find all the things that everyone carries: license, credit cards, pictures of my wife and kids, and some cash. But if you look deeper, in some of the crannies, you'll find two things no one else has: my first pay stub, a tattered, faded beauty from the *Tallahassee Democrat* newspaper from September 1977, and a snippet of a portfolio run from the lowest day of my life, October 8, 1998.

I keep these talismans with me wherever I go, because they remind me why I got into stocks and why I had to stay in stocks no matter what, because the opportunities are too great *not* to be in them. The $178.82 I made that first week as a general assignment reporter in Tallahassee serves as a reminder to me that a paycheck is almost never enough to make a decent living on *and* to save up for the necessities of later life. That torn and bedraggled stub, with its $30 in overtime and oversized take by the federal government, keeps me honest and reminds me where I am from, how I never want to go back there, and how hard work at your job isn't enough to make you rich. You have to invest to make that happen. If you invest well you should almost always be beating the return you get on your day job.

The other smudged rectangle of paper in my wallet, the one that obscures the right-hand corner of my wife's picture, bears a series of cryptic numbers: 190,259,865; 281,175,544; and 90,915,674. The last number has a big black minus sign right after it. That's a cutout from my daily portfolio run on the most disastrous day my hedge fund ever had, October 8, 1998, a day when I was down $90,915,674— that's right, more than $90 million on the $281 million that I was supposed to be managing. I had "lost" almost half the money under my management in a series of bets in the stock market that hadn't yet paid off, to put a positive spin on an unmitigated decline. At that moment, everyone—my investors, my employees, the press, the public— *everyone* had written me off, except for my wife, whom I had worked with for so many years and who knew never to count me out. "You've had it, Cramer, you are gone," the collective brokerage chorus told me.

Not two months before I had been on the cover of *Money* magazine as the greatest trader of the era. Now I was wondering whether I could survive the year. With just two months left, I had to find a way at least to make back that $90 million if I wanted to stay in a business that I had thought I was born for. Most hedge funds don't come back from those kinds of titanic losses.

Using the very same techniques and tactics I will describe here, I methodically made back all of the money I had lost to date that year, and by December I had returned to a slim profit for the year. I finished up 2 percent, a $110 million comeback in less than three months. I averaged $1.4 million in profits every single day. Yet I still waived my management fee of $2 million because I didn't think I deserved a penny given how I had almost broken the bank. I still don't think I deserve to get paid for a comeback, because I dug my own hole by not following my disciplines and my rules, by succumbing to a lack of diversification and to inflexibility, those two assassins of capital.

That snapshot of how close I came to failure reminds me how important it is to stay investing and trading stocks *no matter what* because they are just too lucrative to stay away from for any long period of time. It also serves to remind me of how humbling this business is and how important it is to adjust course, for I had been sloppy and blind to a changing market during that catastrophic year. Had I not been flexible and willing to change strategies, I would never have come back.

In the very next year after my near-cataclysmic debacle, I made more than $100 million. The following year I made $150 million, again using the same rules and techniques I will describe here. I had plenty of help in the $100 million year: the market was terrific, easy, almost straight up. But in 2000, the biggest year, the $150 million year, the market peaked and crashed, yet I still profited supremely because you don't need the market to go up to make money. The fact that almost every mutual fund lost money in my biggest year is not a statement about my stock-picking prowess but evidence that if you are disciplined, use common sense, and take advantage of all the devices and tools out there, you can profit no matter what. Or, as I say at the end of my radio show every day, "There's always a bull market somewhere" that you can make profits from.

But you have to stay in that game to find that bull market. In the end, when all else fails, "Stay in the game" is the only mantra that's worth repeating. It keeps you from picking stocks that can wipe you out. It keeps you from speculating on situations that are worthless. It keeps you from borrowing a lot of money, known as margining, and hoping that stocks will make a magical move upward. It keeps you from wallowing in worthless penny stocks. It keeps you from trying to make a killing in tech. And it stops you from averaging down on bad stocks, because stocks aren't like parents when you get lost at the mall; they don't always come back. Staying in the game is the ultimate lesson. How do I know this? Because it is what I have done. I have been able to make big money when big money could be made because I didn't get discouraged or fed up or desperate when times got tough. I didn't do anything illegal or silly or unethical to stay in the game because I knew that when the game eventually turned, I would be there to pounce on what was to be gained. Staying in the game makes sense rationally and empirically because, over the long term, we know stocks outperform all asset classes. The reason more people don't get rich with stocks, though, is that people can't seem to stay in long enough to win. They get bored, tired, frustrated, defeated, or reckless. They get discouraged. They get beaten by the unnerving and jarring and humbling process not of investing but investing *successfully.*

My methods are designed to keep you from getting discouraged and quitting. Staying in the game is key, it is everything, and if you can't stay in the game then you have failed. And I have failed. I can't let that happen.

But before I take too much credit for the system and methodology I used to keep me making money, I have to give credit where it is due, to my wife, Karen, the woman the Street called the Trading Goddess for her manner and her proficiency in managing money and barking orders to dozens of brokers and traders. Karen was a professional institutional trader before I met her. She was responsible for taking me to the next level. She took a kid who had an eye for spotting undervalued and overvalued stocks, then she grafted on a set of rules, all of which are included in this book, that have seen me through the darkest hours and allowed me to outperform even when I don't have a great set of stocks on hand. She is like a master card player who can turn a good hand into a great one with a couple of tosses and a keen sense of what's in the deck. In fact, on the day that my portfolio "run" dripped with $90 million in red ink, she had to return to the office to reinstill the rules and disciplines that I had forgotten in the three years since she had retired. She again drilled them into my head, so they now tumble out here almost by rote.

Mrs. Cramer's Rules, the Rules of the Trading Goddess, make up a large portion of this book. Like me, Karen had no formal business school or accounting training. Like me, she lived from paycheck to paycheck until she found her true calling, making money in the stock market from scratch. Unlike me, she had no fundamental knowledge of how business worked or how to read a balance sheet or how interest rates control what you will ultimately pay for a stock. She always regarded those skills as overrated. What she understood was discipline and skepticism: the discipline to cut losses and run winners, and the skepticism to see through the hype that surrounds us on Wall Street. She understood better than anyone I have ever met that stocks are just pieces of paper representing shares of companies and no more than that. She knew that you could have conviction about where stocks could go and how high they could go, but it was only discipline that saved you when things didn't work out the way you thought, and she knew that things don't work out the way you think they will far more often than you would like to believe. Sure, the pieces of paper we trade are linked, albeit loosely, to the underlying entities that issued them, but in her eyes it was always important to recognize that everyone, from the media to veteran Wall Streeters, places too much importance on this linkage, which is frequently severed by rumors, by larger market forces, and, of course, by short-term imbalances in supply and demand—all of which can be gamed effectively. Occasionally stock prices are linked irrationally to the high side, as in Japan in 1988–89 or in this country in 2000, and just as occasionally they are linked to the low side, as in September 1982, when the great bull market began; in October 1987, after the stock market crash; and in October 2002, the most recent important bottom that is restoring wealth through equity appreciation in this country. Karen taught me to spot these tops and bottoms, formidable skills that I know I can teach you. I spend considerable time fleshing out those top- and bottom-calling skills in this text so you can do the same without me.

The Trading Goddess also taught me the difference between investing and trading, and how not to confuse them. Karen was—and I remain—an opportunist, one who is not bound by any particular investing philosophy beyond the need to adjust to the vicissitudes of a turbulent market so you are not knocked out of the business before the good times return. Callers and e-mailers are always asking me if I am a trader or an investor. I always respond the same way: what a stupid and false dichotomy.

In the interest of putting this question to rest forever, let me tell you up front why the trader/investor distinction makes no sense. This is not pro football, where you play offense or defense, where specialized skill sets predominate and no one is a generalist. Managing your own money is like playing hockey, where everybody has an opportunity to defend and to score and everybody is expected to take that opportunity. Sometimes stocks are making radical moves in days, as they did in the 1999–2000 period, and you have to capture those moves. If you frowned on those opportunities because they were too "trading oriented" or because you only like to buy "value," you might have missed some huge profits. If you stayed dogmatic, dug in your heels, and insisted on owning overvalued stocks that had already made great moves, you could give it all back. Both of these so-called "strengths" are actually weaknesses, inflexible weaknesses that will doom you to substantial losses at various points in the cycle.

Critics of mine dwell on my bullishness in December 1999 and January and February of 2000, the peak of the last bull market, or the bubble, as some insist on calling it. But the leaps stocks were making in that contained time span have not been and may never be replicated again. In that market the goal was to make those trading gains and go home, as I did with my March 15, 2000, RealMoney.com piece saying to take things off the table, four days after the exact top in the NASDAQ. Rather than feeling guilty about some who stayed in too long, I prided myself in recognizing that the market had changed for the worse in the spring of 2000, after the greatest run of all time, and you had to switch direction, no matter what your previous pronouncements and beliefs had been. You had to stay flexible to be conservative, to be prudent, to be commonsensical and keep your gains. Wall Street gibberish about being "in for the long term" or "only interested in stocks that trade for less than their growth rate or their book value" is just plain recklessness. You have to be willing to change your mind and your direction. Nowhere in the commandments of investing is it written "One shall not change one's mind even if it may be wrong." Businesses change, they become good, they go bad. Markets change, they become good, they go bad. You can't be blind to those changes without losing money or risking being blown out of the game. But you must swear to stay in no matter what. It's not flip-flopping if you like WorldCom when the business is good and hate it when the business goes bad, even though I was accused mightily of flip-flopping, for example, when I tossed aside WorldCom in the $80s after owning it for more than five years. Had I not "flip-flopped" and booted the stock to kingdom come, I might have lost everything I had made in that stock and then some. You must roll with the punches of investing, bobbing and weaving when the underlying businesses falter or fade.

We all like to think of ourselves as conservative investors, but one of the Trading Goddess's most endearing and enduring traits is to recognize when buying, instead of staying in cash, is a conservative strategy and when holding, instead of selling, is the riskiest strategy of all. We'll explore in another section the arsenal of both short- and long-term tools and of using the downside of the market to make money, because, again, that can be the most conservative style available.

Most important, the Trading Goddess taught me to be unemotional and commonsensical about the direction of stock prices. While sports analogies help the business come alive, we can't root for stocks and stick with the home team. There is no home team. While dogma may pay in politics, it's a killer in stocks. While religion is important, hope and prayer are best left elsewhere when it comes to your money. They aren't valid here. While science has made tremendous strides in hundreds of areas of life, the stock market is not a science. It is just a humbling collection of pricing decisions involving the supply of equities and a level of demand mitigated by greed and fear, two animalistic, psychological components. Those who try to quantify it, measure it, and use mathematical formulas to tame it will in the end be chewed up and eaten by it, as the biggest gang of Nobels under one roof, Long-Term Capital Management, a moronically reckless hedge fund, showed when it lost billions and went belly-up in 1998. There are forces and emotions that determine how markets function that are not susceptible to academic logic. Often to figure out how that market is valuing things we have to go outside the balance sheet and income statements, because the emotions of the market can blind you if you are constrained by those. If we simply limit the debate over how stocks get valued to price-to-earnings multiples or price-to-book valuations (don't freak out, I'll explain those, too, in a way that you will at last understand), the market will often seem completely and utterly full of baloney and impossible to understand. But I will teach you how to make sense of all the markets we have seen, how to understand the underlying patterns, and how to know when to avoid stocks or to short them, and to know when the sages and pundits simply can't be trusted when they say, "Stay away, the market's too dangerous." In still another section of the book I will present my biggest mistakes, with hysterical and humbling simplicity, so you will never make them. As I like to say, I've made every mistake in the book, so you don't have to make any. I am your laboratory. I have done the failed experiments and can show you the results that will keep you from doing them. I detail them here in ways that will make you remember when you are about to make similar costly errors so you stop before the red ink cascades through your portfolio.

Yes, stocks are pieces of paper, but they can be bought and sold with a level of emotionless precision that I can prep you for that will work in any kind of market. Broom the dogma, cultivate the discipline, open your eyes, and let's check out the basics in a way that contains—heck, that busts—all the Genuine Wall Street Gibberish that clouds so many minds trying to fathom why stocks go up or down every day.

2

GETTING STARTED
the
RIGHT WAY

The proliferation of investment information has never been greater. We have tons of people telling us what to do. We have lots of experts telling us how to get started and what you need to know before you buy and sell. Yet they presume a level of knowledge that most of us simply don't have. Unfortunately, plenty of novices immediately get clobbered making amateurish mistakes because they don't understand the basics. These mistakes make neophyte investors feel that the game is rigged against them or that they will never succeed on a regular basis. Many of you got started during an era when everything worked, when the economy was strong, interest rates were low, and stocks went up pretty much every day. Homework was anathema to profits because it kept you out of the most promising short-term situations. That level of perfection had been previously unheard of and is unheard of again. Now people feel that things are simply unfathomable. I think the opposite is true: Stocks can be fathomed, but you need the basics, and the basics weren't taught during the heyday of the late 1990s when so many got into buying and selling stocks. And they certainly aren't taught at any level of school in this country.

I know there is always frustration out there among the first-timers because many of you e-mail me or call me at my radio show, *Jim Cramer's RealMoney,* and ask me if I used to lose money regularly when I started. In fact, many of the millions of people who got their start in equities during the boom, bubble, and burst of the late 1990s to 2000 are convinced that the business is a sucker's game and that you might as well just turn it over to someone who is a professional.

But we are a profession without standards. The media, always so eager to tout any manager regardless of credentials, particularly if he is a good talker, never let you know that most of the "professionals" out there are rank amateurs themselves, often with much less experience at handling money and much more experience in sales than you. The astounding progression of individuals who first got clobbered by buying any old piece of trash online and then tendered their money to mutual fund charlatans, who then sold them out to wealthy hedge funds, is enough to make anyone throw his hands up in disgust about the process. You see why individuals reach the conclusion that handling money well in any fashion is simply impossible. The individual has experienced a fleecing that I wouldn't wish on the most shaggy of sheep in the dead of summer.

First, let's clear up a couple of misperceptions about the business of investing. I always thought the buying and accumulating of stocks looked easy. But once I started, I learned about the hazards of commissions, about the changing nature of markets, and the vagaries of the brokerage business. I learned that it seemed impossible to know enough to buy or sell anything right. No one could ever know enough to pull the trigger with any confidence; the task was too daunting.

And of course, when I started, I lost money. Big money. I would go on colossal losing streaks where literally everything I bought went down. I experienced tremendous ups and downs that were psychologically debilitating; often I just wanted to return to the confines of whatever paycheck I was drawing and learn to be content with that income. But I always believed that stocks could be mastered if someone would just show me the landscape, if someone would explain to me the real pitfalls and give me the real rules, not the ones that I read in books or heard about on TV or saw in articles about the market. I call what I knew the Mistaken Basics. They are why, in part, I come to Praise Speculation, Not Damn It.

Part of the reason that I failed so dramatically when I first bought stocks is that I, like everyone else who has ever bought a stock, believed in conventional wisdom about stocks. In fact, I can sum up the doctrine I foolishly believed in with three rules:

1. Buy and hold because that's how you make the most money.

2. Trading is always wrong, owning is always right.

3. Speculation is the height of evil.

I guess it is only fitting in a book written by a successful investing iconoclast that the first thing we do is demolish these three shibboleths. They are blights on the investing landscape, idols that must be smashed before we go a step further. So, let's do it.

First, the concept of buy and hold is a beautiful thing because it presumes a level of ease and a level of perfection that we should all strive for. What could be better than a philosophy bedrocked in patience and conviction? Unfortunately that level of conviction about pieces of paper—all that stocks really are, and don't you ever forget it—is impossible. Patience, while a virtue, can turn into a vice when you sit there and watch a good company go bad and hold on to its stock anyway under the guise of prudence. I can say with confidence that an unmodified program of buying and holding stocks will definitely smash your nest egg worse than a McDonald's cook whipping up a fresh batch of Egg McMuffins. Buying and holding is actually a bizarre misinterpretation of the long-term data that I have quoted about why you need to stay in the game. Given that no asset class has beaten equities over any twenty-year cycle, it is natural to assume that if you buy stocks and hold them you get to beat all other asset classes.

However, the foremost academic on this particular issue, Jeremy Siegel, a Wharton professor, blanches visibly when he hears the distillation of his work interpreted as a recommendation to buy and hold stocks. Siegel's work shows that if you buy and hold *good quality stocks that often pay dividends,* you get the benefit of the cycle. In fact, the dividend portion is the reason why stocks outperform bonds, and not vice versa. Take it away, and you fail to win. Just buying and holding any old stocks, Siegel will tell you, can be a ticket to the poorhouse.

That's why on *Jim Cramer's RealMoney,* I have changed the superficial buy-and-hold mantra to the more arduous "buy and homework" doctrine, meaning that the real homework begins after you have bought a stock. Just buying and holding Sunbeam, Enron, WorldCom, Dome Petroleum, and Lucent, each at one time the most heavily traded stock of its era, was a recipe for certain disaster. Homework, or the spadework that I describe to you in my chapter on what constitutes homework, would have gotten you out of all of these stocks before the damage and the rot set in. Again, not buy and hold, but buy and homework. If you are going to make big money in the market, only with homework can you be sure that your stocks qualify as good quality stocks that can pay a dividend.

Second, the idea that trading is somehow evil is ingrained in most individuals almost from the moment they begin to invest. Stubborn adherence to this point of view has led to more big losses than any other strategy I know. Trading, meaning the rapid or short-term buying and selling of stocks, is something that can prove to be entirely necessary if you are to be prudent and lock in gains when the market takes stocks past their logical extremes, which happens quite frequently in every generation of stocks. If you chose to never sell because, say, you are afraid of the tax man, or because you despise paying commissions, you need to get your head examined. When I got into this business, it made some sense *not* to sell. It would routinely cost you several hundred dollars in commission to trade more than a couple of hundred shares. When combined with the spread, the difference between the bid and asked, for all but the most liquid or heavily traded stocks, a diminution of return was almost a given. A quarter of a point of spread, $200 in commissions, and gigantic taxable gains might have turned a substantial gain into a moderate loss on a trade. But that was then, this is now; we are in a whole different ballgame. Taxes these days are incredibly low even on short-term gains, because ordinary tax rates are much lower than they used to be. Trades that would have cost hundreds of dollars in commissions will now be done for about seven dollars by any discount broker. The liquidity of almost all stocks is pretty terrific since the advent of decimalization, where stocks trade in penny increments. You no longer get nicked for quarters and halves on the buy and sell. Pennies, just pennies separate almost all of the places you can buy and sell stocks. They just don't eat into the profit anymore. You can't use them as an excuse not to take a profit. In fact you have to be a fool not to sell to lock in at least some of a big gain these days lest it be taken away. The old bias against trading, however, remains as people simply don't know how little friction there is between the buy and sell these days.

Finally, the bias against speculation has taken on mythic proportions. I don't know of a soul besides me who thinks that speculating can be a handy tool on the road to riches. Yet I know that all of my biggest gains, my largest wins, came from pure speculation, which I define as making a calculated bet with a limited amount of capital that turns into a monster home run. I believe that speculation is not only healthy and terrific, but is vital to true diversification. You must be diversified to stay in the game when things go bad. (More, later, about how diversification is the only free lunch in the business.) But diversification without speculation is stultifying and can mean the difference between your losing interest—which is unforgivable—and your paying attention. Speculating, particularly when you are younger, is not only prudent, it is *essential* to making it so you don't have to be totally dependent on that darned paycheck to become rich. I believe in my heart and in my head that if I had never speculated I would be working as a lawyer right now, perhaps proofreading some indenture somewhere in the middle of the night trying desperately to stay awake as others made the money. You've got to build in speculation as part of diversification. It is a crucial component.

I play a game called "Am I Diversified?" every week on my radio program. I ask people to read to me their five largest holdings. When they have done it they have to ask me whether they are diversified. I feel so strongly about this notion that I have taken to asking why people don't have one stock bet that could make them significant amounts in a short time. I want to see speculation for a portion of even an older individual's portfolio, albeit only a name or two—a small percentage—to keep you interested. Given the nature of the potential losses I don't want someone who will need the money for retirement to speculate with more than a fifth of his portfolio. You have to make taking a chance a part of your arsenal. I know this pro-speculation view runs counter to anything you have ever heard or read, but this is how I made it big in the market, this is why I was able to beat the market even when I was just starting out both as an investor-hobbyist and then as a professional at Goldman Sachs before I went off on my hedge fund. Of course a portfolio of nothing but speculation is like a diet of nothing but bacon and cheese; it will kill you. But speculation in moderation is no different from enjoying some so-called fattening foods in an endless bid to stay on the healthier regimen. The current wisdom, though, is either buy and hold whatever strikes your fancy as solid, even if it isn't, or turn everything over to someone who doesn't care as much as you do about either capital preservation (no defense) or capital appreciation (no offense).

Understand that I love to invest. I love to buy and do homework. I have owned some high-quality stocks for years and years and years. Yet I always do the homework still. And I always speculate when I am able to speculate, either through the use of options (which I'll explain later) or through the use of small-dollar acorns that I think can grow to be tall oaks or, even better, to be taken over by larger oaks long before they go through the slow process of growing up.

I know that academics and those market professionals who believe that stocks are priced perfectly don't believe that you can make large amounts with small investments in a short period of time. They think such situations don't exist or that they are flukes, luck. Because they don't believe in them and because you often search for them and fail, the tendency, the belief, becomes ingrained that there is no quick way to make big money.

Let me give you an example of a situation I stumbled on in my younger stock-picking days—an example of what some would say was just rank speculation but I say was a legitimate opportunity—that might show you why I believe in speculating wisely. This opportunity came when I was younger and had almost no money to speak of, precisely the time to speculate the heaviest because you have your whole work life to make the money back if things don't pan out.

At Harvard Law School, I managed in my spare time to work for Alan Dershowitz, helping to get the supremely guilty—at least in my view—Claus von Bulow acquitted on procedural grounds. The job paid well, more than eight dollars an hour. Despite being phenomenally bored with my law school classes—to this day I regard them as pure torture—I made it my business to go every day. I would check in on the markets every hour via the phone booths located outside the classrooms, usually reserved for homesick kids calling their mothers after a particularly brutal grilling or exam. That spring, 1984, the oil patch had heated up. Getty Petroleum had just gotten a bid. I had made some money speculating in some call options, which for a little money provide the right to be able to capture the upside above a particular level of stock, in the Conoco battle the previous year and in Sinclair Oil, another target, not long after. I had small positions—several hundred dollars' worth of money I had saved from the Dershowitz chores—in both oils and was drawn to the group. At this point I was also managing a pool of money for my friend Marty Peretz, who had found me via my answering machine. I had such a hot hand picking stocks while attending classes that I began recommending a stock a week on my machine. Only later, in my third year at law school, did I discover that such a touting system was a violation of the 1940 Investment Advisor Act, but I hadn't taken that class yet, so who knew? Marty tried to reach me to write a positive book review for the *New Republic*, which he owned and edited, on behalf of a mutual friend, Jim Stewart, a terrific author, and got discouraged when I never called him back. After three straight weeks where he said I had made more money for him than any other person alive in the thirty years he'd been buying and selling stocks, he handed me a check for $500,000 over a cup of joe at the Coffee Connection. I ran his money side by side with my little pool of cash. I told Marty that I thought our next big hit would be Gulf Oil; it just seemed too logical. I purchased us small amounts of Gulf call options (again, the right to make money if a stock reaches a certain level). I had decided early on that call options, if you can handle their risk, were the ideal method of speculation for a small investor because the downside was limited and the upside was bountiful. (More on how calls work and how to master them later in the advanced section of the book.)

One day, while I was in class, Chevron launched a bid for Gulf Oil. I was gleeful after I called in and discovered I had had my first big hit. I had been discouraged when I had initially lost money for Marty, but this Gulf Oil deal put me in the black with him. I wanted to give his money back and just trade for myself—I hated the responsibility of running other peoples' money and still do! But Marty wouldn't hear of it. Now we were back where we started, and I was feeling better about myself.

That spring I had been taking Antitrust with the giant of antitrust, the late Phil Areeda. Most of law school was a valueless blur, but this guy was a master. I still recall his classes, among the few I took seriously, because he was a great teacher. We were working on a unit on Standard Oil and the origins of antitrust law. I always sat in the back and said nothing. If I was ever called on, I always passed, lest I look like an idiot. But I was taking it all in. I thought, You know something, this guy Areeda knows what the heck he's talking about. Most of the professors were a bunch of left-wing, dogmatic blowhards. But Areeda was in the game.

Right after the announcement of the bid, and the concomitant move up of Gulf, the oil giant's stock started slipping. One day during a break in class, I checked in with my broker, Joe McCarthy from Fidelity, and heard the disturbing news that Gulf had fallen back almost to where we had first bought the calls, on chatter that the government was definitely going to block the Gulf-Socal (as it was called then) merger. I was so distraught I didn't even notice that the break was over and I slunk back into class late, several minutes after intermission had ended.

It was obvious that I was tardy. Areeda hated that. He was too much of a gentleman and I was not enough of a scholar not to feel bad about coming in after class had started. At the conclusion of the class, I went up to him to apologize for my slothfulness. Areeda knew I was one of those students who couldn't care less about law school, but he knew I was interested in business. I took a chance. I said, "Professor, I was late because I own Gulf Oil and my broker says that the deal won't go through."

He looked me in the eye and he said something I would never forget: "It's a done deal." I looked at him the way a man looks at the piece of glass he just found in his backyard that he now realizes is a diamond. I said to him that I had real money riding on this one. Was Justice going to block the deal?

"Not a chance," he said. He knew the players. He knew Reagan's people wouldn't block it.

I asked him again.

He said he didn't have any more time to waste. If I had done my homework, which I obviously had not, I would have known that the decision was in the bag. I left the class and bet the farm for me and for Marty on Gulf Oil, wagering just about every penny I had in the bank, some $2,000 at the time.

Justice approved the deal soon after and I made a fortune for Marty and enough for myself to pay for law school and college (I still owed substantial amounts from college) and emerge from school free and clear. Two thousand dollars turned into twenty-five thousand just like that. And an indebted student who expected to labor for years to free

himself of that indenture was freed before he graduated. I had speculated and I had succeeded.

Would I endorse this view if you called me on my radio show or
met with me privately for a consultation? Yes, if you were young
enough that you could afford to lose it all and still make it back. No, if
you were older and speculating the same percentage of assets I did,
which was just about everything. I want you to speculate, but as you
get older, you don't have the rest of your life to make the money back
from the paycheck side of the ledger, so, naturally, you have to scale
back and take smaller risks. But as a small percentage of assets and
with a hunch like I had with Gulf, absolutely. These kinds of informed
bets are the best kind of investments, because the risk, the downside, is
limited, and the reward, the upside, is monumental. I know, I know,
you won't always have the insight of some Harvard antitrust professor, but these kinds of home runs, while not as frequent as singles, do
get hit every day in this business.

Why is this kind of short-term thinking so antithetical to most investors? How did we get brainwashed into buy and hold forever? I
think that the literature on the topic is very much responsible for the
misapprehensions about speculation, buying and holding, and trading. All investing literature has one thing in common: It refuses to
admit that great investing, long-term or short-term, has much in
common not with science or mathematics, but with *gambling*! There,
I said it. We are wagering on the direction of stocks, both long and
short. We are wagering in a way that we hope will allow a little bit of
money to grow into something huge. We are betting that we can evaluate merchandise and figure out which can win, which places, which
shows, and which loses. We want more winners than losers; if we get
more winners than losers we will grow rich. Once you admit that it is
wagering, and that you have to monitor the jockey (the manager) as
well as the horse (the company) as well as the track (the stock market),
then you can make some sense of what you are up against and know
which rules do and don't apply.

That's why it is no coincidence that (until now) I always recommended one text to those trying to figure out how to beat the market. One book, besides this one, that can change your view of investing forever. It's not *Reminiscences of a Stock Operator* by legendary trader Jesse Livermore (written under the pseudonym Ed Lefèvre), even though that's a real hoot. Nor is it something by value investor Benjamin Graham, nor the Peter Lynch books, which are excellent, nor the Bill O'Neill books, although I would come to like them later.

In fact, it is not a stock book at all. It's *Picking Winners* by Andy Beyer, the premier horse-racing columnist in the country, who until recently penned a column for the *Washington Post*. Yep, a handicapping book. Because the two, horse-race betting and stock betting, are so alike that the wagering rules he lays out apply to both. Beyer excels in handicapping horses; I excel in handicapping stocks. Beyer's main lessons, besides the basic need to be a good speculator, are vital for you to understand, and I will give you a variety of ways to master them. They seem simple, but in the reality of stocks, it will take plenty of practice and homework for you to use and maintain them:

1. If you learn from mistakes you will not repeat them.

2. Only go to tracks where there aren't a lot of good players so you can clean up. (The analogy here is only to invest in stocks where the research and information flow aren't perfect and lots of minds aren't already trying to figure it out.)

3. Only bet on situations where you have total conviction. Leave the rest to others; you don't have to play. You don't have to invest in everything that comes down the pike.

Now, let's analyze how these three rules apply to stocks. First, amateurs must realize that much time must be spent doing homework (I will show you what homework entails) and learning the stocks you own. Approach it like a job. Investing can be a hobby, but trading can't. Even Mrs. Cramer, who is a fabulous trader, has failed miserably as a part-time trader, although her investing skills are still top of the heap.

Second, while you can't be an expert on everything, you can learn a few stocks well and profit handily from those. I will show you where to find them, but you still have to do the homework when you get them.

Most of all, recognize that you have to have an edge, something different that you can bring to the party. I will show you some methods you can use to gain an edge in your investments, using commonsensical approaches to the businesses around you.

To get there, you must have a basic understanding of what stocks are, how stocks work, and why they go up and down. You have to know how they work before I can give you the rules, show you the mistakes, and explain the best ways to find the best stocks, and, finally, how to speculate in ways that could make you rich without a lot of money, both basic and advanced methods. Only then can you make the wagers, both short- and long-term, that fit the rules that Beyer outlines. Only then can we benefit from his handicapping wisdom.

We assume so much in this business, we who own and trade stocks. We assume that you understand what a stock is, what it represents, and how stocks figure into the capital structure. Those are blithe assumptions. I know this because I have seen people confuse shares of a stock with something that is almost tangible, something that is palpable, and that misconception leads to a level of certainty and lack of accurate skepticism that can betray you in a heartbeat. So let's take a second to explain where stocks come from and where they fit into the investment picture. Those who have been investing for years should still pay heed because you may assume certain things, too, that may not be true.

First of all, all companies need money, especially companies that are trying to grow. They can get money in a couple of ways. They can go to the bank as we go to a bank to get a loan such as a mortgage. The collateral for the loan might be the inflow of cash the company expects (the receivables) or it might be the worth of the company itself. A company can issue debt, or bonds, that it pays interest on over time, and then, when the debt is due, it pays back the principal.

If the owners of the company are willing, or if some of the owners want to get money out of the company, the company can issue common stock shares in the enterprise. A company's capital structure can be made up of shares that are issued to the public and bonds that are issued to the public.

We all assume that the common stock the company issues represents the real ownership of the company. We proudly talk about how we own shares in the company and are therefore somehow "owners" of the company, as if we were all members of some grand club that owns the clubhouse. The first thing I want to do is disabuse you of that entitlement. When you own stock, you do have a fractional interest in the company if there is no other element in the capital structure, that is, if there is no debt. But beyond the danish and O.J. that you might get if you attend the annual meeting, owning stock itself entitles you to nothing. Worse, if the company has debt, the debt holders are senior to you and have more power than you. I call these folks the bond bullies. As long as the company is doing well, the bond bullies behave themselves and let the stockholders run the company. However, if the company loses a lot of money, to the point where it can't pay the interest on the bonds, the bond bullies take over. I stress this because in the period from 2000 to 2003, many common stock shareholders were wiped out and bond holders took over companies. The common stock shareholders in many cases did not know what hit them. They thought they owned the company. So, remember, you only own it when things are good. When things go bad, you don't own anything but the piece of paper that the common stock is printed on, and you probably don't even have that because almost all stocks these days are held electronically, with no certificates issued.

The saving grace of stocks is that they can only go to zero. Don't laugh, I've owned some stocks that were so bad that it was a blessing they stopped at zero. Each share of common stock is theoretically worth something, a fractional share of ownership. But if you go to the company to redeem your shares to cash out of your ownership, the company will tell you that while it issued the shares, it won't take them back from you. Companies aren't department stores of shares. You have to sell those shares to someone else. In fact, the company can issue more shares at any given time to dilute your ownership in the enterprise. It can also buy back those shares if it wants in the open market, if it chooses to shrink the number of shares outstanding.

Why do people own stock if the company won't take it back? Why is it worth anything? I know people who have traded stocks for years and years who have never asked themselves that, yet it's a tremendous leap of faith to understand why an electronic entry of shares that can't be taken back to the company is worth anything at all.

The answer is really twofold: There is an enterprise value to the whole company that can be bought or sold and can grow over time from the retained earnings of the company, and there is an income stream (known as dividends) that can come from the shares when the company is prosperous. If you own a stock that pays a dividend you could be getting both the income stream and the value of an appreciating stock. Most companies, however, don't start out as dividend payers. Many other companies have no intention of paying a dividend because they want to reinvest earnings to grow the company and don't want to return any capital to the shareholders.

Why are we given this opportunity to participate in the welfare of a public company? Why do companies go public, or sell shares to investors? What is the stock made of and what determines its price? Let's look at it through one situation I know well, one that is somewhat typical of the process, although each company, of course, is different from others in its own way. Let's look at TheStreet.com, a publicly traded company that I own a ton of shares in. Marty Peretz and I started the company in 1996 by putting in $100,000 every month. It didn't begin to generate any revenue until 1997, but then advertising on the Web took off like a rocket and we needed money both to pay people and to expand. The money we needed was beyond what Marty and I could afford. Frankly, while we were growing revenues, or sales, nicely, we were losing money hand over fist. We had no profits, which are sales minus expenses and the cost of the goods sold, but we had two revenue streams, subscription and advertising, and we had a brand, which had some amorphous value. When we had burned through all of the money that Marty and I were willing to invest we had to raise money from other individuals, known as venture capitalists. They gave us money not because they were our buddies—far from it—but because they hoped to get more than their money back when the company was sold to another company or if it went public. We were in it to build the company, they were in it for the payoff. That's a fairly typical situation for young, growing companies.

After we burned through the venture capitalists' money, we raised money from a couple of other companies, notably News Corporation and the New York Times Company. They, too, gave us their capital in return for the right to have shares when we issued them. We could have gone to a bank, but I don't think any bank would have lent us money because we were losing too much money as it was. But because of the fascination with the stock market at that time, we hired a banker, Goldman Sachs, to tap the public's dollars. We knew people would buy shares in our enterprise for the reason they buy shares in many enterprises: They hoped we would one day either return a profit or be bought by another company for more than they paid for their shares. One of Goldman Sachs' main jobs was to raise money for us through an underwriting, or initial public offering (IPO). Everyone thinks he understands this underwriting process intuitively, but as one of the people who has worked on IPOs, from the entrepreneurial side to the sell side, I can tell you they are rather mystifying. Unless you are a serial entrepreneur, you probably will only go through the going-public process once, if you are unlucky enough to go through it at all.

I was hopelessly naïve. Here's the way it really works. Management of the company, which is typically clueless about Wall Street, has a meeting with the banker's corporate finance department, which draws up the documents for the offering and structures the deal, and the syndicate department, which prices the merchandise. The investment banking people tell you how many shares you are going to have outstanding and how many of those shares the company will float publicly. The syndicate person tells you what price those shares will most likely be issued at. Our syndicate people told us that they looked at companies comparable to ours and said that given how much in sales we had—we had no profits—and how much money the New York Times and News Corp. had paid, the company should be worth $250 million dollars. The figure wasn't totally arbitrary—the New York Times and News Corp. had valued it similarly, although it sure was hard to figure out why it was worth anything given how much it was losing. Then the investment bank said, arbitrarily, that the company's ownership would be divided into 25 million shares. Of that, 19 million would be owned by the original investors and 6 million would be sold to the public. I give you these numbers because there is no magic to the number of shares a company has. Goldman could have said we were going to have 100 million shares and 24 million would have been issued to the public. It could have said we would have 200 million shares and 48 million were going to be issued. That's just how it works. The total share count matters tremendously only as a way to figure out how much earnings per share there are. Of course, TheStreet.com wasn't close to having any earnings per share, but you can still figure it out by taking the overall loss we were having in a year and dividing that by the number of shares to be issued, so you can compare TheStreet.com's earnings per share to those of other companies.

I initially owned 50 percent of the company with my cofounder Marty Peretz. When we invited the venture capitalists in, our 50 percent stake was diluted to about 30 percent each. With each new round of financing, we gave up more of our claim to the enterprise. By the time we contacted Goldman Sachs, my stake had been diluted to about 16 percent of the enterprise, since each new buyer was entitled to shares and the company issued shares to some of the people who worked there in addition to salaries. You may think that 16 percent is way too little versus where we started, but it is part of a much bigger pie than we started, so I was quite happy with the percentage.

Goldman Sachs then conducted what is known as a road show, where it flies management to a bunch of cities to stir up demand. We already had a ton of demand for the shares before we started, so the roadshow was a complete waste of time and should have just been done over the Web. But theoretically you want to explain to people in person what the company does and what it plans to do. In actuality, the merchandise—the shares the company is issuing—was "hot" merchandise, meaning that everyone was clamoring for the darned stuff and we could have just as easily sold shares on eBay, but that's not how it works, unfortunately.

It is during this period that people at the company write the prospectus, or selling document, which tells you what the company does, how it is doing financially, what the backgrounds of the people involved are, and then gives you a huge list of reasons, or risks, that tell you why you would be nuts to buy the company. It's a funny way to do business, but, as I have said from the beginning, there's a lot of nutty, counterintuitive things about Wall Street that often are there just to confuse you and make you need someone who can help you—for a fee, of course. Most people throw the thing away immediately, but the prospectus can be an immense source of information about a company. You don't need to keep it—they are all online now, reachable with a keystroke.

After the company's top officers have been on a plane visiting a dozen cities, the merchandise gets repriced by the bankers to take into account the stirred-up demand as the deal gets closer. For me, this was another totally eye-opening process. While we started the trip thinking we would get $10 a share, the price got lifted seven times, the final bump to $19. It was only later that I found out that the plan was always to have it priced at $19 because that's the price Goldman thought would work best for everyone—the buyers and the company selling the shares. We insiders were restricted from selling for eighteen months, and then we were allowed only to dribble out stock slowly, so as not to crush the offering with too much supply. At this point we were only allowed to buy more on the deal, not sell any stock. If we had been allowed to sell stock, that would be considered "secondary" stock, not "primary" stock, which is just for the company.

Because the system for initial public offerings at the time couldn't really factor in all of the market orders, the company ended up selling 6,350,000 shares at $19. The stock opened, however, at $63, nowhere near the $19, as demand totally outstripped supply. Brokerages aren't allowed to issue more supply than they originally promised and so many uninformed folks in the public foolishly used market orders to buy. They ended up buying stock for 20, 30, and even 40 points more than they thought they would because they used the dreaded market order system. Never use it, as I will explain later, when you can use limit orders. Those who got the stock from Goldman Sachs at $19 on the actual offering mostly flipped the stock at those inflated prices and pocketed the $63 minus the $19 they paid. What a huge windfall for the customers and what a monster shortchange for the company! But there are no do-overs in this business. Even though, in retrospect, we could have sold many more shares at a much higher price, the company still had to pay Goldman Sachs 6 percent of the proceeds for this one-day sale.

Once the deal is done, the company has almost nothing to do with the shares again. The shares that come public, and then, in time, the shares of insiders such as the venture capitalists and the corporations and the founders like Marty and me, are free to be traded, although insiders can only peel them out slowly since there are tightly regulated rules for how much stock you can sell at one time—again, so as not to overwhelm the market. The price of the merchandise is reset every day through trading by the public, in this case on the NASDAQ, where companies can be listed that don't make money—you have to make money for a year before you can list on the New York Stock Exchange. While there are differences in how stocks trade on the two exchanges (the New York Stock Exchange uses what is known as a specialist system with humans manipulating the supply and demand, while the NASDAQ trades electronically from computer to computer with no human middle man), those differences are virtually irrelevant to all but those who trade in multiple thousands of shares, so we won't need to address the pros and cons here of the two systems. Suffice it to say that once the deal goes public, the public sets the price from then on. For us at TheStreet.com, we had to watch the sickening slide from opening day at $63 to $1 a couple of years later, although it has since bounced back to more reasonable prices. You should remember those prices whenever you hear a silly academic say that the pricing system of stocks is "perfect," meaning that it prices in all data precisely. Within a period of two years the brilliant "market" valued TheStreet .com at both $1.2 billion and at $20 million. That's a lot of room for the savvy to make money and the naïve to get shafted.

3

HOW STOCKS ARE MEANT

to

BE TRADED

Now that you know the process that companies go through to become public, it's time to figure out how we—you and I—should value them. Determining a company's value tells you what's worth buying. Deciding what's right to buy and what's right to sell, and the best ways to do so, are the fundamentals of investing. Doing it correctly and intelligently can make you very rich. Doing it in an uninformed way, the way the vast majority of people do, can make you poor unless you get lucky. This book is about taking as much luck and hope out of the equation as possible.

People ask me every day what a stock they own is worth. They almost always say, "I bought TheStreet.com at ten dollars and it is now at four dollars. What should I do with it?" I tell them immediately, I don't care where a stock traded, I don't care about the past, I don't care where you bought the stock, the only thing I care about with a stock is what's going to happen next. I must say those words a dozen times a week on my radio show because most people don't grasp this simple concept that determines just about everything you need in order to know whether a stock is going to go up or down: the future.

People are constantly trying to bring up the irrelevant when they talk stocks. Maybe you bought the stock well, maybe you bought it badly. It shouldn't influence your decision. They want to mention what went through their minds when they bought it and why they bought. I don't care about that either, because it obviously didn't turn out right or you wouldn't be referring to where you bought it and mentioning how you are down on it.

I'm driven so crazy by this web of meaningless alibis that the only time I take individual questions about individual stocks on my radio show is on Fridays when we play "The Lightning Round." I forbid callers to say anything but the name of the stock and I take it from there, telling them up or down, buy or sell, based strictly on what I think is going to happen in the future. That's because owning stock is a bet on the future, not the past. You must buy into that notion or you mustn't buy stocks yourself.

I didn't always feel this way. At one point, no doubt like you now, I was completely caught up in the notion of my "basis," the technical term, both on Wall Street and with the IRS, for the price I paid for a stock. If my basis for Maytag, say, was $34, and the stock was $28, I would let that unrealized loss get in the way of the decision-making process, because, I, like you, hate to take a loss. Of course, the situation is already in "loss mode" as I like to call it, a loss to anyone but you because you hold out hope that should play no role in the process.

In fact, I would let this basis factor so mar my judgment about the future of Maytag that I wouldn't be able to think clearly about whether I should give up on the position or buy more. I would say, "Maytag, I'm down six, maybe I have to buy more. Maybe I should be bigger, 'cause I'm down." Or, obviously, "Maybe if I buy more I can make it right even if I'm wrong now!" Lots of that kind of logic swarmed in my head when I was starting out.

This pigheadedness about my basis—in the face of obvious facts about how bright or poor the *future* of Maytag would be—made my wife go ballistic. The Trading Goddess knew that the future was all that mattered, and she knew I was being blinded to it because I was down six bucks when I reviewed the piece of merchandise on which I was "long," or owned. In those grand old days of trading together at 56 Beaver Street in downtown Manhattan, a floor above the steak joint, Delmonico's, a downtown fixture, she would insist we get off the desk multiple times a day and go to a bare office located right above the kitchen of the restaurant. There, with steak fumes wafting in and threatening to embed themselves in our clothes and our nostrils, she would go over each position slowly and methodically, reciting each name from our position sheets. After each stock she would ask me what I thought and how I would rank it on a scale of one to five, a one being a stock I wanted to buy more of right now and a five being one I needed to sell pronto.

These sessions were extremely painful because there would be a dripping tone of sarcasm when a stock had obviously gone awry. She was always exacting in her methods; these weren't lovey-dovey klatches between husband and wife, believe me. They were discipline camps. I would try to think clearly about each position she would enunciate, but invariably I would be blinded by my basis. I just couldn't get past the decline from where I bought the darned thing. My judgment was stymied by the stigma of unrealized loss that each negative position carried.

Then one day, we got off the desk and went to the steak room, as I called it, and she handed out the sheets as always but the basis, the price I had paid, was whited out. That's right, she had grabbed a bottle of Wite-Out and painted over every price that I had originally paid for the stocks. "There," she said, "now you can think clearly."

Of course, when we got down to the Maytag position, I was able, at last, to measure Maytag for what mattered, the future, not what I was letting matter, the past, the 6 points I was down on the position. When not faced with the tether of history, I immediately admitted that Whirlpool and GE were kicking Maytag's butt and that we ought to just face the darned music and dump the stock.

From then on, she routinely whited out all the bases of every stock from our position sheets. And our performance increased dramatically. Lesson number one: When it comes to buying or selling a stock, don't tell me where you bought it, tell me where it's going. That's all that matters when it comes to buying or selling a stock.

Besides the past, people are way too hung up on price, the dollar amount you have to pay per share. Most beginners, but also many people who got in during the heyday, the bubble, when everything was working, don't even realize what "price" is, so let's explain that first before we explore whether we are paying too much or too little for a stock.

When you get a quote, or when you look at a stock's closing price in the morning papers, you are seeing the exact last price at which the merchandise—and this is just merchandise—changed hands. That doesn't mean it's where you can necessarily buy the stock. Stocks trade in bids and offers—you hit the bid, or sell it there, or you take the offer, or buy it there. The uninitiated use the terms "buy" and "sell," but we never do that on Wall Street; we say "take the stock" or "hit the bid." That's because we are intent on getting the job done. "Buy" and "sell" are amorphous terms, too amorphous for most professionals, but good enough for those who are just trying to buy small amounts, typically less than 100 shares. Any more than 100 shares and you are going to have to learn that "buy 200 shares of Nortel" is simply taking your life into your hands. Here's why. "Buy" and "sell" mean "buy at the market" and "sell at the market." Only amateurs and fools enter market orders. Our ridiculous system of buying and selling stocks is predicated upon your being ripped off by whoever gets that market order. And you will be. If you enter a generic market order, the order can be matched with another customer within the system or brokerage you are trading in, at a price perhaps at least surprising and at most entirely disadvantageous to you. Especially when the merchandise you are buying is illiquid or "trades by appointment," meaning that it is difficult to find multiple buyers and sellers. When I was just starting, trading stocks out of phone booths or sneaking out of law school classes to place orders, I always used market orders and rarely did the order ever work to my satisfaction. I always felt I was getting ripped off. It was only much later, after I turned pro, that I realized that I *was* being systematically ripped off—by myself—because I foolishly believed that the system of buying and selling stocks at the market was set up to aid the little guy. Just the opposite. A market order is a license to abuse you, at the behest of a larger client or the brokerage itself trying to "find both sides of the trade" internally so it can get the full commission on both the selling and the buying instead of having to share it with another firm.

So what can you do?

Lesson number two in trading stocks: Always use limit orders when you buy or sell any stock, especially when you are buying in un-seasoned situations, with new stocks or just-issued stocks, such as The Street.com on the day it came public. Decide what price you are willing to pay for a piece of merchandise, and then enter it. Never use a market order. You can determine yourself what you think is right, what you think is expensive, or what you think is cheap, and hold out for it. That's vital, that's what you have to do, and don't let yourself be abused by the system. This "limit" order is particularly important in so-called fast markets, when there is news impacting the stock you are trying to buy, making the merchandise a moving target. You determine the parameters. If I want to buy Nortel and the offered, or where I can buy it, is $3.50, but there is news out—a new contract gained from BellSouth, say, that will jack up the price—then I enter the order this way: "Take two thousand shares of Nortel at three fifty-five." That way I've set a limit on the price I will pay for the stock.

Similarly, if I want to sell Nortel and the bid, or where I can sell it, is $3.48, but Nortel has lost some important business to Cisco that I know will send the stock plummeting, then I say, "Sell two thousand shares of Nortel as low as three forty-five." I make up the price, I give the limit.

That way I buy it at the price I want, and if I buy it at the wrong price at least it's my fault, and not the fault of the system. Nobody tells you not to use market orders because it is in nobody's interest except yours to do so. The broker wants you to do the trade so he gets the commission, but if you "limit" it, the trade might not happen, and then he doesn't get paid. (If the stock never reaches your target price, then the trade isn't executed.) The brokerage wants to cross your order with another order in house to get both of the commissions. A market order lets that happen, but at a price that you might not like. Never use market orders, ever! If this simple point is your only take-away from what I have learned the hard way, you are already well ahead of the game.

Now, how about that price, that last sale dollar amount. Do you know what that price means? If you go to Macy's and there are two cable-knit sweaters, one by Polo made of cashmere and one by Macy's house brand made of polyester and cotton, both selling for $100, you know that something's wrong with the price of at least one of these two items. The Polo cashmere should be $400. The poly-cotton Macy's deal should be $49. We can do stuff like that in our heads. We know bargains and we know rip-offs. We are sophisticated shoppers about things like sweaters at department stores. Alas, if only we were better at buying bigger ticket items like stocks at the malls I shop at every day, the NASDAQ or the New York Stock Exchange.

The reason why we can't spot bargains and rip-offs when it comes to stocks is that the prices we pay aren't "real"; they are simply ratios created by the companies through stock splits and share adjustments that often confuse even professionals but always confuse the little guys. When you buy a cashmere sweater for $400, you know it is worth more than the poly-cotton sweater at $49. But in the stock market—and only in the stock market—a $49 stock can be more expensive than a $400 stock!

We have to understand how these ratios are calculated so you can spot bargains and overvalued merchandise as easily as you can at Albertsons or Wal-Mart or Macy's. Don't freak out at the mention of the word "ratio." I was doing ratios with my fifth grader last night. They are simple division, something that our schools actually teach successfully to all but the socially promoted. You know I am going to get you through this with flying colors, so drop your objections and let's get to work.

To help us understand the real or underlying worth of merchandise versus the arbitrary price per share that we pay, let's stick with Maytag, the washer and dryer company everyone knows, and compare it to Whirlpool, its biggest competitor. Recently Maytag traded at $27 a share and Whirlpool traded at $67 a share. Are they roughly the same price? The beginner, of course, says no, one is $40 more than the other and is therefore much more expensive. Only on Wall Street, where so much is done to confuse the millions of people who shop at our store, is the answer "yes" to the question whether Maytag at $27 and Whirlpool at $67 are the same price. In fact, they are almost exactly the same price, as befits two competitors that duke it out pretty evenly. But you have to understand their price-to-earnings ratios to see through the $27 to $67 disparity. You have to understand the ratio to know that $67 isn't more expensive than $27.

You see, we don't care about the actual price that we pay per share. If Whirlpool, for example, were to announce a two-for-one stock split tomorrow, you would be paying $33 a share, and instead of saying that Whirlpool is selling for $40 more than Maytag, you would say it is selling for $6 more. Or, if Maytag were to do a two-for-one reverse split, so that it was selling at $54, you would think they are selling at similar prices. But share prices are just guideposts that a company can change at will. They don't help you figure out relative worth at all. (Never forget that while splits are exciting, they produce no more "pencil." That's my shorthand for taking a pencil and breaking it in half. You have two pencils, but you haven't created more lead. That's all a stock split is!)

What really matters isn't the price that you pay or that you see at the end of the long column of numbers next to a stock symbol or name in the newspaper stock tables each day. What matters is the price-to-earnings ratio of each stock. You have to take that last price on that line in the paper next to the stock's name, and you have to divide it—come on, take it and just put a line under it—by the amount per share the company earned in the previous year. Maytag earned $2.18 last year. That's a number that can be found by simply inputting MYG, Maytag's symbol, into Quote.Yahoo.com. This will instantly tell you how much money, on a per share basis, Maytag made. (You can arrive at that number yourself, as you used to do before the Web's incredible explosion of free information, by dividing the amount the company earned for the year—that's back to the process of share issuance as we talked about with TheStreet.com—by the number of common stock shares there are.)

Now, you divide $27—the last price paid—by $2.18, and you get 12 (rounded to the nearest whole number). That's the magic number that you need to know, Maytag trades at 12 times earnings. You are paying 12 times Maytag's previous earnings per share for each share that you buy. That's the real price. The (M)ultiple, 12, times $2.18, the (E)arnings per share, equals the (P)rice per share. We express the price as an equation: $M \times E = P$.

You should always remember this equation as a way to understand how we arrive at prices. We take the earnings and we figure out what we are willing to pay for the earnings—the multiple—then we times them and we arrive at the price. This formula can also help us figure out future prices. If we know what the earnings estimates are going to be (E) and we can figure out what we might be willing to pay for those earnings (M) we can arrive at a future price or we can figure how much above or below a stock might be from where it might trade in the future. The multiple allows us to make apples-to-apples comparisons with the stocks of other companies in the cohort.

To put it another way, if we have the price, and we have the future earnings estimates, we can measure whether we are paying too much M or too little M for the stock right now versus its peers. Any change in the earnings estimates (faster growth, for example) or any change in the economic landscape (such as lower interest rates, as we shall see) can affect what M we will pay.

Congratulations, you have just mastered the art of figuring out what a stock is worth and what it might be worth in the future.

Professionals never say, "Maytag's a bargain because it trades at twenty-seven dollars." They say "Maytag's a bargain because it trades at twelve times earnings and yet it is a consistent grower that deserves to sell for a higher multiple." Or professionals might say, "Maytag's expensive at twelve times earnings given its spotty history." The subjectivity is in the comparisons to other equities of similar nature.

Whirlpool, on the other hand, earned about $6 last year and it trades for $67. What does it trade at times earnings? What's its magic number? Divide the $67 by the $6 and you get roughly 11 (again, we are rounding because the precise multiple isn't as important as the approximation). So Whirlpool trades at a multiple of 11 times earnings. Now we have something that allows us to compare the two companies; we have something that explains the *relative* worth of each company's shares. Maytag trades at 12 times earnings while Whirlpool trades at 11 times earnings.

Here's where it gets really interesting. While the Whirlpool at $67 seems almost $40 more expensive than Maytag at $27, when we make the comparison apples to apples, when we break it down by P/E (price-to-earnings) ratio, we see that Whirlpool trades at 11 times earnings and Maytag at 12 times earnings. That's right, Maytag at $27 is actually more expensive than Whirlpool at $67. Almost 10 percent more expensive, despite the prices quoted.

We say, using the vernacular of Wall Street, that Maytag is "one multiple point more expensive than Whirlpool." We are simply subtracting Whirlpool's 11 multiple from Maytag's 12 multiple to arrive at that one-point disparity. Do you know why a $27 stock can be more expensive than a $67 stock? There are many reasons. One is that a Maytag appliance might be slightly better than Whirlpool's. A second may be that Maytag's brand has a better reputation than Whirlpool. A third could be that Maytag's management might be better than Whirlpool's. All of those reasons do matter. But the real reason why one trades more expensively than the other is that one grows faster than the other. All reasons for changes in multiples pall compared to Wall Street's intense growth fixation. The main reason Maytag trades at one-multiple-point premium to Whirlpool is that it grows faster than Whirlpool. On Wall Street we care about growth, growth, and then more growth of the future earnings stream of an enterprise. That's the major determinant of what we pay. The other reasons are quite secondary, despite what you have read or heard otherwise. Growth is the focus, the be-all, the end-all of investing, the mother's milk. Nothing trumps growth. If you understand that seeking growth, or more important, seeking *changes* in the growth rate that may be unexpected by others, is the most important factor to focus on as an investor, you will catch all the major spurts in stocks that can be had. That's because stocks move in relation to changes in growth of earnings at the underlying company. If you can predict or forecast changes in growth in the underlying company—either through management changes, or product development cycles, or changes in the competitive landscape, or through macroeconomic concerns like lower taxes or lower interest rates—you can predict big moves in a stock *before they happen.* That's what I have spent my whole life searching for, and I am living proof that these changes can be forecasted, found, and acted upon ahead of the crowd.

How is growth measured on Wall Street? To chart future growth, you have to start by looking at the pattern of earnings, particularly earnings per share, or EPS. If you pick up the annual reports, or download them online, you will discover that Maytag has been growing its earnings much faster than Whirlpool. In fact, if you do the arithmetic, or if you go to Yahoo! or TheStreet.com or any other Web site and ask for the "quote," you will also get the long-term growth of the enterprise. You will see, for example, that Maytag has been growing its earnings at 9 percent a year, while Whirlpool has been growing its earnings at 5 percent a year. Maytag has been growing its business much faster than Whirlpool. Again, Maytag trades at a higher multiple than Whirlpool, 12 to 11, because it grows its business faster. Wall Street pays a premium for high growth and awards a discount for slow growth. The multiple I have measured reflects past growth, but people on Wall Street presume that past growth can help indicate future growth, and they judge companies accordingly unless the companies make acquisitions, change management, or discover something new and different that can make them grow faster. While not always an accurate predictor of future growth, past growth is a terrific starting point for projecting a company's future growth.

For many this growth fixation seems somewhat alien, if not counterintuitive. We tend not to rate any of the other goods we buy according to how fast they grow. It isn't an ordering principle in other walks of life. We don't buy cars, for example, for how fast they go, unless we are race car drivers. Houses don't go for growth, they go for looks and convenience. We don't choose mates or friends by growth. That's another reason why everything on Wall Street is so counterintuitive: Other than college basketball coaches trying to figure out which high school athletes to recruit, growth is a metric that matters only in the stock market.

We do, however, have a concept that all of us understand in the betting world that is analogous to the multiple we pay for growth. Despite its alien terminology, the multiple is actually nothing more than "the line" as expressed in Wall Street–speak. We take the line as second nature for every bet we have ever made. Anyone who has made even the friendliest of wagers, say, on the Super Bowl, knows that you can't bet on the favorite team without having to spot the other guys something. Teams are not traded even up. Their records matter and they get factored into the price of the bet. There's a favored team and a team that's the underdog. You often have to give or take points. The multiple is our own expression on Wall Street of the spread between the winners and the losers. You have to pay a higher price for growth on Wall Street just as you expect to have to give points to the lesser team in betting on a football game. In sports, the favorite could be favored because it is better coached, has better players, is bigger, or has a history of winning. In business, a company is favored because it has more consistent growth over time. That company is favored, and the cheaper company is the underdog. Just as in wagering, you have to pay up to place a bet on a superior company on Wall Street. The cheaper company, the underdog, tends to stay cheap, just as the underdog tends to lose. Think of the lower multiple as the handicap, the discount factored into a lesser equity that makes it possibly compelling as something to wager on. But only when it gets so cheap as to make it seem that the line between the good team and the bad team is wrong does it pay to invest in the underdog.

Now, let's notch things up a bit and decide how to figure out if the line is right in stocks or whether the market's oddsmakers, all of those buyers and sellers, have created an opportunity because they might be wrong about a company's future. We know that all too often there are imperfections in the line when it comes to sports wagering. Are stocks any different? Let's figure out whether the cheaper of Maytag or Whirlpool is *too* cheap and might be worth buying. Remember, all we have done so far is figure out which one is trading for a higher multiple than the other. We have figured out which one is more expensive and determined that Maytag is one multiple point more expensive than Whirlpool because of its higher growth.

We are looking, in other words, for imperfection. Is there something about that pricing that could be wrong, either higher or lower than it should be? Unlike the supermarket, where there are scanning devices and checkers to be sure the store is selling the product for the right price, our store at Broad and Wall often misprices things. Just like in sports gambling, where we are trying to figure out where the line might be wrong, giving us too many or too few points, we have to exploit the mispricings. Again, Maytag's price-to-earnings ratio is 12 but we have calculated that it grows almost twice as fast as Whirlpool, which has an 11 multiple, or price-to-earnings ratio. I would argue that any company growing twice as fast as another in the same industry should sell at twice the price-to-earnings ratio of the other—not 9 percent higher as it is now—because growth is all that matters. So, in reality, Maytag at 12 times earnings is more of a bargain than Whirlpool at 11 times earnings, even though they are in the same business, because Maytag is doing better and growing faster. Maytag's the steal at a 12 multiple, and Whirlpool's the more perfectly priced. Therefore Whirlpool will be less likely to produce a win. The line seems "wrong" enough to buy Maytag for an investment to bet it will go higher over time, at least as it trades against its competitor. That would be my initial take if people were to call in to my radio show, for example, and ask whether Maytag is a better buy than Whirlpool. Without having any other insight, I would go with Maytag.

The line can be wrong for a million reasons in well-known competitions like MYG versus WHR. But most investors don't look for the "games" where the line is most wrong—in younger, underresearched, and little-known companies. Instead, unaware of Andy Beyer's advice to seek out lesser tracks that don't attract the best handicappers, most investors traffic in only the big races, stocks like Microsoft or Intel or IBM. These are the Kentucky Derby and the Belmont Stakes of my business, the most known and written about, where the line is almost always perfect and very little money can be made. The imperfect line happens only when you stray away from the major players, go to the lesser tracks, in this case the companies worth $2 billion and less, and particularly the $100 million to $400 million companies. These stocks are considered more "speculative" by the cognoscenti, whether it be the talking heads you see on television or the authors of the dry books about finance. Nothing could be further from reality. The most terrible speculations, as defined by their risk-reward, are the big, well-known companies. You can't possibly get a homework edge on them; almost all the news on them is already "in," or discounted. That's why I preach that your homework should focus on the less well known situations, the markets with smaller, young growth companies. Although you must accept the risks that come with less knowledge, the rewards are far greater than with the perfect lines of the established players. Betting on the favorite to win at the Kentucky Derby might ensure a victory, but at a price that doesn't make the reward worth the risk. In other words, the logic behind Andy Beyer's *Picking Winners*—out-of-the-way tracks generate outsized earnings because the line is often imperfect—is analogous to Wall Street, where the multiple is often set improperly for lesser-known, underfollowed companies.

Of course there are other details at work in evaluating companies' stocks besides the rate of growth of the corporation underneath the equity. For example, some of us might be yield-conscious. Given the fantastically low tax rate on dividends—15 percent goes to the government, you keep 85 percent—we might want to compare stocks on a yield basis. Whirlpool pays out 43¢ per share each quarter and Maytag pays out 18¢ per quarter. Again, we do our best to confuse the hell out of you on Wall Street because those two dividends are *equal!* You have to break out that fourth-grade division skill again and add in some multiplication. If you get dividends four times a year, you are getting 72¢ a share for Maytag (18¢ per share four times a year) and $1.72 for Whirlpool (4 times 43¢). You then divide that 72¢ by $27— last price—for Maytag and $1.72 by $67, Whirlpool's closing price, and you get 2.5 percent for both. Their dividends are exactly equal even though Whirlpool seems like it pays more. Again, that's because the dollar amount of the dividend isn't relevant; the yield, as expressed by the dividend divided by the price, is the apples-to-apples comparison.

So, on a dividend basis, these two stocks are equal and we can't differentiate them, although I would argue that a company growing its earnings twice as fast as another company might eventually boost its dividend at a faster pace, too.

Before investing in either company, we might examine their balance sheets. Again, when faced with a security laden with debt versus one with a clean balance sheet, I am going to favor the clean balance sheet, because when the economy turns down, too much debt can be a killer—to the equity holders. But if a fast-growing company with a great opportunity has to take down debt to finance a worthwhile investment, then the case can be made that the company's indebtedness should not be held against it in the competitive derby for your dollars. This brings us back to the price-to-earnings multiple versus that growth rate again as a way to figure out whether Maytag is a better buy than Whirlpool. With dividends equal and balance sheets roughly equal, I will still want to buy the "more expensive" stock, Maytag, because it is only fractionally more expensive (1 multiple point: 12 P/E minus 11 P/E of Whirlpool) but it is growing almost twice as fast. That's simply more compelling than the stock of Whirlpool.

On Wall Street many of the professionals, the analysts on both the buy and sell side who compare companies with one another, simply stop when they calculate the P/E and the growth rate. They make their buy/sell decisions on those ratios. They take the growth rate of Maytag, and they match it against the growth rate of the average company in the Standard & Poor's 500, the ultimate benchmark betting line. They then compare the price-to-earnings multiple of Maytag to the price-to-earnings multiple of the S&P 500. They use the same process we used to calculate Maytag's price-to-earnings ratio. They figure out the "average" multiple that all of the stocks trade at. They average all of the P/Es together, and they use that as the benchmark. Recently, the average S&P 500 stock traded at 22 times earnings. So Maytag's price-to-earnings multiple is substantially lower than the S&P average. But Maytag also grows more slowly than the average company because the average company in the S&P 500 grows at about 9 percent a year. So while Maytag is cheaper than the average company in the S&P 500, as expressed by the P/E, or price-to-earnings multiple, it deserves to be cheaper. Most Wall Streeters declare that Maytag is "fairly valued" versus the S&P index because it doesn't grow fast enough to be attractive; it is therefore not much of a bargain even if it is a bargain versus its competitor Whirlpool. If it traded at a smaller multiple and grew much faster than the average company in the index, then it would be a huge bargain. If it traded at a large premium to the multiple of the average stock but grew much slower it would be much too expensive to buy. That's the kind of calculation that highly paid, I would say overpaid, people on Wall Street make every day.

You often hear some talking head on TV say, "Maytag's expensive." That calculus is almost solely based on the exercise we just went through. If they didn't use shorthand, what these people would be say-ing is, "When you calculate the growth rate of Maytag, and the price-to-earnings ratio of Maytag, and you compare it with the average company as represented by the S&P 500's growth rate and multiple on earnings, you don't find Maytag particularly compelling." Or, to analogize back into sports and betting, the "line" on Maytag is accu-rate. There's no "steal" there, nothing that makes you feel Maytag's a great bet.

All of this makes sense in the world defined by Wall Street. But does it make sense in the real business world? Ahh, that's still another story. In the "real world" Maytag could be worth $40 a share if Electrolux de-cides it's worth that and adds Maytag to its business collection. In the real world Maytag could be worth $50 a share if General Electric de-cides it can't let Electrolux have the property. In the real world these aren't pieces of paper, they are companies that throw off cash and profits and can be used to augment the earnings of other companies. Businesses have a value to Wall Streeters and a value to Main Streeters. The Wall Streeters care about growth; the Main Streeters care about enterprise value and how much it would cost to buy the whole com-pany. Wall Street loves to be bound by simple calculations like growth rates and prices of a company. All that gibberish about "overvalued" and "undervalued" or "fully valued" comes from comparing the price-to-earnings ratio and the growth rate of the average company to the price-to-earnings ratio and growth rate of the S&P 500 index.

Go back to the example of the two sweaters at Macy's. Wall Street is addicted to finding the mispriced anomaly, the cashmere sweater that is priced the same as the poly-cotton alternative. Unfortunately, the big cap part of the market, like the mall, doesn't allow for such obvious bargains, so most goods seem "fairly" valued to most participants be-cause that cashmere item gets spotted by the millions of buyers out there and gets bought, even if it is buried in poly-cotton offerings.

Unfortunately, this kind of calculation, while intelligent and ra-tional, won't make you rich. Too many people, smarter and more knowledgeable than you, can look up these kinds of data and make these comparisons. So, while we want to understand how valuations work, we don't want to be trapped by them if we want to get rich. In fact, just the opposite: We must exploit the anomalies that this rigid arithmetical approach to investing creates every day. We don't want to invest to stay even with others; we want to invest to beat others at the contest of making money.

At one stage in my career I wanted to be an artist. I remember studying fine arts at Harvard, taking a course on modern art affectionately known as "Spots and Dots." In that class, the professor described how modern art didn't want to be bound by the four walls of the canvas, that artists like Braque and Picasso hated being bound by the canvas and actually attempted to make their art more like life itself, which is hardly two-dimensional. They placed things on the canvas to make them come alive.

I think that the analogy of modern art holds up well in the process of picking stocks, and it is one of the reasons why I regard myself as almost always able to pick out big winners among those stocks that are considered overvalued by Wall Street. While I accept the simple equation that $E \times M = P$, I refuse to be bounded by it. I want to think outside the walls of the earnings and multiple, outside the confines of simple earnings analysis to ascertain which companies are growing fast enough to own.

I run a public portfolio called ActionAlertsPLUS.com. Unlike every other commentator in the country, I don't mind showing what I am going to do beforehand so you can run ahead of me. And I love putting my money where my mouth is, which again distinguishes me from all of those talking-head reporter types who swear a vow of stock abstinence, which then makes them incapable of figuring out the process but certainly allows them to claim "honesty" in their ignorance. Frankly, I would rather be smarter and wiser and disclose my positions candidly up front than be divorced from the process. You can't be any good if you aren't a practitioner; you just don't get enough practice. You need to be in the hunt to find great stocks or you shouldn't be commenting or telling people how to do it. I know it may look to some that I am corrupt because I praise stocks I own, even though I tell you that I own them. But think about the logic of it: I champion the stocks I own because I like them enough to put my money behind them. I champion stocks I own because I think they can make me money and you money, too. By similar logic I knock stocks I don't own because I think they are too rich and you could lose money if you buy them. I try to explain this all of the time on radio and TV. Nevertheless, people confuse my motives and believe that I am picking on bad guys and pumping stocks I own so I can make more money. If only life were that simple and if only I were that powerful! You spot bargains in the store the way I spot bargains on Wall Street, except that when I buy a bargain on Wall Street I am telling others and hoping they will take advantage of it, too. (I have established rules banning myself from taking advantage of any pop I might create by freezing my actions for five days if I mention a stock on radio or TV, and I won't sell a stock for at least a month after I buy it.) I regard myself as simply an oddsmaker trying to determine when the line is absurd and wrong.

Recently, for my ActionAlertsPLUS.com account, I had one of my biggest hits ever, AT&T Wireless, which you could have shared with me, and gotten better prices than me, if you had subscribed to that site. (You get better prices because I send out an e-mail about what I am about to buy to give you a head start before I buy it.) In a matter of weeks I had a double in AT&T Wireless that was accessible to all who read me. I am not bound by the two-dimensional thinking that hamstrings all of the high-paid analysts on Wall Street. I am not constrained by the growth mantra, as measured by the price-to-earnings multiple, even though Wall Street is. I see the piece of paper that I am trading and I remember that there is a business underneath it that the paper can lay claim to as long as the business is solvent. I recognize that stocks trade and, at times, companies trade, too. The stock trades on Wall Street, but the company trades on Main Street. Some companies are so huge that they trade only on Wall Street. Those are the acquiring companies like Exxon or Microsoft or Intel or Pfizer or General Electric. They are too big in terms of their market capitalization to be taken over by anyone else. You can only trade their stock and their stock will be valued traditionally. You will always have to figure out whether the line on Pfizer or the line on GE is too expensive or too cheap to hold on to the stock. That's the best kind of analysis for stock in a company that is too big to be bought by another company. Obviously these better-known companies have more perfect pricing, and it takes a bountiful market to move them up faster than other stocks, given their size and their well-known-ness. How these stocks move up or down is discussed in a later chapter.

But when a company is even the second or third largest in an industry, then the whole shooting match, the control of the company, can trade. A takeover can occur that gives you an instantaneous win.

At the time that I issued an alert to buy AT&T Wireless, it was the third-biggest wireless company in the country. That was right before it was acquired by Cingular, a company put together by BellSouth and SBC Communications, two of the biggest landline companies out there. Before it was acquired the stock of AT&T Wireless had dropped from $32 to $6. I hated the stock in the $30s, when all of the analysts loved it because they thought the company had tremendous growth ahead of it. I thought the other companies in the wireless phone business would eat its lunch.

When the growth at AT&T Wireless faltered, in part because of poor management—something that the analysts who made the faulty estimates didn't take into account—the stock took a header. It went to the twenties, to the teens, and then to the single digits. When it got below $10, one analyst after another made the calculations we did earlier for Maytag—in other words, looked at the growth of AT&T Wireless's earnings and the price-to-earnings multiple—and decided that it was too expensive relative to the growth and the P/E of its peers and of the S&P 500. All seven of the major analysts were constrained by the growth mantra. They were considering AWE (its stock symbol) as a piece of paper, a stock, not as a company with an ongoing business.

Although I care about the apples-to-apples valuations of AWE versus the S&P 500 index and versus the other stocks of the players in the industry, just as I care about the P/Es of Maytag versus Whirlpool, I am not willing to be bound by such two-dimensional thinking when it comes to the actual enterprises the pieces of paper represent. I grew to love AT&T Wireless, the company, even as its stock was marked down by the market, because, unlike the counterintuitive thinkers on Wall Street, I actually believed the company was growing cheaper as it went down in price. No, I am not being cynical or sarcastic. As a stock price goes down, the business becomes cheaper as an enterprise, and we must never forget that ultimately these are enterprises we are trading. Wall Street loathes stocks as they come down because it thinks of them only as ratios versus the growth of earnings. I, on the other hand, love stocks as they come down, because I know the enterprise underneath may not be deteriorating as fast as the stock price. Just as in the mall, I am always trying to spot merchandise that is being marked down below its potential. Or, if we were talking about buying homes, I can see the value of a fixer-upper to someone with deep pockets even as others just think the home looks like an eyesore and has little worth. I am always on the hunt for damaged stocks where the merchandise underneath isn't that badly damaged—not damaged companies, but damaged stock prices. That's where the biggest anomalies among the established companies can be found. That's where the line is most wrong, among the visible but fallen stars.

How I came to buy AT&T Wireless, this fixer-upper of a stock, is somewhat typical of the kind of commonsense analysis that I do, that you can do, but that isn't done on Wall Street. My ten- and thirteen-year-old girls and I absolutely love the Fox show *American Idol*. We think it is tremendous that these talented youths duke it out in front of a panel of terrific judges, yet ultimately we decide who wins with our votes. Unfortunately, every time we call to vote on our faves, we get a busy signal. Every morning, I drive "the bus" to the middle school, taking my daughter and picking up kids along the way. It's the time when I find out things I should know but never did during the days when I used to go to work at my hedge fund at 3:45 a.m. so I could trade in Europe. I got tired of hearing how everyone else in the car was voting and getting through and I wasn't, so I asked one of the girls how come she didn't get discouraged by the busy signals that I kept getting. Why, she explained, she text-messaged her vote. I told her that I wanted to text-message, too, and she told me you had to have an AT&T Wireless phone to text-message.

Ah-hah, now that's a gimmick. That day at work I pulled the file on AT&T Wireless and I saw that it had a huge installed base that happened to be growing by leaps and bounds in part because of this *Idol* promotion. The "file," just so you know, was simply the current quarterly report plus the most recent news clippings I found in Factiva and the most recent Wall Street reports that I found on FirstCall, all publicly available data that once was available in real time only to the richest and largest of mutual funds and hedge funds. I wanted to buy AT&T Wireless, but I could tell that these analysts didn't know why the numbers were so strong. Not one analyst alluded to the Fox promotion that was driving so much traffic to the company, traffic that I figured would certainly stop or diminish once America's most popular TV show finished for the season. I waited until the show ended and then watched as the numbers slid and the sign-ups, overinflated by the television show that probably none of these analysts watched, dropped precipitously. I noted the decline but still did nothing because I knew that come that November (2003) the FCC would force the carriers to adopt wireless portability, meaning we could easily switch carriers without losing our phone numbers in the process. Sure enough, when November and December rolled around, the complaints about AT&T Wireless were horrible. The other carriers did much, much better.

It didn't hurt that I went to a bunch of AT&T Wireless and Verizon Wireless stores to hear the complaints about the former and the praise of the latter. That kind of research, while anecdotal, steels your resolve that you are operating in the right direction. I still do it; you can do it, too, if you have the time and inclination. It isn't must-do, but it does help to verify your thinking.

Of course, Wall Street listened too, and then began the sickening process of downgrading the stock from hold to sell, one analyst after another, as the weaker, non-*Idol*-inflated numbers collided with the poor service of AT&T Wireless sales centers during the portability switch.

But, I recognized that the brand name and the franchise weren't losing their cachet as fast as the stock was losing its valuation. It was only a matter of time before management would get fed up and realize it couldn't compete with the other players. These managements are made up of humans who make the calculation every day whether they should go it alone or cash out, succumb to others for a higher price than where their shares trade. They want to get rich, too, either short- or long-term, and if their stock isn't going up because the business isn't growing fast enough, they can elect to sell and take the money and run. As each analyst, seven in all, downgraded the stock to a sell and it fell from $9 to $6, I issued alerts saying that you should buy more. When the stock got to $6, I said double down, that this franchise wasn't nearly as damaged as the stock itself. Managements don't like looking stupid. They can and do recognize that their job is to make money for shareholders, although it takes an honest management to realize that it can make money for shareholders only by selling out. It does help, though, that management often has incentives to sell out, as was the case with the bountiful options package that was readily available for all to see in the AT&T Wireless proxy, the voting documents for the directors of the company. Remember Andy Beyer's rule number 3: Only invest in situations where you have total conviction.

What Wall Street didn't realize was that instead of being bound by the two dimensions of price-to-earnings and price-to-growth rate, there was a living, breathing entity, an actual business, that could be sold to the highest bidder. There has never been a case in history where a company that is not the first or second largest player in a five-

or six-company competition didn't succumb to a takeover by one of the other players that sought to become the premier largest player in order to take advantage of the tremendous economies of scale—for example, advertising and technology spending—that accrues to number one.

Sure enough, I had to wait only a few weeks before the initial inquiry came. And then another and another and then another again. Next thing you know, while every analyst had a sell on it, there were bidders willing to pay low double digits—all the other players out there.

Boom. Fifteen. That's right, I caught a $15 bid from $6, as the takeover war played out. The analysts caught nothing except scrambled egg on their faces.

It was all ours because we refused to be bound by the two dimensions of the canvas. How clueless was Wall Street? Even the best analyst on the stock, the Morgan Stanley fellow, who downgraded the stock at $7 on fears of wireless portability, upgraded it at $14 after the bid! How silly is that?

If you stay bound by the canvas of the stock, as the Morgan Stanley analyst did, you are always going to miss the bigger picture of the underlying entity. Wall Street cares about the growth of earnings, while businesspeople on Main Street care about the business underneath and how much it can add to their own earnings streams. That's why they will boost their own stock's worth by buying a fixer-upper.

There is no magic to pricing imperfections and finding bargains. You just have to know which streets to shop on and remember to compare the prices on Wall Street with Main Street before you buy.

4

SOME
INVESTING
BASICS

You now know how to buy stocks and how Wall Street and Main Street value merchandise. But what should you be buying and selling? What should you be owning? Should you own stocks at all? How many? For how much money? And for what purpose—for retirement, for fun, for college? How do you build your portfolio?

First, I hate one-size-fits-all answers to questions about you. We are all different, we all have different needs and different incomes, different worries and concerns. On radio, for example, I am always happy to answer questions on the relative worth of stocks, performing the exercise we just went through with the Maytag versus Whirlpool calculations. But those calculations don't help you if you don't have an investment strategy in the first place.

The most important reason why we invest, the most important reason why we will always invest, is that we don't make enough money in our day jobs to get us through the rest of life. We have to put money away, we have to save, because otherwise when we are done working and we don't have income coming in, we won't be able to afford life itself. But we also save because we know that if we can augment our incomes we can have more fun, or give more money away, or buy things that we otherwise couldn't afford. We can save to help buy a house or a car or any other large-ticket item. And we also save to give to others in our family, for our children, and for the cost of schooling.

I mention all of these obvious needs because the methods I advocate for each are different. When we are saving for retirement, that's Job One, so to speak, and we can't screw it up. The standards are higher and the risks we take are lower than for any other task because we must have money once we stop working. The other kinds of savings, because they simply augment current paychecks, don't require the conservative strategies that retirement money does.

We consider these two streams, the necessity stream (strictly for retirement) and the discretionary stream, as very different animals. Something that is right for the former could be extremely stupid for the latter. Complicating things further is the fact that we do different things and make different choices depending upon how old we are. When you are younger you can take far greater risks than when you are older because you have more time to make the money back from your paycheck. You also have more time to let the great cycle of stocks—in any twenty-year period high-quality stocks that pay dividends have outperformed all other asset classes—work for you.

Let's take the retirement stream first. It is vital that you start saving for retirement as early as possible. I had this drummed into my head, correctly, by my father, and to give you the true sense of how important it is, let me tell you a story.

Because of some reversals in my life, notably that someone—never caught—stalked me while I was a reporter living in Los Angeles two years out of college, I had the misfortune to live in my car for much of 1978 and 1979. Even though I had barely enough money to eat and pay the Allstate liability bill—I waived the collision!—I still managed to put away $1,500 toward retirement. That's how important it is to start saving early. I put the money with Fidelity and the compounding of that $1,500 would be enough for most people to live on for several years of retirement. The logic of equities through thick and thin is that powerful.

I tell people that the younger you are the more important it is that you take even bigger speculative risks with that money because even if you get wiped out you have nearly your whole working life to make it back. That's why I favor the single most aggressive strategy available, accumulation of high-growth equities either through mutual funds or through your own selection—more on that later—until you are in your thirties, coupled with a percentage of assets devoted to speculation. When you get to the thirties, I like to throttle back the risk level to stocks that pay dividends or have the prospect of paying dividends within the near future and cut back the speculation. In your forties, I like to introduce bonds into the mix. Bonds don't allow much growth of income; they are more a preservative of capital, a place to hold money with a little bit of return to be sure you have it for later. Depending upon when you need the money, I alter the equation. If you want to retire at sixty, I would put more than half of your retirement money in fixed income in your forties. If you intend to work for years after sixty, I would put much less in those placeholders. Your fifties begins the big shift toward more and more fixed income. And finally, in your sixties, unless, again, you keep working, fixed income should dominate. Your opportunities to grow your money are now limited and the reward isn't worth the risk.

I mention the example of living in my car and saving for retirement because I am such a conservative when it comes to the later years. So many people call in to my radio show and say that they want to take more risks, that they want more aggressive investments because they didn't save early. Others in their sixties want my blessing to keep the vast majority of their assets in stocks. But I never bend on this. Here's why. I recognize the vulnerability of equities and the fallibility of my own judgment. Let's wind the tape back for a second to the spring of 2000. While I sensed that equities were overvalued, had I blessed a nontraditional, nonprudent course of action—staying in equities, particularly the kind of equities people were drawn to in that era—I could have wiped out people if they overstayed their equity exposure. You never know when it is going to be the spring of 2000 again, and you can't allow your judgment to be swayed by the chance to make more money in stocks than they might allow. The desire to let it grow over time, to let the dividend and income streams come your way, is what should drive retirement investing. Only as you get closer to needing the money should your caution take hold so that you don't let a lifetime's worth of savings be wiped out by a swift downturn in the market right before you need the money.

What I tell people, though, is that for the second stream, the discretionary stream, the money not cordoned off for retirement, the money meant to augment the paycheck for other needs, the stakes are much lower. Consequently, you can take bigger chances with this portion of your assets. With discretionary investments, risks predominate and rewards can be outsized. With this stream you can and must speculate with at least a portion of your money, perhaps as much as 50 percent when younger, in your twenties, and then dropping back by 10 percent every decade, but never falling below 10 percent, if only because that's what you can afford to lose without damaging your necessity money. It is with this money that you can take chances. It is with this money that you can and should be trying to make yourself rich with some excellent outsized risks that could give you giant returns. There you can take as much chance as you would like and I will most likely bless it, as long as you follow the rules I lay out in subsequent chapters. You can put this money in the riskiest of ventures, provided you are willing to do the homework first. There I want you to seek out small-cap speculations, provided you follow my rules of good speculation. There I want the steak, the fat, the stuff you love but the traditional financial books say will be bad for your financial diet. They are dead wrong. They are as wrong as all of those doctors that pooh-poohed the Atkins diet over the years. I need you to become fascinated with the market with some of those assets of yours, the more so when you are younger. The younger you are the more speculative you can be!

That people don't routinely look at these two streams as entirely different kinds of money, so to speak, with radically different rules, drives me crazy. The mistaken conflation of the two streams leads people to be far more risky in their retirement and way too conservative in their discretionary pool choices. So, if you learn one takeaway lesson from this chapter, it is the need to think and act very differently with these two rivers of potential wealth. People who want to speculate in their retirement streams, particularly when they are older, will not get my blessing. People who *don't* speculate with their discretionary pool of capital are similarly making a huge mistake, provided they follow my rules on speculation. Mind you, this view is radical in its commonsense approach. Every other text I have read admonishes against speculation at all times. I think just the opposite. I want to build it in, provided you follow the rules of speculation, so that it is a tamed beast that can grow into something huge, then be stopped out before it can destroy your hard-earned capital.

Cramer's Law of Time and Inclination

Should you be running your 401(k)? Should you be managing your discretionary pool, or should you hand it off to others?

The federal government, in fits and starts, has made saving for retirement a priority. It has created various confusing programs such as the IRA and 401(k), allowed us to take control of the non–Social Security portion of our savings, in a tax-deferred way. The tax-deferred nature of the programs makes them imperative. If you don't have an IRA or a 401(k), by all means set one up this very minute to take advantage of the power of allowing your money to compound without your worrying how to pay the tax man. You must have a good menu of offerings to choose from and you shouldn't have to pay high fees to be in those investments.

It's terrific that we have been given control over some of our savings. But it is terrible that the government has given no instruction about how we should control it, no rules to follow, and no training about how to do it. We have all been made our own personal portfolio managers by the IRA/401(k) revolution, but we haven't been given a dime's worth of education about how to be a portfolio manager. We teach kids in junior high and high school tons of things that are completely irrelevant, but we don't educate them one whit about how to take care of their own portfolios. It's flabbergasting to me to watch my kids read and learn about the Etruscans or about the hypotenuses and the order of the planets but nothing about stocks and bonds and portfolios! It drives me up a wall! Worse, the people whom the government wants us to rely on, the people in the financial services industries, have failed us mightily in instruction. In fact, I would argue that many of them have done their best to try to keep us in the dark, to make us less effective as clients or portfolio managers so we can be more reliant on them and they can make more money. I preach this every day when I say let me be your coach, let me show you how you can be your own portfolio manager, and if I can't do that, I know I can teach you to be a better client. You have to be one or the other, though, better client or better investor. There is no alternative. So let's see which one you are.

I like to build portfolios for both discretionary money and retirement money, with the former consisting of a diversified group of stocks as well as some speculation built in, and the latter being strictly common stocks when you are younger and then gradually moving to more fixed income as you go up in years.

What determines whether you are in shape to build a portfolio? When a caller asks me for help in managing or building a portfolio, I always tell her that I won't even help until she tells me if she has the time and inclination to manage money herself in a diversified fashion. I need to know both because not everyone can be a portfolio manager; some of us are always going to need the help of others who are professionals, either because we don't have the time to do the homework, or we lack the inclination to learn how to measure companies against one another to find the bargains that make for great investments. So let's explore these two great variables—time and inclination—in the context of building a diversified portfolio to see where you fit in.

When I speak of time, I am speaking of the time to do homework on your portfolio. I will detail what the homework entails later, but suffice it to say that I think the rigors of the market demand one hour per week per stock to stay on top of it. (I have found that to keep up with all of the pieces of information publicly available for each stock, you need that much time. It is a shorthand measure, but I have clocked it over and over again and it almost always turns out to be right no matter how known or unknown the company might be.)

When I speak of inclination, I mean the desire to do the work. I believe the rudiments are so easy—you have already performed the most difficult task in calculating the multiple—that I have confidence that if you have gotten this far into this book you have the smarts to do it.

It's the inclination that trips people up. I always say that you need the same amount of time to keep up on your stocks as to keep up on your local sports teams. The problem isn't the time; it is the desire to do the work. If you don't have that natural inclination, you won't spend the hour per "team" that you need to follow. So, you have to ask yourself whether you like this stuff enough to stay on top of it. (If you don't have the time or inclination, then you need help. I explain how to get help in a later chapter, so don't get disgusted or discouraged. There are many ways to skin the investment cat.)

Now, you might have the time and the inclination to spend a couple of hours a week on your investments, which would be fine if you only had to own one or two stocks to get rich. But because of the third point, the need to diversify, you won't be able to spend just two hours a week on building your own portfolio. Diversification is the bedrock of portfolio management. Every Wednesday on *Jim Cramer's Real-Money* I play "Am I Diversified?" You dial 1-800-862-8686 and I ask you to give me your top five stocks. Then you ask, "Am I diversified?" I then play the "Hallelujah Chorus" or some funny jock jam if you are, or I give you the buzzer they use on *Jeopardy* if you aren't.

I play this simple game because diversification is the only free lunch in this whole gosh-darned business. Remember, owning stocks is a fallible process. You must never forget that these are pieces of paper. Pieces of paper can go down the drain as quickly as toilet paper if they are the wrong ones or we get into the wrong market.

That's why we have to diversify. When markets are going up, and when whole sectors are roaring, diversification seems like a huge drag. Why bother? When it is sunny, who the heck needs an umbrella or a raincoat? But when it is raining or stormy, or we get a hurricane like we had in the bear market of 2000–2003, diversification is your shelter, your virtual brick house that can't be brought down by the elements.

Diversification is also a weapon, a weapon against the malfeasance and the criminality that can engulf the investing process if we are not careful. You know how my game of "Am I Diversified?" came about? Do you know why I insist on playing it every Wednesday week in and week out? Remember the people who testified in front of Congress after the Enron debacle saying that their nest eggs were wiped out because they had kept all of their assets in Enron stock? They had all of their eggs in the Enron basket, in some cases millions of dollars in this one stock. The day that they testified, I happened to be talking on the radio about how badly I felt for these poor souls who had each lost hundreds of thousands and, in some cases, millions of dollars in Enron stock for their 401(k)s and their IRAs. My wife, the Trading Goddess, happened to be listening. She called in and let me have it. Just took me apart. She said how dare I feel bad for people who had millions of dollars and then gave it back in the market. How dare I feel bad for people who weren't smart enough to diversify and were so greedy as to not take the care to put their eggs in different baskets. I was just encouraging that kind of behavior for others when I could have been using their intellectual laziness and lack of knowledge about the value of diversification to drive home the point about how easily avoidable such heartbreak is. She was furious that I put the emphasis on the government's screwup in not catching Enron earlier. Diversification, she said, assumes that the government will screw up and not protect us. It presumes that companies' execs will at least let us down if not loot their own enterprises. When she was through with me, I said, Holy cow, I better appease the Trading Goddess and find a way to make diversification come alive on the show, pronto. So we now play "Am I Diversified?" every Wednesday, and while it may seem hokey, it works.

Diversification is not only our greatest defense against chicanery, it is also our lone defense against the fizzling out of whole companies and whole sectors. We can't afford to put too much money in any one area because that whole area could wipe out our wealth.

I know, this too seems counterintuitive. How could we not want all of our money in the hottest sectors? Why would anyone want to put money in places that aren't hot, that aren't working?

History, however, tells us how wrong that kind of thinking is. When I got in this business, I used to review portfolios that were made up entirely of oil and gas holdings because, well, it was 1982 and wasn't oil going to $100 a barrel? Those portfolios would have been wiped out by the decline in oil to $10 that happened soon afterward had I not diversified these portfolios to less "hot" areas. Similarly, in the mid-1980s, the hottest stocks by far were food stocks. The great consolidation of the food stocks was occurring at the exact same time that the entities were going global. General Foods, Kraft, and Pillsbury were soaring. These stocks were insulated from the tremendous Japanese incursion that was occurring in manufacturing. Nobody wanted Mitsubishi ketchup; these food stocks were the lone safe spot as the Japanese wiped out much of our manufacturing base. I would see people whose portfolios looked like aisles two through seven in a Safeway or an Albertsons, for heaven's sake. That presumed that food was going to stay a growth business forever. Sure enough, by the 1990s, the food stocks had become stagnant. They have now underperformed for two decades, mooting the compounding process. They are barely investible because they have so little growth. You invest in them only for takeovers, and that's not a sound investment strategy. Those who have been betting on a Campbell or a Heinz takeover for the last decade or two have suffered horribly while other enterprises have generated both large capital gains and bountiful dividends.

Of course, for the last decade all anyone wanted was technology, but we are now seeing the drawbacks of a portfolio made entirely of four or five of the great tech stalwarts of the 1990s. Owning those stocks now is like watching paint peel! Those who flee from all tech to all pharmaceuticals might have their portfolios wiped out by drug importation from Canada. Each sector at one time or another faces potential extinction. So we spread our stocks among many baskets.

While this seems counterintuitive given how much we want to be in the sectors that are in favor, we understand the hazards of concentration all too well. Would we really accept a diet, for example, that consisted only of Porterhouse, T-bone, chuck, and sirloin? Would we like a diet made up of bread, cake, pasta, and oranges? Of course not. We know how unhealthy those would be. It's the same with stocks; we need a balanced diet of stocks at all times.

For many people, though, this diversification concept slips right through their fingers. People call me and say, "Jim, I own Cisco, Dell, Intel, Microsoft, and EMC—am I diversified?" When I ask them if they are serious, they try to tell me that they think they are diversified because they own a networker, a personal computer maker, a semiconductor company, a software company, and a storage company. Heck, those stocks are as interrelated as a kneebone, shinbone, ankle bone, and footbone, for heaven's sake. These stocks all trade together.

I know that on a day when the NASDAQ, where a lot of tech lives, goes up 2 percent, you are going to feel like you are running with ankle weights if you own only one tech stock, but it is the two-ton weight on the downside we must fear, not the ankle weight when things are going well. And if you don't know the difference between these companies, if you don't know what they do for a living, then you don't have the time and inclination to do the homework necessary and you have to hand it off to a "professional." I put quotes around the word, though, because I can tell you that most "professionals" aren't much better about this stuff than you are. In fact, they amateurishly set up and run funds that claim to be diversified but are no more diversified than the mock tech portfolio I just described to you. They claim the defensive power of diversification, when, in actuality, they are faux-diversified, owning a ton of stocks that will trade as closely as if you had Super Glued them together. They know this flaw, but if they can shoot the lights out for a quarter or two, and they usually can, their marketing departments can make hay out of your money while the sun shines, and the portfolio managers are paid by the dollars they take in, not by what they make for you.

How many stocks does it take to be diversified? I have found that you have to have a minimum of five to capture true diversification and protection from the undesirable elements. It would be terrific to be able to have as many as ten positions to really ensure diversification, but then you will be bumping up against the time and inclination requirements that I have already detailed. More important, more than fifteen stocks and you have simply become your own mutual fund, something I hear about often in the portfolios people talk to me about on radio or send to me via TheStreet.com. If that's the case, if you insist on fifteen or more stocks, you might as well hand off your money to one of those mutual fund fellows, although the costs, in fees, will be prohibitive unless you select a passive model, such as an index fund, which doesn't allow the manager to trade at his own discretion and charges you a higher fee, often for nothing special at all!

For retirement, I don't want to include speculative stocks, but for the discretionary stream, one of the five choices should be speculative, and perhaps as many as two or three of the five can be speculative when you are in your twenties or early thirties and you can make back the money in the event your investment fails.

How Much Do You Need to Get Started?

Given that you need at least five stocks in the portfolio to take advantage of the free lunch of diversification, how can you build a diversified portfolio of stocks for, say, less than $2,500? That leaves each position with no more than $500 per stock, making it so you simply can't own enough of any good stock north of $10. That's no good. You run the risk of owning five highly speculative stocks in small dollar amounts, and that's not acceptable. The only way to get enough of each stock with that little money is to be in an index fund, an exchange-traded fund like a Spyder (a stock that represents the S&P 500), or a mutual fund. If that's all you do have, you would do best to skip to chapter 7, where I evaluate those offerings for you. Of course, you can still own stocks if you have less than $2,500, but you cannot be diversified, and I care too much about diversification to approve a portfolio of fewer than four high-quality stocks and one speculative investment. (When you get to that $2,500 mark one day, then you can call your own porfolio's tune.)

But if you have more than $2,500, you can easily build a diversified portfolio that can allow you to make excellent money over time. I believe that $500—five positions each for a total of $2,500—of virtually any stock is enough to start out with, provided you add to the positions over time with new money.

How do you build that portfolio? You need to find stocks that will go up faster and more consistently than other stocks. I will show you how to do the homework to find them and then how to do the homework to maintain them—remember it's buy and homework, not buy and hold, that matters. And you need to buy them right, through methods that I will also detail when I talk about how to accumulate stocks correctly and sell them right when they go wrong. Staying on top of your portfolio, pruning it correctly, selecting new positions—these are the fundaments of the process and I love teaching them. I promise you will learn to do it just as I do and that you will enjoy it as I do. So don't despair because you think right now you don't have the time and inclination. My methods, I believe, are so much fun and so compelling that maybe you will be willing to give up that one sports event or TV show or movie to focus on getting rich beyond your salary. Believe me, it is worth it like nothing else in the world.

Lately some academic studies have shown that mutual funds can diversify too heavily. Two University of Michigan professors recently quoted in the *New York Times* studied funds that were more widespread in their holdings versus others and found that these managers underperformed those with concentrated holdings, thereby contradicting long-held notions of the virtue of diversification. Indeed, it is true, if you are an active manager of other people's money, you can indeed be "too" diversified. But that's not an important consideration when you are running your own money. We need to worry about having enough stocks to be diversified because it protects us from owning one stinker that takes down our whole portfolio. But we don't want to be so diversified that we are mutual funds ourselves. That's why I think that ten to twelve positions is the maximum for hobbyist investors, but being "overly" diversified is almost never a bad thing.

What Is the "Homework"?

When I say we no longer believe in buy and hold, that we have adopted a new regime of buy and homework, what does the homework mean? People ask me this question more than any other when I tell them you need an hour a week per position that you maintain. What am I looking for? What do you need to see? What can be seen? Is the "homework" even possible, and does it assure success?

First, understand that ever since the passage of Regulation FD, a rule set up to benefit you—and to hurt the full-time professionals like I was—everything that can be seen, everything that can be known about a company without being an insider, is available to all. And, candidly, it is all you need to make the right decisions. You will never have all the information you need, but this public data will suffice.

When I first got into this business I had to spend a tremendous amount of time just trying to find current information about companies. I used to have to go to the midtown Manhattan library to read old microfiches of quarterly reports two quarters after they were filed.

Research about companies was simply nonexistent unless you were rich enough to be a client of a major firm. Given that I wanted to get rich, it was a vicious Catch-22: Only the rich could learn which companies were worth buying!

But now everything's changed. Every quarterly report is instantly downloadable from the SEC's Web site for free. Almost every research firm makes its research readily available online, either on its own site or through Multex, which is owned by Reuters. So, the public documents and research are all right in front of you. No excuses.

I also used to have to get as many as twenty local papers a day to stay on top of the companies I owned. I would have to go through each business section every day to see if there was news about the companies. Now Google or Yahoo! or Factiva make all articles everywhere instantly available for free, or for a small fee. You can go to the Web site of any local paper in America and get data on a company that otherwise was totally unavailable unless you subscribed to the hard copy of the newspaper. And this data is perhaps the single most important stream of data because good investing is often local investing. Local investing, or at least simulated local investing, that is, looking up what is said about your company in its local paper, gives you one of the best information edges you can have.

When I broke into the business, working for wealthy families and small institutions, if you did enough commission business with me I might be able to get you to see a management presentation where you could get insights on companies nobody else would get. Those closed meetings are now illegal. Every meeting where anything of any materiality is discussed is webcast, again for free. You can't know something I don't know. It's not allowed.

Further, I used to be able to call management teams and speak to high-level executives about how their business was doing, something you could never do. Now I can still make those calls, but management can't answer them. They will be fined or prosecuted for talking to anyone without talking to everyone. There is no offline insight that some have that is denied to others.

Finally, when a company reported results, it used to hold a conference call for selected institutions and shareholders to brief people about how business was during the quarter and to give projections for the future. Now they still hold the calls, but everyone has to be allowed on them. There are no closed calls anymore.

That's the good news. The bad news? You have to read every report, from the quarterlies to the annuals, you have to read every important article, you have to listen to all of the conference calls, and you have to read the analysts' reports. That's the basic homework you have to do. The calls can be up to an hour and a half in length, but they provide the best information possible. Listen to them *before* you buy, although I have almost never heard of an individual investor who listened to two or three conference calls before he bought. I would never own a stock unless I had listened first. This information is too vital.

I know that seems excessive. But you would do much more research if you were going to buy a car or a home, and yet, a stock is every bit as big an investment. All of this work can be done on the Web, so there really are no excuses.

What are you looking for? What will you learn on a conference call that you wouldn't learn otherwise? You are looking to see how a company is doing, you are trying to take the company's temperature. When companies report, you are looking for clues about how fast the company is growing as measured by sales or revenues (they are the same) or how profitable the company might be—that's the earnings per share. If your company is a young company, you are looking for fast revenue growth. If your company is older, it should have been able to figure out how to monetize that growing revenue into earnings, and then into dividends. Old-line companies should be trying to maximize the cash they take in (the cash flow) to reward shareholders. Some buy back stock, others pay dividends. Given the low tax rate on dividends now, it could be especially important to you to find stocks that do pay or can pay good dividends.

How can we tell if a company is doing better or about to grow earnings faster than we would have expected? The rate of revenue growth matters, but just as important is something called the "gross margin," or how much profitability each sale can generate. I know that this focus may seem a bit alien to you, but the simple way to look at it is to think about shopping at your supermarket. You know if you are buying a can of all-white albacore tuna for $1.40, and it cost the store $1.40 to buy the can it is selling, the store's taking a beating. If it is buying the can for $1.00 and selling it for $1.40, then it has a hefty profit margin. But if it then spends a lot of money on labor and plant and equipment and advertising to sell it to you, the business could still be a loser. And the store doesn't make it up in volume. A company has big margins when it can charge what it wants for what it makes. What determines that? Competition, cost of the items to make or procure, and the cost of doing business in general.

Some businesses are high-margin businesses because they have little competition. For example, Microsoft has little competition for Windows, save Apple Computer, so it makes a ton per Windows. In fact, it made so much that the government declared it a monopoly and tried to break it up. Intel makes a ton of money per microprocessor, almost 60 percent of the sale of each Pentium chip is profit. That's because, again, it has little competition. Utilities have no real competition, but not a lot of growth, either. Cable companies have natural monopolies, but those can be invaded by alternative methods of program delivery—satellite dishes—that can take down gross margins and destroy profitability. Some businesses, however, such as supermarkets, have tremendous competition and razor-thin margins. Other businesses, such as the basic materials businesses, can have hefty margins when their products are in short supply because there aren't enough plants making the products and then have terrible margins when the industries build too many factories. Still other businesses, such as drugs, have patent protection that gives them a hefty payout for seventeen years on new drugs but then, when the drugs go off patent, they are almost worthless to the companies. Some businesses have big profit margins only when the world's economies are booming. Those are "cyclical" concerns. Some businesses, such as farming, or road building, or military spending, or aircraft building, have big profit margins when their own business cycles catch fire. Others have profit margins regardless of the world's economies. These are called "secular" growth stories, independent of the cyclicality of economies. People will use Dove soap or drink Coca-Cola regardless of how strong or weak the economy is. People don't skip taking medicine when they are sick unless they can't afford medicine, and most developed societies won't let that happen. This secular-versus-cyclical decision, as we shall see, is at the heart of a great deal of good investing and can generate tremendous outperformance if you catch the right moment to shift or rotate between secular growth and cyclical booms.

Each business has what is known as a metric or a series of metrics that measure how it is doing versus its peers. For the cable industry, for example, the enterprise value per subscriber; for hotels, it is the average revenue per room; for airlines, it is the average revenue per seat. In retail the measurement that gives you the best thermometer reading is the same-store sales, which compares how much business a store did last year versus this year. Restaurants are measured the same way. These metrics give a true measure of growth. Total revenues, on the other hand, could be augmented by new stores that are added to the mix. For technology, the metric is the gross margin per product sold. For financials, it is the net interest margin, or how much money was made on each dollar that the bank or insurance company or savings and loan had in assets.

If you are going to buy a stock in a business, you must find out what metric or metrics are important—always pretty self-evident from reading the research—so you know how your company measures up. If you don't understand the metric that an industry measures itself by, you haven't done enough homework to buy the stock. Go back and do the work until you do know. If you can't figure it out, you have not mastered the process enough to do it yourself, or you have chosen a stock from a group that is too hard to understand and you will not make the right move when the market goes against you, which it invariably will.

Let's go back to our Maytag-versus-Whirlpool example. If we are looking at revenues and revenue growth, that's simply the price of all the washers and dryers Maytag sells times the number of units sold. Pretty easy. Given that there is nothing magical about selling washers and dryers, one can suspect that unless Maytag invents some wholly new device, its product will be heavily dependent upon how well its consumers are doing. (And, by the way, I mean wholly new and spectacular. Maytag just began offering home soda and beer machines, vending machines, a terrific line extension from its normal vending machine brand, but it would have to do ten times the business it is doing ever to budge the multiple upwards.) Maytag is hostage to the economic cycles worldwide. If it wants to grow profits, it has to find a way to make each washer and dryer more cheaply. It can't just raise the price per unit because the competition in the appliance business is too fierce. Maytag is what is known as a cyclical business, because it does well when there is a cyclical upturn in the economy. Drug stocks, on the other hand, don't need cyclical upturns to grow. We call that kind of stock a "secular" growth stock, meaning it has its own growth levered to its products. The simple way to think about this is to view the companies as products you might or might not buy. You can't afford to skip taking medicine just because it is expensive, but you can withhold purchase of a new washer or dryer if you aren't doing well. That set of calculations happens to 300 million people in this country all of the time, which is why we are willing to pay a higher multiple-to-earnings for the growth of drug stocks than we are for the growth of washer and dryer companies. One can't be deferred; one can. One has protection from competition, the other is extremely competitive. You want to buy the latter only when the "line," or multiple to earnings is so out of whack with the growth prospects that you are compensated for the vicissitudes of the consumer and the economy.

Remember, when you do the homework, you are trying to measure how the company is doing—how the company is doing versus its peers and how the company is doing versus all of the companies out there as measured by the S&P 500. While there are many components that can be measured, the main thing that your homework should identify is whether your company is growing faster than the average company. Once you can measure that—with information easily available in the management's discussion and analysis section in the public documents or even on Yahoo! Finance, TheStreet.com, or a host of other sites—you have to compare it to the average growth of the S&P 500. Then, you have to compare its P/E multiple to the P/E multiple of the average company. A bargain is a company that is growing sales and earnings faster than the average S&P 500 company but sells for a lower multiple than the average. An expensive stock is one that sells at a P/E premium to the averages but grows slower. I would almost always turn my back on a company that has the latter, but be intrigued by one that has the former.

If everyone is doing the same calculations, you might ask, how can there be any bargains? Aren't stocks perfect indicators of the future, as the academics insist? And, you might be wondering, how can you be better at this stuff at home than I can be as a professional?

First, remember the market cares more about future growth than it does about past growth, and to anticipate future growth you need insight that not everyone has. (Don't worry, I will give you my tips for how I have spotted future growth ahead of others for years.)

Second, the market's constantly throwing sales that allow you momentarily to find merchandise that is growing faster than the average company for less cost than the other company. In other words, if you are patient, and if you can keep the bat on your shoulder and let the pitch come to you, you will be able to buy stocks more cheaply than you should, which is the essence of good money management, whether it be done by pros or by you. Waiting for a company's stock to go from expensive to cheap because the market is throwing a sale may be the smartest thing you can do when you are building your portfolio. Similarly, when the market takes one of your stocks from cheap to expensive, paring back your holdings is essential so you can pick up some more of the stock when it inevitably becomes cheaper again.

Make Sure You Are Investing in Viable Companies Before You Measure Growth

Of course, it would be simple if the only thing we cared about is growth of earnings and sales. But we also have to be sure that the enterprise we are buying is financially sound. On my radio show I must refer to the balance sheet of the companies I talk about dozens of times per hour. I like companies with no debt and I don't like companies that have a lot of debt. When you have too much debt you can't pay the bills if your business runs into trouble. When you can't pay the bills, the creditors—the bond holders or the banks—take over the equity. It saddens me that so few people understand that if you just look at the "equity side"—the number of shares times the dollar price—you don't get the full enterprise picture. You must also consider the debt. A company like a Revlon or a Nortel or a Lucent looks incredibly cheap if you simply multiply the stock price times the shares. When you factor in the debt, though, it's not nearly as cheap as you think. That debt does matter. It can choke off the "healthy" business you think you are buying. Yet I must have gotten dozens of calls a week from people who owned the common stock of WorldCom or Kmart before they went bankrupt and thought they would be entitled to something. They didn't understand that they were holding a two of clubs against the bond holders' aces.

Don't be mystified by this stuff. It is easier than you think. If you are making $40,000 a year and you have payments of $40,000 a year in credit card debt and mortgages, you know you can't make it without having to file for bankruptcy. Same thing with companies. Companies present balance sheets every quarter that tell you whether they are taking in more than they are paying out in interest or not. When the companies do their conference calls, they also post their balance sheets on the Web or make them available to you so you can make judgments just as I am suggesting.

Of course, some businesses take down a lot of debt as part of their regular enterprise. Merchants take down debt in the fourth quarter so they can have lots of goods to sell at Christmas. Airlines take down a lot of debt to buy planes. Cable companies borrow a lot of money to build out cable systems.

That's fine, as long as they are taking in enough money to pay back the debt. Given that I am an extremely conservative investor, I rarely own the stock of companies that borrow a lot of money. I like companies without a lot of debt. The reason is self-evident: It is much harder to lose your money when you invest in companies that don't borrow money or are not extremely leveraged. When companies borrow money, either in the form of bank debt or a bond sale, the collateral is, well, you! Your shares. Your ownership shares. The bond bullies strip you of your ownership rights and take over the companies when things go bad. That's why you must be vigilant about doing the homework. You must be sure that you aren't investing in something that could be taken away by the bullies because they have the legal right in bankruptcy to do so. I know this seems very basic, but when things turned bad in the economy, I listened to caller after caller on my radio show who had no idea that their shares could be crushed, literally made to disappear, as the ownership of the company switched from the common-stock holders to the bond holders and the banks.

We don't study corporate finance in high school or college. We don't understand the capital structure of companies. But we do understand mortgages and credit card debt. I am sure, if you are a bank officer, that there will be situations where a heavily indebted individual, one without a good income, is a good risk for a mortgage or a MasterCard. But the odds are against it, so you most likely pass up the opportunity. Same with stocks. I am sure that my method, which favors companies without a lot of debt, is going to steer you clear of some incredibly good situations, real home runs that you will regret not owning as they go over the fence. But unless you accept that an indebted company is purely speculative and it takes up your speculative spot in a diversified portfolio, I will always tell you to say no to the investment. As I say all of the time on *Jim Cramer's RealMoney*, it takes only one really bad investment, one totally belly-up situation, to ruin your profits from all of the good stocks. And, believe me, as my old boss at Goldman Sachs, Richard Menschel, would remind me endlessly, there are no asterisks in this game. You can't say, "Well, I would have had a great year if it weren't for WorldCom," or "Without Enron, we would have made good money." Menschel drilled into my head the need to avoid the clunkers that can wreck all the good work of a diversified portfolio. Too much debt almost always crushes a company before it can make you enough money to merit the investment. Avoid the bad balance sheets, and most of the problems that befall investors will never visit you. Isn't that worth missing a one-in-ten shot that comes back from indebted hell?

In essence, the reasons you do homework are both offensive and defensive. The offensive portion is to identify companies that have the ability to grow earnings faster than the market thinks but are priced below what the market multiple is at the moment. You are trying to discover the unknown value of companies before others discover and exploit their value. You are also trying to identify whether everyone knows all that is good about your stocks and whether the company is more than fully valued versus others in the market. The defensive portion involves staying close enough to a company to see that it has fallen off the wagon and is beginning to take down more debt than it can afford. That, too, is readily obvious to those who do homework, but not to those who buy and hold. It is the latter situation that must be detected before it destroys all of the good elements of your portfolio. Remember, you have to play both defense and offense in order to turn small amounts of money into large amounts.

Before we leave the notion of homework, let me tell you what is not homework. Looking at the chart, the graphic demonstration of where a stock has gone, is not homework. It can tell you nothing. Some think it is the sole compilation of all investing thought and from it you can divine the next move. That's preposterous, and I have the tire tracks on my back to prove it, for I have been short, or have bet against, many a failed chart only to be hit by a huge takeover and a subsequent wipeout. In investing a picture is not worth a thousand words; in fact, it is worth almost nothing. A chart is *never* enough to buy a stock from. Never. Don't be conned into believing that looking at a chart can suffice for homework; it simply can't.

Similarly, the commodity "tools" that brokerage houses try to portray as proprietary and therefore somehow generating an edge for you are meaningless in the real investing firmament. When you see a brokerage ad with people talking about how the "tools" are all there to pick stocks, you should run, not walk, to another broker. There are no "tools" that generate buys and sells, just hard work and research—which tools, if anything, will obscure. The reason why these brokerage houses advertise tools is that they don't provide any real research of any value but have to try to lure you in with some pretense of specialty.

Not to praise Wall Street research too much; as I have said many times, some of my biggest gains were made betting against Wall Street research. But the one thing that Wall Street does excellently is create primers about industries that allow you to help figure out the metrics. Before I ever buy a stock in a new industry I always do my best to locate the research primers from whatever houses have written them, whether it be nanotechnology or the clothing or restaurant industries. I need the benchmarks to make educated decisions. So do you. You can use Yahoo! Finance and TheStreet.com to find them.

Once you have decided to focus on a single stock for your portfolio—for either your retirement or discretionary account—you have to figure out mentally what's the risk-reward of that particular equity. You have to make a judgment about what the market will ultimately pay for a stock using the P/E parameters outlined earlier. Risk-reward analysis defines the short-term stock picking that professionals do, and I want you to understand the motivating forces behind it. Assessing the risk is a question of assessing the downside. Assessing the reward is a question of assessing the upside. The upside and the downside are created by two different buying and selling cohorts that you must understand in order to figure out the analysis correctly. The value guys create the bottom; the growth guys create the top. Fortunately, because I am chameleonlike in nature and inherently unwilling to be anything but flexible, I understand both teams, the value team and the growth team, and I can tell you what constitutes wins and losses for each team. People are always calling my radio show and asking how I judge the risks and rewards of individual stocks. I tell them that I like to think about where the value guy will begin to buy a stock after the growth guy has given up on it, and when the growth guy will begin to sell the stock because the growth is slowing or no longer accelerating at an attractive enough level for the growth stock buyer.

I boil it down on my radio show to something quick and dirty: "Three up five down, or ten up, three down." That's because I like to know the upside and the downside before I buy so I know if I can handle the pain. But let's go through the exercise of how I judge the risk-reward in real life so you can do the same.

Recently a caller, Bob, asked me which I liked more, Rite Aid or Walgreens. He wanted my blessing to buy Rite Aid over Walgreens. I could tell that he would have vastly preferred me to recommend Rite Aid because, as is so often the case, it was simply more tempting because of its small dollar amount: Rite Aid was at $5.31 and Walgreens was roughly $30.

I told him I couldn't go there. I mentally calculated the upside and downside of both and concluded that Walgreens was the cheaper and less risky of the two and the better stock over the long term.

Here's how I did it. First, I took a look at the long-term growth rates of both companies, just as I taught you to look at Whirlpool versus Maytag. Walgreens is growing earnings at 15 percent, Rite Aid is growing earnings at 12.5 percent. WAG's growing faster than RAD. But when I calculated the price-to-earnings multiples of the two—remember that's how we figure out what's expensive and what's cheap, not by assessing the $5 that RAD trades at and the $30 that WAG trades at—I discovered that Rite Aid is trading at 40 times earnings while Walgreens is trading at 25 times earnings. Given that Walgreens earnings are growing 20 percent faster than Rite Aid's, it simply makes no sense to me—and will make no sense to the big money that controls the marginal prices of stocks—that you should be paying a huge 15-point multiple premium for Rite Aid. The upside, set by the growth buyers, won't allow Rite Aid to trade much higher. The growth buyers will, indeed, be willing to pay more than 25 times earnings for Walgreens' consistent growth, because we have seen multiples of up to 40 times earnings for long-term consistent growth, especially at a time when other companies are having a hard time growing. (That's the upper limit of what disciplined growth buyers are willing to pay. There is always someone willing to pay any price, and later on I will talk about how to game those folks, but right now we are trying to do traditional risk-reward.) Given that Walgreens is slated to earn roughly $1.30, I could see the stock trading at an upper limit of 40 times earnings, or $52 a share. That's a sharp 70 percent gain from $30 a share where the stock was when Bob called me.

Now let's consider the upside of Rite Aid. It is already trading at the ceiling of what good, disciplined growth players will pay, 40 times earnings, so I think the reward for the stock is roughly where it is selling now. It is more than fully valued by the growth guys already. No gain.

Once we have quantified the upside, as defined by the growth buyers, we have to consider the downside, where value buyers would step in to stem the decline. As I have often described, most market players care about growth, but there is a smaller, yet still very disciplined cohort that actually likes to buy stocks as proxies for the businesses underneath. These are called value buyers, and they are the potential trampolines, or at least safety nets, that will get under a stock after it disappoints and create a bottom betting that something good—takeover or turnaround—will happen to the company the stock represents, and to you if you simply buy the stock cheaply enough.

These buyers look at abstractions such as the book, or replacement value, of an enterprise, or what other companies have been willing to pay for similar entities in the same industry. Given that Walgreens is the largest drugstore company in the United States, it is unlikely that it can be taken over. So what the value buyers in a WAG would look for is a time when the stock is getting shelled, perhaps because of short-term considerations, like a missed monthly sales number or a weak Christmas, or a market sell-off in general, a time when they can get this fine grower for below its long-term growth rate. The way these folks think is, "Okay, Walgreens grows at 15 percent. If I can ever buy that stock at a P/E that is at a slight premium to that growth rate, instead of the excessive premium it sells for now, I could patiently wait until the growth-stock buyers realize what they are missing and they bid the stock up again."

Again, I expect Walgreens to earn $1.30 a share. Knowing that value guys start early and then buy as a stock goes down, I would expect the value buyers to show up at around 17 times earnings, or about $22 a share. That would put the downside of Walgreens at about $8 below the current price, which is a lot, but on a percentage basis, which is what matters, you are looking at around a 25 percent potential decline before the cushion sets in.

When will the value buyers settle in to stop a decline in Rite Aid? I expect Rite Aid to earn 26¢. Value guys would step in when the multiple is, again, at a small premium to its 12.5 percent growth rate. Using the same haircut I gave Walgreens, that would mean roughly 14 times earnings, or $3.64.

Now, let's recap the risk-reward so far: I see Walgreens as having 22 up and 8 down, a fantastic risk-reward. I see Rite Aid as having nothing up and around a buck and a half down. That's not an acceptable risk-reward ratio versus Walgreens.

Wait, it gets worse. We have only looked at the equity side of the balance sheet. I then did the balance-sheet analysis of Walgreens versus Rite Aid, which is incredibly important to let you be sure the bond bullies won't one day be in charge. The key to balance-sheet analysis, as always, is to figure out what kind of interest the company has to pay each year on its equivalent of a mortgage it might have taken out. Sure enough, Rite Aid has to pay $330 million in interest. But it only has $284 million in operating income. That's not a sustainable situation.

Walgreens, by contrast, has no debt. That means the risk-reward ratio I outlined on the equity is probably too kind to Rite Aid versus Walgreens because the value buyers might not be as tempted to start buying at $3.60 if there is a bond bully waiting in the wings to take the company away from them.

So far everything's pretty quantifiable. But I also like to factor in what I know about some other variables, variables involving the industry and the management of the two companies. These also assess future growth and help flesh out the "exact" nature of those earnings estimates that I was using to calculate multiples. They are necessary additions to the process because they inject real world concerns into an otherwise sterile arithmetic competition.

I know, for example, that the drugstore business is already "over-stored," meaning that it is a mature industry. I know that because a quick search of the articles about the industry—a necessary part of anyone's homework—shows me that many of the players in the drugstore industry have nowhere to expand. Perhaps Walgreens can move into the food business or Rite Aid the dry-cleaning business, but that's not been in their skill set so far. I also know that JC Penney is selling Eckerd to CVS, which means that the competition is about to get even tougher because CVS is, like Walgreens, an excellent outfit. I can also see from the clips that Wal-Mart says it wants to enter the drugstore market, and we know that Wal-Mart laid waste to the supermarket business when it chose to go in, so who knows what havoc the big chain can cause drugstores.

That could mean that the highly indebted player, Rite Aid, might not even be able to make it. Walgreens, with its clean balance sheet, is also known as a well-run, stable enterprise when it comes to management. There's been very little turnover during its most recent past. A quick look at Rite Aid, though, shows pretty consistent turnover—including some because of criminal prosecutions—again a real negative.

All these subjective and balance-sheet tests tell me that if anything, the $8 down/$22 up analysis I have done for Walgreens is probably conservative on the downside and the upside, whereas the downside of Rite Aid may be even greater than the buck and a half that I thought it might be, maybe as much as $2–3 more, given that no company will want to buy an indebted Rite Aid if it looks as though the company might have to declare bankruptcy because it can't pay its interest. Remember, in that situation the common stock gets wiped out, crushed. What you own will be gone.

So, it all gets translated like this: "Bob, the risk-reward of Walgreens versus Rite Aid is simply so much better that you can't afford to risk buying Rite Aid. You may have a very compelling reward with Walgreens."

Could I be wrong? Of course, there are multiple factors that are involved in the process that I haven't taken into account. Maybe Walgreens is having a better than expected quarter right now and it could be worth even more. Maybe Rite Aid could attract a takeover bid simply because lots of companies do stupid things. Maybe Wal-Mart buys Rite Aid, even though that seems unlikely because WMT is known as a disciplined buyer, and paying north of $5 for RAD is undisciplined, to say the least. There are always unknowable facts in the investment process, always, but we can't let them undermine judgment to the point that judgments can't be made. Because then we might as well put the money in the bank. For the purposes of Bob's query, I am confident that I have offered him the best judgment that can be made. Notice, Bob has made up his mind to own shares in a drugstore chain. It is not my job to talk him out of such an industry. It is simply my job to portray the risk-reward as best I can.

When I make these calculations, I am doing so only against other members of the drugstore cohort. In real life, nothing exists in a vacuum. But I would be doing the same calculus for Rite Aid versus, say, the S&P 500. I used the S&P 500 as a benchmark, not just to figure out what the whole market is doing, but also to figure out what I should pay versus individual stocks. If Rite Aid is cheaper than the S&P 500 but growing faster than the S&P 500, then indeed it is a bargain. But if it is more expensive than the S&P 500 and is growing slower than the S&P 500, then it should be a sell, not a buy.

That's the basic daily decision-making process on Wall Street. These risk-reward parameters will work for any stock and are excellent for comparing one stock to another. But how do you find out when stocks are about to embark on their runs? How do you find out, for example, if Walgreens is about to journey to $50 instead of languishing at $30? How do you find the trigger, the catalyst for such a move? And, more important, how do you find stocks that can defy traditional risk-reward parameters, situations where there could be, say, 100 points up and 10 down, or even 300 points up and 20 down? How do you find the 10×ers, the super growers, without putting too much capital at risk in the process?

How can you spot gains of all varieties, from the small 3- to 5-point gains that can be fabulously winning on an average annual return basis, to the 20-, 30-, and 50-point gains that might disappear soon after or might continue on indefinitely? That's the subject of our next chapter.

5

SPOTTING STOCK MOVES BEFORE THEY HAPPEN

What makes stocks go up and down in price in the time we own them? How can we figure out which stock is going to go up *before* it goes up? How do we figure out which stocks are going to go up the fastest so we can capture those bursts? Aren't these more important questions than whether we like the "fundamentals" of a Computer Associates or the management of a Microsoft? Aren't these the real goals we're after, not just the reshuffling of the S&P 500 deck?

I asked all of those questions during the interviews when I was trying to get a job at Goldman Sachs out of law school. People would talk to me amorphously about how high-quality stocks went higher and low-quality stocks went lower. They would relate the management of the company and the prospects of the company to the stock price and hold up examples of how the decline or advance in fundamentals always seeped into the price of the stock, either immediately or eventually. I took it all in but still was confused about how a stock pushed from 10 to 11, or fell back from 11 to 10. The so-called obvious case of the fundamentals guiding the stock's movement just didn't seem self-evident to me, and it may not seem self-evident to you. The moves, at least short-term, seem almost random, not based on the fundamentals.

Then one day, I annoyed a senior executive of the firm with my incessant questions about what causes a stock to go up a point. I just couldn't figure out how it all happened. He then called me over to his Quotron—that's what they were using then—and said, Okay, watch Stride Rite. He then hit up SRR and it showed the bid price (where the stock could be sold) and the offer price (where the stock could be bought), both of which were clustered around 7. He said to me, "You want to see a one-point gain; you want the anatomy of a one-point gain? Okay." He punched in a light on his keyboard and said, "Buy me fifty thousand Stride Rite at the market." Next thing I know the stock is tearing toward $8, careering toward it like a moth to a two-hundred-watt bulb on a hot summer evening. It was only after the exec said, "Okay, that's enough," after about 30,000 shares had been swept and the stock stopped at $7.50, that I recognized how easy it could be to move some stocks. It was the essence of supply and demand. The exec had created demand that could not be met by the sellers "on the books," so the specialist was letting the stock climb until it reached a level where sellers appeared.

Of course, most stocks aren't as illiquid, meaning there are many more sellers and buyers at all different levels, than Stride Rite had that day. But you get the idea. Demand and supply determine the minute-to-minute pricing of stocks, and if you blitz a stock with demand, unless it is one of the larger companies, unless it has more than $100 million in market capitalization, the level I think where you first get some real-time liquidity, you are going to produce your own anatomy of a one-point gain.

In the real world, the day-to-day world of stocks, there are many forces that can affect the pricing of an equity. The first and most basic is the sheer act of buying and selling a stock that doesn't have much volume. That's where we move stocks with our own buying. That won't happen very often to you as a smaller investor.

Even at the height of my firm, Cramer Berkowitz, I managed only about $450 million for a bunch of wealthy families, a pittance compared to the major mutual funds and some large hedge funds that control the marginal dollar that determines stock prices at the end of the day. I mention this to drill into your head the importance of considering supply and demand of the stock at all times. That's because way too many people get confused; they think we are trading the actual companies themselves, that the pieces of paper we are trading, investing, owning, are some sort of redemptive right, a coupon that will give you certain cents off, or an ownership right that will allow you to have a chunk of the brick and mortar if not the cash in the treasury of the joint. Untrue. These are, in the end, simply pieces of paper, to be bought, sold, or manipulated up and down by those with more capital than others. All other investment books stress the linkage between the stock and the company. Me? I stress the abject lack of short-term linkage and the opportunities that such an unconnectedness presents. While it is true that over the very, very long term—say your lifetime—stocks should indeed reflect the fundamentals, over the short term, the twelve- to eighteen-month time frame that is most applicable to most owners these days—like it or not that's how long most stocks are held—the fundamentals of the company play only a part in what moves a stock up or down. In fact, I believe the reason that so many professional managers and amateurs fail to beat the market or make big money is that they are way too hung up on the largely artificial linkage, short-term, between a company's health and the health of the stock. I think that deep down they like the linkage because it makes them feel that they aren't gambling with their money (or their clients' money). They think that if they stay focused on the fundamentals they have turned gambling into investing. I wish I could be so glib. I wish I could focus only on the company and not the stock, because it would be much easier. But it would also be much less lucrative.

Remember my litmus test: I am trying to get you to buy stocks that go up quickly, in a time frame that matters to you now, and get you to avoid stocks that go down rapidly, that could wipe you out. If I can do that I can help you become wealthy. But if I choose to ignore that short-term direction of stock, I am leaving endless amounts of easy cash on the table for others to pick up, and that's just not going to allow me to outperform others and grow wealth in time for it to be used. If we lived for hundreds of years and didn't need the money for eighty to one hundred of those years and if we were incredibly rich to start, we could overlook these short-term bull markets quite easily. Yet, to me, it is just plain unrealistic and far too paternalistic to think and act otherwise, even though the vast majority of the practitioners out there ply this pristine but impractical advice.

More important, finding out when a stock is about to have what I call a Game Breaker move requires only some knowledge of the company and much knowledge about the way stocks work as they go about the process of growing. There will be lots of stocks that we will see move up by a billion dollars or more in capitalization—a totally catchable move—without any real, discernible change in or development at the underlying company. I have seen stocks tack on $500 million in market cap simply by saying that they are now nanotechnology stocks, not just technology stocks. I have seen fortunes made by adding a ".com" to a company and fortunes made by taking a ".com" off the name of the company. In each case these were fathomable moves. Remember the diet analogy: I don't care how we catch the moves, whether it is with carrots and melon and broccoli, or whether it is with steak and bacon. I just want us to catch the darned moves. Again, I know this is heresy. No investing text advocates trying to catch these moves. No market professional wants to be affiliated with these moves because they can be short-term in nature and they resemble gambling more than "investing." But so what? If we can catch Taser or Netflix or eBay or Yahoo! while not wholeheartedly believing in them long-term, if we clearly mark them as the speculative entry in our diversified portfolio, why should we not take the dozens of points that can be offered by these situations? Why can't we snare them? Why must we be bound by, for example, a bear market in most equities if there is a bull market in some speculative enterprises that we can capture with buy-and-sell disciplines?

To me, the landscape looks like this. First, there are undiscovered companies with undervalued stocks—that's where most of the Game Breakers come from. Then there are discovered companies with undervalued stocks—that's the small-cap-to-mid-cap phenomenon, where some great gains can still be had regularly. Then there are discovered companies with fully valued stocks—that's where the vast majority of money managers play. We can make money in that cohort, but it's very difficult to make big money. I think of the gains from this segment as singles and doubles rather than home runs. Finally, there are undiscovered companies with fully valued stocks, the most dangerous sector of all for most undisciplined investors. That's where most of the speculation occurs and why most people lose money speculating. The typical uninformed speculators are buying stocks already exploited by the process of discovery. Once a stock is discovered, it is difficult for it to stay undervalued. And once a stock is fully valued, a whole new set of rules applies if you are going to make money investing.

All of these situations require disciplines: a buy discipline, which allows us to figure which quadrant we are in—for if we are in the discovered/fully valued quadrant we must be quite disciplined—and a sell discipline, which requires rigorous departures from stocks that we desire to keep.

How different are the quadrants? You need a market dislocation to buy in the discovered/fully valued segment, but you can act at will in what you will regard as a venture capitalist style in the undiscovered/undervalued segment. Each cohort is different, but none is more dangerous or risky than the other, provided you sell right in the early stages and buy right in the later.

We know that hoped-for future growth in earnings propels stocks. So, it is natural that we begin to believe that the catalyst for a big move requires a recognition that there is more growth to come than anyone knows.

What I have learned in my many years of trading and investing is that there are many different types of moves to be caught, and only some of them lend themselves to the traditional analysis that I outlined, say, in the Walgreens versus Rite Aid example. In fact, I think that the WAG vs. RAD is, in many ways, the most pedestrian, least exciting point gain to try to catch, even as it might be the easiest type to try to nab before it happens. Given my predilection for flexibility, I like to have metrics and doctrines and methodologies at hand to discover the secrets behind moves in all four groups—undiscovered/undervalued; discovered/undervalued; undiscovered/fully valued; and discovered/fully valued.

For some, these metrics might seem strange. Most stock pickers think of groups as small, medium, and large capitalization. But capitalizations can lie. Some stocks are large cap that shouldn't be. Some stocks are small cap, but not for long. If we want to make big money—the purpose of this book—the cohort that makes the most sense to look at is the undiscovered/undervalued, even as the graybeards would no doubt thumb their noses at these stocks, despite the likelihood of finding the next Starbucks or Home Depot or Comcast—all incredibly speculative at one time—among them.

Indeed, let's not kid ourselves. When you are buying the discovered stocks of discovered companies, you are simply doing handicapping and risk-reward work as we performed on Walgreens versus Rite Aid. But when you are trying to find the next Game Breaker move, you are strictly embracing speculation because, by nature, you are on unproven and subjective grounds. The earlier you move, the more your actions resemble gambling. However, as is so often the case, the earlier you pounce, the greater gain you can have. Once again, the investing that looks the least like gambling produces the most humbling returns, while the investing that seems much more like wagering produces the heftiest of returns. That's why this book not only doesn't frown on speculation, it insists that a part of your discretionary portfolio be dedicated to it.

The types of gains that can be had using this method are similar to those of another form of investing: venture capital. You place a series of bets on a bunch of long shots—that's what VCs do—and you recognize that many, sometimes even most, will not work, but that the winners will more than make up for the losers. Amazingly, because of the asymmetric nature of losses—stocks stop at zero when they go bust—the losers can't possibly wipe out more than what the winners, with their infinite potential, can make. Further, when my trading rules for speculation are adhered to rigorously, you end up with a truly bountiful combination where your winners are allowed to run and your losers are stopped out *before* they get to zero. That's because the stocks that go from unknown and undervalued to unknown and overvalued exhibit similar characteristics that we can flag in order to exit before they flame out.

Let's take the different techniques and rules I use for each cohort and discuss how you can spot the big moves in each size of stock before it happens.

I am going to give you the traditional large cap analysis first, to walk you through the way that most managers do their thinking. Given that the vast majority of conventional stock picking involves choosing among higher quality blue-chip stocks that either pay dividends or can pay dividends, I want you to be grounded in the traditional methods and type of moves that can occur.

The reasons behind traditional moves of large cap stocks can be grouped into two logical catalysts:

1. Rotational catalysts: Decisions by portfolio managers to shift from group to group depending upon the macro backdrop: weak-to-strong economy or strong-to-weak economy, as dictated by the incredibly important actions of the Federal Reserve. These catalysts involve switching between secular growth *stories* and cyclical (smokestack) blastoffs that must be captured if you are to make money in all kinds of markets.

2. Estimate revision catalysts: Given the need all managers have to try to figure out where the biggest future earnings gains are going to

come from, we must be able to detect when companies' estimates are going to rise. We have to be able to spot product cycles or demand cycles before they occur so we can profit from surging estimates.

Once you have mastered these traditional stock-picking method-ologies, I will show you how to spot undervalued stocks and undis-covered companies before others do so. That's where the biggest gains can be had. The disciplines involved in the undervalued and unknown stocks are completely different from those involving large capitaliza-tion entities. That's because most of the small caps *never* get to be big caps or even transition through to mid cap, yet they are still fertile places to look and explore and exploit.

Only after that discussion will I identify the rules you will need to trade and invest in all of these stocks correctly, as well as show you the mistakes that I have made in trying to exploit this methodology so you can learn from them.

The Secrets of Successful Large Cap Investing

As a successful hedge fund manager, running hundreds of millions of dollars of capital, I had to be sure that I could get in and out of stocks and be able to change my mind and direction without clipping huge percentages off my performance. The only stocks that allow that kind of flexibility are large capitalization stocks. As an individual, you are not so restricted. By the nature of the smaller size of your individual portfolio, you need not dwell in the house of the large cap. Neverthe-less, that is where most people feel most comfortable selecting stocks, so we need to master the ways of making as much money as possible in this cohort.

Most discovered stocks do nothing but mimic the market. They trade largely on the underlying specific businesses and on the progress of their sectors in the overall domestic and worldwide economies. In fact, for discovered stocks, I find that sector analysis and specific stock analysis each explain about 50 percent of the moves. In other words, knowing a business cold may not be as important as knowing how the sector is doing and how it performs in a given economic cycle. Whirlpool and Maytag are never going to trade like biotech companies no matter how great they are at washer and dryer making because the appliance sector only grows at about the same pace as the gross domestic product. There are a limited number of product modifications that Maytag or Whirlpool can add to spur growth before the sector overtakes and then stunts that growth. You don't have such an inhibiting course in biotech, where the drugs themselves define the limit. In other words, catching a Game Breaker move in Maytag or Whirlpool or most cyclical stories is difficult unless the world economy is growing at a huge pace, a cyclical theme such as a housing boom has ignited, or the company gets a takeover bid. But other industries, tech and biotech classically, are uniquely prone to these Game Breaker moves. I like to have a mixture of all of these kinds of situations with at least one entity, the speculative entity, where a Game Breaker move is more likely.

Sector thinking is so ingrained among the "big boys" at the mutual funds that they tend to determine the marginal prices not of businesses themselves—they don't take over anything, just the stocks—so that if you try to buy a good company in an out-of-favor sector you are most likely going to lose money until that sector comes back in favor, which will have little to do with the company's intrinsic fortunes. We call this the "best house in a bad neighborhood" thesis: No company, no matter how good, can truly transcend its sector.

I am not as concerned about sectors and companies right here, though. I am concerned about finding stocks that have catalysts, that are about to move, to put on huge point gains. All my life I've been fascinated by the ability to catch "the big move" in a stock, that spurt that makes you all the money there is to be made in a stock. Capturing that spurt was my specialty. (Remember that example of getting Gulf Oil before the takeover clearance? That is the outsized move we are trying to catch.) It is not enough to know Maytag versus Whirlpool on an earnings basis. You have to know what makes Maytag or Whirlpool break out of the range that either will most likely be trading in most of the time. You need to figure out when Maytag is going to make that move, that multi-billion-dollar market capitalization move, that makes the stock worth so much more than it is now. Figuring out that inflection point, that catalyst, knowing when a stock goes from dormancy to action, from caterpillar to butterfly, is what you've got to be able to do if your stock picking is going to yield extraordinary results, results not bound by the S&P 500 or the Dow Jones or the NASDAQ 100. If you aren't soundly beating those indices, you might as well hand off your money to the mutual funds.

Remember $E \times M = P$? That simple equation is what drives the vast majority of stocks. The E is the earnings, or more accurately, the earnings estimates of a company. The M is the multiple, what multiple of those earnings estimates people will pay for a stock. P is the price of the stock. In other words, if you know what a company could earn and you know how much people value those earnings, you will be able to figure what price the stock is selling at. I know multiplication seems pretty easy. Solving for M is as simple as dividing the price by the earnings per share. Think back to the work we did on Maytag. If Maytag is going to earn $2 a share and it sells for $30 a share, the multiple the market will pay right now is 15. So, let's take that a step further. There are only two ways a stock should be able to obtain a higher price in the market: The earnings can go up *or* someone will pay a higher multiple for those earnings. So if Maytag is going to earn $3 per share instead of $2 and the multiple stays the same, the stock should trade to $45. If you knew or could build a thesis that Maytag might be earning $3 instead of $2 and the stock was at $30, you would know you are going to make money buying that stock because it will eventually go higher when the new earnings are reported.

Unfortunately, figuring out how Maytag is going to make $3 instead of $2 is not something that can be easily done by reading the documents and looking at the business model. Think about all of the things that go into making those earnings per share. If you are going to predict that Maytag's estimates are a dollar too low, you have to know that Maytag's products are going to sell at a much better than expected level or that Maytag is going to make its products more cheaply than anyone thinks and sell them for more money than anyone thinks, or that Maytag's got some newfangled product that no one knows about that is going to make it a fortune. New product introduction, better sales, better margins—this is the stuff of higher earnings estimates, and if you can predict them, you are going to land a big win.

But what if instead of the earnings estimates changing radically, the M changes? What happens if you can figure out that the multiple is going to get bigger? Remember, if "E × M" equals the price of the stock, then we should be trying to predict when the M is going to get bigger even if the E is going to stay the same or go up just slightly. Let's say you know that Maytag's going to earn $2, etched in stone, but you believe that people should pay more for that $2 than the 15 times that they currently pay. Maybe you think Maytag should fetch 20 times earnings. That means you think the multiple is too low and should expand to a much higher level. If you are right, you could have a gigantic hit, as the stock would proceed to $40.

At Cramer Berkowitz, where I compounded at 24 percent year after year with no down years, I specialized in trying to determine whether the multiple was going to expand or contract on the same earnings. I spent most of my time trying to develop models and methods that would predict that the M would go up, often in conjunction with work that showed that the E was about to increase beyond what people expected.

I did this because it was obvious to me that if I could figure out which companies were going to beat expectations, I could get in front of large moves before they happened.

Fortunately, understanding why a multiple will expand or grow is something that anyone with common sense and a keen eye for what matters can learn to do. Unfortunately, the vast majority of people, including professionals, have no idea about why a multiple will expand and don't even think it is possible to figure this out. These people are wrong. Given that I have repeatedly managed to predict multiple expansion, I know it is not only possible, but, given the directives I am about to describe, it is actually easy.

The first reason a multiple expands and contracts is the macro concerns that have nothing specifically to do with Maytag, Alcoa, International Paper, or any discovered company with a fully valued stock. Some in the business call this "top down" thinking, meaning that if you have a view of the nation's economy—and you always have to have a view if you are going to pick stocks with any consistency before they move—you can predict the direction of the multiple.

Let's stick with Maytag for a moment, because it is, in many ways, a perfect proxy for the macro elevation of the multiple. If the economy is heating up, or, more importantly, if you believe that the economy may heat up because the Federal Reserve is going to cut interest rates—something that always stimulates the economy—you should be betting that Maytag's multiple is going to expand. So, let's say the economy is growing at 2 percent and the Fed is not happy with that growth. And let's also say that Maytag is supposed to earn $2 a share. You can bet that that multiple is going to expand above 15 with an easier Fed. Will it go to 16 or 17? Perhaps, if the Fed steps on the gas. If the Fed cuts in small increments, I think you will see people "pay up" for Maytag, or pay a heightened multiple. If you think the economy is going to expand to 5 percent growth, I think you might be looking at a $40 stock, because with that level of growth there will be buyers willing to pay 20 times earnings, because you can see a similar multiple increase in past economic expansions. You can measure that multiple simply by looking at where a stock has traded in the past and what it has earned in the past. Some of that expansion is predictable—people will now pay 20 times because by the time we get to the next year, the stock might be earning $3 in an economic expansion. They pay it now because they know that when we get to $3 the multiple will be 15 again, the average multiple of the stock, except the stock will now be substantially higher because of the E's gains. The way I look at this process is to say that the M anticipates the E, and if you can shift your portfolio toward stocks that should have a greater E when the economy is *about* to expand, you are going to find yourself riding a wave of multiple expansion to higher levels.

What if you think the economy is downshifting? Maytag's multiple will most likely collapse as it anticipates a decline from the $2 in earnings power that we thought it had. I could see the multiple go down to 10 times earnings or even 9 or 8 as it has in past slowdowns and recessions. Of course, when it gets there, when the economy slows, it might turn out that Maytag really earns only $1.25 and it is back at that same 15 times earnings. Maytag would be a "short" in such an instance. (I'll explain shorting techniques in the final chapter.) The M fluctuates in anticipation of the downshift or upshift in the broader economy.

The P/E multiple of all sectors responds to the giant macro picture, which is why it is so important to stay focused on where you think the economy is headed. Remember, I am not saying that you must have a view of the economy to own stocks, I am simply pointing out that if you don't have a view you won't be able to capture the spurts that are caused by multiple expansion or contraction. But I think the gains that can be had by this method are so significant that it is important to try to have the larger picture in the back of your mind when you are selecting stocks.

How important? I had a chart above my desk at my hedge fund at all times that showed what should be bought based on multiple expansion and what should be sold based on multiple contraction. That chart derived from the accelerations and decelerations of the economy. I call this chart, by the way, my mental "playbook" because, as in sports, it tells me which "players" to insert in the lineup, or the portfolio, when the economic circumstances demand changes. On my television show we spend a tremendous amount of time trying to divine the next two to three percentage points of GDP (gross domestic product) precisely because of the point gains that can be had through multiple expansion or contraction based on that macro performance.

My chart, which looks like a wave, shows the ebb and flow of the economy and what works and what doesn't depending upon where the waves are going. Let me walk you through this. You need to know this if only because it explains what is known as "sector rotation," the driving force behind most days of trading in and out of groups of stocks that you see. Such trading drives the shorter-term performance of everything from Avon to Zimmer Holdings.

The chart starts at −2 percent with the economy expanding back toward flat-lining; zero to 7 percent growth. That's a classic recession condition. In a recession, the Federal Reserve can be counted on to cut interest rates on the short end, where it controls them, rather dramatically, as it has done in every recession since World War II. The longer-term rates, which are not set by the Federal Reserve, also drop as the demand for money declines.

At any given time, the market is churning toward the next possible outcome. When you get to a recession, the stocks that have maximum multiple expansion—the stocks with the highest multiples—are those of companies with recession-proof earnings: the drug companies, the food companies, the soap and toothpaste companies, and the beer and soda companies. At a slowdown's depth, but *before* the Fed takes any action, these companies' stocks are prized possessions because they still deliver the E in the E × M = P equation. (The cyclical companies are missing their estimates like mad at that point in the economy.) The M expands to what is known as a "peak" multiple right at this point in the recession. So, if Procter & Gamble, the quintessential "recession-proof" company, normally sells at 20 times earnings, it might sell at as much as 25 or even 30 times earnings, depending upon how desperate the market participants are for growth at any cost.

Now, let me tell you what confounds most market players. Just when you think that P&G can't go down, just when you think that the M is going to keep expanding past where it has ever gone, that's precisely when you have to switch horses and get on the most depressed horse, the cyclical horse. No matter how many times I explain this stuff in my columns and on my radio and TV shows, it always comes as a shock to people because it seems so counterintuitive. But when I walk you through it you will see not only why it makes the most sense, but why it is incredibly easy to predict and to catch the gobs of points that come with it.

Right when you think that only P&G can deliver earnings, the Federal Reserve floods the economy with low-priced money to head off a serious downturn. Remember, the Fed can control both the printing presses of dollars—through the reserve levels it allows banks to carry—and the price of those dollars, by setting low rates for how much it costs borrowers to take down that money.

For individuals, who live and die by mortgage rates that don't fluctuate that much or by credit cards that never fluctuate, the lower rates may mean nothing. But for companies that are constantly making decisions about deploying capital, the sudden decline in rates acts as a spur to investment and demand. I have found that stocks anticipate that money spigot by about six months. In other words, when you think the Fed is about to become accommodative, to start slashing interest rates, that's when you have to leave P&G and focus on the "smokestack" companies that are cyclical in nature, companies that actually make things that are discretionary, as opposed to the necessities from P&G. Again, it always helps to think of this process in terms of stocks. So, let's take P&G versus Maytag. As the economy slows down or shrinks, the market anticipates the Fed's actions. It anticipates that what currently may look bad for Maytag and look good for P&G is going to switch. So, in my wave chart, I would have "sell PG/buy MYG" because I was anticipating that while the E for PG is going to stay steady, the M would shrink, while the E for MYG is about to get better, and the M would therefore begin to grow. That's the opportunity to make the most money in Maytag; it's also the moment when you should anticipate losing money in P&G.

Remember, I always try to distinguish Wall Street from Main

Street. In real life, business at P&G remains constant. The company doesn't do any better or worse depending upon the Fed; we just "pay up" or expand the M because we trust the E so much versus all of those cyclically dependent companies.

At Maytag, however, the lowering of rates is a big event. The stock acts accordingly and anticipates that things are going to get better.

The reason why most people don't understand this process is that right at that very moment, the shift of, say, −2 percent going to 0 percent in the economy, Maytag seems incredibly expensive. Again, the process of the market seems remarkably counterintuitive. At the bottom of the economy, Maytag, which normally might earn $2, could make, say, only $1. As that downshift occurs, Maytag's stock gets crushed. If Maytag might have been at $30 when the economy was booming, I expect it to go down to $20 when the economy rolls over. That's the multiple contraction phase at work. (Why doesn't it pay even less than that? Because in the end, Maytag, the stock, can be bought by another company, one that wants Maytag's earnings for another cycle. The intrinsic worth buoys the stock of the company. That's the AT&T Wireless example in chapter 3. Market players are so fickle and care so much about future earnings that they often forget that these pieces of paper represent real companies and those companies are sought after by other real companies if the stocks of the potential targets trade through intrinsic value.)

Because stocks anticipate the fortunes of their companies, the collapse of Maytag the stock occurs *ahead* of the collapse of Maytag the company. Unfortunately, throughout this process of decline, the analysts who follow Maytag constantly reiterate their buys of the stock saying it seems so cheap based on the past earnings or on the earnings they are predicting. This moment is the most dangerous one for you as an investor. I have seen so many individual investors get burned at this juncture because a stock will seem so tempting as it comes down because it seems "cheap on the earnings." That's because they think both the E and the M are constant and that when multiplied they should equal a higher price. The siren song goes like this: "Maytag, which will make $2, is now trading at only 12.5 times earnings; it should trade at 15 times earnings, so buy it." The analysts don't respect the power of the cycles enough.

Me, I step aside, or at my old hedge fund, I would be shorting—or betting against Maytag—furiously as I would recognize that the E would soon fall apart, making a mockery of those who are looking at the past. During this freefall period, the analysts are slashing their estimates, and with each estimate slash the stock goes still lower. The estimate slashing collectively drives even more money to the PGs and out of the MYGs as the market seeks safety of earnings and flees earnings at risk.

That keeps happening. PG keeps getting pumped up and MYG keeps getting punished until the estimates for Maytag finally reflect the reality of the company's true fortunes. Of course, that's when the analysts who have been recommending Maytag all the way down because it appears to be so "cheap" on the $2 they are expecting at last cut their estimates down to $1. Because the process of analysis as practiced on Wall Street is so flawed, the analysts downgrade the stocks. That's right, all the way down they kept reiterating their buys, saying how cheap the stock is, trapping you in Maytag for the horrible slide. But at the bottom, they cut their numbers and then they say the stock is no longer cheap—the E is cut in half, making the M look really big and expensive—and the analysts take the stock to a hold or a sell. If they don't do this, their investment policy committees will make them downgrade the stock because Maytag is now too expensive on next year's earnings versus other stocks the firm is recommending.

That's precisely the moment when I cover my short or begin to buy Maytag. At that price and after that decline, I can predict that the Fed will take action to stimulate the economy. I can also predict that the intrinsic worth of a Maytag will buoy it. I would also expect that the dividend of Maytag, which might have been not meaningful at $30, could support the stock at $20. It is true that in a really tough recession

Maytag might have to cut the dividend, but it can't cut its own intrinsic worth to another company that might want to own Maytag's business.

The reason why all of this processing seems so difficult is that with cyclical stocks, stocks hostage to the economic cycle, you must purchase them at precisely the moment when the M is highest. That's the opposite of what you do for noncyclical stocks. Noncyclical stocks must be *sold* when their M is highest.

Here's how the process plays out. As the economy downshifts, the stock of P&G goes up as market participants seek safety and pay more for P&G's earnings power. They sell Maytag because they recognize that Maytag's earnings power is too iffy. But once the economy shows significant deceleration, you have to have faith that the Fed will cut rates and start the expansion again, so you pay a super-high multiple for Maytag just when you must sell P&G at its super-high multiple. The process then works in reverse. As the economy improves, the analysts who deserted Maytag at the bottom and slashed estimates now have to take up their earnings estimates for MYG. Maytag begins to look cheaper and cheaper to them as the E is coming back in the $E \times M = P$ equation.

For me, as someone who anticipated the economy expanding, I now ride Maytag up, perhaps back to where it was, as the earnings estimates expand. During this period, one by one, the analysts come back to the stock and begin to recommend it. How do I know when to get off Maytag? I could, again, anticipate the slowdown that eventually occurs in all cyclical economies, but I have a much easier way. I sell it when all of the analysts love it again and start talking about how Maytag deserves an even higher multiple than 15 on that $2. I have captured the big move; I let others have the rest. In fact, that's when I tend to start embracing Procter & Gamble because at the top of the cycle nobody needs the safety of a PG, and its M shrinks.

So, you can see, as the wave progresses, from −2 percent to 0 percent to, say, 2 percent growth, I am riding MYG and shunning PG. As we get to where I expect the economy to peak out, 3–5 percent, I am selling MYG and starting to shift to PG. When we get to that 5 percent, I expect the Fed to put the brakes on, slowing the economy, and the process of the crushing of Maytag and the expanding of PG begins anew as PG will make its estimates despite the Fed's forced slowdown.

I don't mean to limit the discussion to Maytag and Procter. Some stocks, known as secular growth stocks, can transcend almost all cycles because they grow so fast. Yahoo!, eBay, and Amazon, for example, face few of the pressures of the Maytags or the P&Gs because they have organic growth that isn't dependent on interest rates. These kinds of stocks—which are few and far between—don't get caught in the cyclical pull. I consider them "unsinkable" against any tide, even if their growth can't last forever.

But the vast majority of stocks at these various stages in economic growth are just like men on a chess board: They advance or decline in predictable patterns that can be gamed. When I anticipate that the economy is about to reverse waves because of the Fed and go from soft to strong, I buy Dow Chemical and DuPont and I sell Coke and Pepsi. When I see the economy acting too strong I begin to anticipate the process of M compression and I lighten up on my Phelps Dodges and my Alcoas as the Fed starts tightening. Again, it will seem counterintuitive to most outsiders because at the top of the economic cycle these big cyclical companies are making money hand over fist, but you must anticipate that such profits can't last and you must jump ship when the M is the smallest, just when all those analysts are telling you how cheap things are getting.

This sector rotation is perhaps the single most difficult part of the investing process because the notion of selling cheap and buying dear is totally antithetical to the beliefs of most investors. Yet it is a total article of faith with me to the point where it will seem that I am recklessly buying the most overvalued cyclical stocks and mindlessly selling the cheapest cyclical stocks.

I love sector rotations and have gamed them for years and years. Near the top of every economic cycle I reach into what I call my fridge and medicine chest stocks, all of which have been thrown away because no one wants dowdy old Procter or General Mills or Colgate when things are booming. And just when things look most terrible I banish all that stuff that you buy at the supermarket and the drugstore and I load up on the big uglies the market gives away. That's how you let the market work for you to catch the biggest sector rotation gains.

If this method strikes you as something you could do at home, you need not be limited to individual stocks to exercise it. While I have a predilection toward individual stocks, both the sector exchange traded funds and the Fidelity sector funds can be used to move in and out ahead of sector rotations.

Let's go through the typical scenarios of the wave of the economy so you too can anticipate the ebb and flow correctly when you are picking stocks. These scenarios are preciously important for those who are trading discretionary money for big profits, but less important for those playing the twenty-year investment cycle with retirement money. The classic texts all repeatedly deemphasize these cycles, but I have talked to thousands upon thousands of investors and they all have one thing in common: They don't like to lose money even if it means that they can make it back on the next cycle.

If the economic waves are coming in, meaning the economy is getting stronger, we have to monitor the Fed as soon as the GDP growth gets above 4 percent. That kind of growth rings bells at the Fed that it is time to cool things off, that it has to tighten—even if the Fed says otherwise. Am I calling the Federal Reserve governors or the chairman liars? Not really. But the Fed's job is not to figure out this stuff for you, it is to keep prices stabilized, and the governors send out multiple false signals. Just pay attention to the growth rate and don't listen to what they say, because you know what they will do. We can forecast what they will do based on what they have done in the past. When the economy heats up you will begin to see all things financial—real estate investment trusts, savings and loans, banks, insurers, brokers, mortgage companies, and homebuilders—trade down. It is ritualistic and can't be ignored by anyone trying to make bigger money than the market it-

CYCLICAL INVESTING AND TRADING

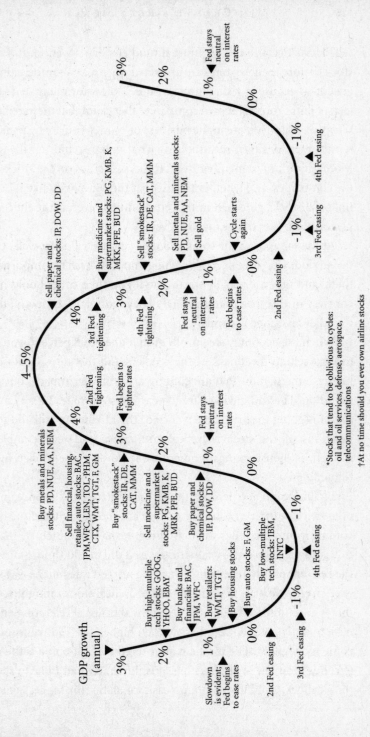

GDP growth (annual)

Slowdown is evident; Fed begins to ease rates

2nd Fed easing

3rd Fed easing

4th Fed easing

Buy high-multiple tech stocks: GOOG, YHOO, EBAY

Buy banks and financials: BAC, JPM, WFC

Buy retailers: WMT, TGT

Buy housing stocks

Buy auto stocks: F, GM

Buy low-multiple tech stocks: IBM, INTC

Fed stays neutral on interest rates

Buy paper and chemical stocks: IP, DOW, DD

Sell medicine and supermarket stocks: PG, KMB, K, MRK, PFE, BUD

Buy "smokestack" stocks: IR, DE, CAT, MMM

Fed begins to tighten rates

2nd Fed tightening

Sell financial, housing, retailer, auto stocks: BAC, JPM, WFC, LEN, TOL, PHM, CTX, WMT, TGT, F, GM

Buy metals and minerals stocks: PD, NUE, AA, NEM

3rd Fed tightening

Sell paper and chemical stocks: IP, DOW, DD

Buy medicine and supermarket stocks: PG, KMB, K, MKK, PFE, BUD

4th Fed tightening

Sell "smokestack" stocks: IR, DE, CAT, MMM

Fed stays neutral on interest rates

Sell metals and minerals stocks: PD, NUE, AA, NEM

Sell gold

Fed stays neutral on interest rates

Fed begins to ease rates

Cycle starts again

2nd Fed easing

3rd Fed easing

4th Fed easing

*Stocks that tend to be oblivious to cycles: oil and oil services, defense, aerospace, telecommunications

†At no time should you ever own airline stocks

self. That's because the big mutual fund elephants want out of these stocks before their earnings are impacted negatively—or the estimates get cut—because of rising interest rates. I know for many that's a big leap of faith. You might own companies that claim that they aren't rate sensitive. But if you are in the business of money you are by your very nature rate sensitive, regardless of what you say and tell investors. More important, remember that this book focuses on the stocks, not the companies, and whether the execs at the companies like it or not, financial stocks go down in this environment even if the businesses perform at better than expected levels.

At the same time, the techs and the cyclicals will react well during this period. The price of money, while important, isn't as important to them, and they are usually starting to fill up their order books nicely courtesy of the growth in the GDP. They "correlate" properly; this is why they are called cyclicals!

When the economy steamrolls even higher, to 5 percent, you have to start selling the stocks of the retailers and the autos because the higher interest rates that are coming are going to impact consumer spending. That drag will cause the earnings estimates to get cut and the M is going to shrink in advance of the E! You can still add to the positions of the deeper cyclical companies and tech companies, though, as their earnings momentum is slower to be broken by Fed tightenings.

By this point, at 6 percent, the Fed should have hiked once, maybe even twice or three or four times. If we are at 6 percent and the tide is coming in and the Fed is still tightening, we have to anticipate that the tide is about to go out—dramatically, as it did in 2000 and 2001 when the Fed sent us into recession by moving interest rates all the way up to 6.5 percent. We have to begin to sell the cyclical stocks and the techies that we accumulated when the economy was just accelerating and we have to anticipate that even as rates go higher, the Fed will soon become too vigilant. The moment after the third tightening is the most perilous moment in all investing. It is the time when I like to stay on the sidelines, build up maximum cash for all but the longest-dated of my portfolios (my 401[k] and my IRA), and wait. Cash, not even bonds, is king at these junctures. In fact, because the Fed is raising rates regularly at this point, the price you get for your cash, for your money that is being kept in the bank, is beginning to look attractive, especially against the dividends that won't keep up with the Fed rate hikes. Cash is king. I like to presume that after the fifth or sixth tightening, the Fed's actions will have the desired effect. That's because, with short rates so elevated, it becomes prohibitive to build up inventory of just about everything, from stocks with margin loans to copper, plastic, wood, or any other kind of inventory. The business cycle shuts down at high rates because businesses can't afford to borrow to take down merchandise to sell. They also can't afford to bet that if they order a lot of stuff to sell they will do well, because the price of that stuff increases due to inflation. It is the inventory cycle that gets busted by high rates. It always happens. It happened in 1994 and in 2000, the first time with what was known as a "soft landing," meaning that the economy braked nicely, and the second time in a hard landing, where businesses quit taking down any inventory and sales just stopped.

It's at that moment when the economy still appears to be roaring that I switch to buying the most boring consumer staple stocks, the ones that do best without economic strength, the Procters and Kimberlys and Colgates. Then, when these stocks are all at their fifty-two-week highs for several months—it does last that long—when the m's are steepest on them, you sell them, sell them hard, and buy the homebuilders, the real estate investment trusts, the brokers and insurers and the mortgage companies and even those retailers that you threw out when things got too hot. Their time on the wave is now at hand as the tidal process begins again.

For the most part, the mental playbook that I have now put on paper for you rules. The playbook is so powerful that if the big market participants even think there could be rate hikes ahead, if they even *smell* rate hikes, they are going to sell whole groups because they anticipate the decline in the economy. It is incredibly important to have a sense of where you are in the economic cycle if you are going to pick stocks even for the long term. Otherwise I predict you will get discouraged when you buy Coke and expect it to ramp up only to see Alcoa and International Paper taking off every day while Coke and other growth names languish.

These patterns are burnished into the thinking of all big-time portfolio managers; when these elephants move, they move stocks with them. To ignore their activities—especially when they are so easily predicted and anticipated—is a tremendous waste of money for all investors, short- or long-term. Given that you can set your clock to these patterns, why not take advantage of the big GDP cycles and make some good money at the expense of the elephants who simply can't help themselves. Except for takeovers, their movements are by and large the most important catalysts for large-scale moves in stocks.

The second and by far the most difficult way to predict a big move is to try to figure out possible changes in the E portion of the $E \times M = P$ equation for an individual stock away from the broader economic cycle. This is the method that the vast majority of people on Wall Street—sell side, buy side, hedge funds, mutual funds, strategists—try to live by and, predictably, it is the hardest and least rewarding. Put simply, every brilliant mind on the Street is playing in this field. It is, I am afraid, an almost Sisyphean task and not just because of the bruising competition.

For the longest time, I was able to chat with the chief financial officers of companies to see how their businesses were doing versus their competitors. With this information I was able to build models that showed me what companies might really earn versus what Wall Street thought they would earn. Sometimes I would divine that companies were going to report upside surprises, other times I could figure out when there would be shortfalls. It was never perfect because no CFO was allowed to talk to you during "quiet period" when they were within five weeks of the end of a quarter.

Still, when the companies reported their real earnings, Wall Street was surprised to the upside or the downside and I would sell my stock into the upside surprises I predicted or cover my short into the downside. There were tremendous and quick profits to be had using this method.

But several years ago the SEC decided that these private conversations should no longer be allowed between private citizens and the CFOs or the CEOs. The SEC passed a rule that said there had to be fair disclosure of data to everyone simultaneously or that no one could get it. That meant that nobody could do homework working with the company to build a better model than anyone else, and the possibility of predicting surprises with help from the company ended for all, including the sell-side analysts who used to cozy up to and have special relationships with management.

That was a bummer for me as a professional, but it has proven a boon to me as an individual investor. Now I know that no one has an edge over anyone else at least as far as what the company might tell them legally. That doesn't mean, though, you can't predict the surprises. It is just either more cerebral or more time-consuming and requires a lot more research.

For example, when I was just starting at Goldman Sachs I was able to catch a big earnings upside in Reebok simply by noticing that Reeboks didn't stay on the shelves during the aerobics boom in the 1980s. Sure, I had to go to a dozen stores and chat up salesfolk to ask, but that's still legal. You can still build a model from the ground up. It just takes a tremendous amount of time and energy to do so, too much time and energy for anyone not doing the research full-time.

Similarly, I had the greatest short of my career by staking out a couple of Gantos, a now-defunct retailer, on several key Saturdays and noticing that no one was buying. My dad and I stationed ourselves right next to the register weekend after weekend for a month at selected Gantos and tallied how much—or in this case how little—was really being purchased. I was able to predict an astounding decline in earnings as the analysts took as gospel from management that the company was doing well. Those big store registers never lie. That's still fair game, too.

But that kind of difficult and time-consuming research is beyond the abilities of most, but not all, everyday investors. The more realistic approach to gaming the E is to try to anticipate *spending* cycles, particularly capital expenditure cycles, and ride the stocks from undervalued to overvalued as it dawns on other market participants that a big earnings cycle is at hand.

For example, the airline business is notoriously cyclical, with a seven fat year, seven lean year cycle almost etched in stone. Boeing, one of America's best companies, has been fairly good at predicting cycles through its own order book. When I detect that Boeing sees a cyclical upturn, I load up on the stocks of all of the companies that make parts for Boeing, all of which tend to be through the floor at the bottom of the cycle. I buy the stocks of companies that make fasteners or screws (Fairchild) or seats (BEA Aerospace) or cockpit instruments (Honeywell) and I wait until they see the orders and then the earnings that those orders provide and then, when everyone starts touting the stocks—usually at least a year into the run—I begin to scale back the holdings and sell into strength. It's tougher than it sounds; I start to sell when all of the analysts are furiously raising estimates and the stocks are expanding by leaps and bounds. But you must sell that strength gingerly, scaling out into the strength so as not to get caught at the top. The keys are to have lean enough inventory of the merchandise when the big Wall Street store is giving it away and have enough inventory so that you have enough to sell when your wares become ultrafashionable again.

There are many big economic cycles like the one in aerospace. Semiconductor equipment cycles, for example, are long and easily playable. When the semiconductor companies begin to do well, they raise money in the public markets to buy equipment. These companies can't resist doing so. You then have to buy the stocks of Applied Material and KLA-Tencor and Kulicke & Soffa and Novellus. However, once Wall Street starts raising too much money for these equipment companies, it is time to leave the table.

My favorite cycle to play is the telco equipment cycle. Here you have an extremely competitive industry that has lean and fat years. When these big telephone companies are flush they always begin to buy equipment, and you can predict that the earnings estimates for the Nortels and the Lucents and the JDS Uniphases will soar. But when the companies start to get too competitive and the returns aren't there, or when they merge, they will cut back dramatically on equipment spending and the stocks get crushed. You can't judge these vendor companies by the managements; they almost never see it coming and have been known to blow analysts and investors out of the water regularly. You have to watch the customers themselves, the SBC Communications and the BellSouths and the Verizons and the Vodaphones and Nippon Telegraph & Telephones. When they are doing well, that's when you buy the telecom stocks. When they are doing poorly, regardless of what the vendors say, you must sell.

There are many cycles out there that are worth playing. Pharmaceutical companies are constantly introducing new drugs, some of which sell exceedingly well, boosting profits dramatically. And of course, the takeover cycle that I anticipated in the oil patch with Gulf Oil can make you a fortune if you are in a group that's about to consolidate because there are too many players. As I write in 2005 the oil cycle is very much "on," particularly for the under $1 billion equity names. You could have thrown darts at the participants in that cycle in 2004 and crush the S&P 500's return.

In these methods of predicting big moves, the multiple expansion-contraction process and the predictable sector spending cycle technique, it is the anticipation that matters. Once everyone realizes what you anticipated, it is time to take profits.

That makes investing, by the way, a much more lonely and difficult process than most people think. You have to love stocks when people hate them, you have to leave stocks when people love them. That's the most puzzling thing in the world to do because you will always feel alone and isolated. It is amazing, but those are the feelings I always have in my gut before I make the most money. Because I am so public with my ActionAlertsPLUS.com account, I am constantly selling what's hot and buying what's not, feeling the heat of the investing public telling me how wrong I am. I will know, though, that that's when the biggest gains are about to occur. The day I don't hear the cat-calls is the day I know that I have already missed the big chance for big money.

For many of you, this whole notion of catching cycles of any kind might just not be worth the effort. You simply want to own high-quality stocks all the time and you don't have the time or the inclina-tion to make the switches or play the cycles. It is too labor intensive for you. Or you find it too difficult to fathom the changes and make the calls. That's okay, you can still do fine, maybe even as well as the mar-ket, *but you will never beat the market* and you will never catch the big moves that can make you rich in a shorter time than the long-term stock cycles will allow.

So let me tell you a story that might change your mind and get you to think more about these cycles. When I started my hedge fund in 1987, I was determined to buy the most consistent growth companies I could find. I was determined to avoid the rotations, to buy and hold good-quality companies and make money over time. I figured that those growth companies would continue to increase in value over time because the market loves growth so much. Isn't that what great investing was supposed to be about? Don't heed the short term, think long-term!

After two months of running my hedge fund I found myself down 9.9 percent. Unbelievable. I was being taken apart, just annihilated by my growth stocks, like Heinz and Merck and General Mills and Coke. My partnership had a "down 10 percent" clause—I go down below 10 percent and I have to give the money back. It's pretty frightening when you are about to lose your livelihood because of your poor perfor-mance; it concentrates the mind about the cycles like nothing else.

What was working? Why, Phelps Dodge and Dow Chemical and Alcoa. These stocks were killing my stocks. I thought it was incredibly unfair given that these big metal and chemical companies didn't have real growth over the long term, certainly not any growth in excess of the rate at which the gross domestic product of the United States was growing. Their rallies seemed absurd. Didn't any of the buyers understand how they would eventually be led astray by PD and AA? Didn't people just want to buy and hold the great growth companies? Isn't that the best way to get rich?

At the time my girlfriend, Karen Backfisch, was on the trading desk of Steinhardt Partners, where every day she was taking down 500,000-share blocks of Alcoa and Phelps Dodge and Georgia Pacific and International Paper. She read me the riot act when I told her that I was sticking with my consistent growers. She explained to me that the market only likes "consistent" growth during an economic downturn or when the economy is doing nothing. Its first love affair is with "inconsistent growth" during one of its periodic explosions. She traced out a chart for me that I have been using ever since and that you can find on page 115. Put simply, when the economy is growing between 1 and 3 percent, you should own all of the Coke or Pepsi you can get. You should load up on the Pfizers and Mercks and Heinzes. When the economy is growing at a 3–6 percent clip, though, you have to own the cyclical stocks because they will have the best year-over-year comparisons. My future wife convinced me that most people who determine prices in the stock market have no real knowledge of history. They simply look at the number that is reported, and when they see PD .86 versus .38 (as in Phelps Dodge earned 86¢ this quarter versus last year when it earned 38¢), the market will go crazy for Phelps Dodge regardless of whether it will slip back to 38¢ or not by this time next year. While she was, of course, being a tad glib, to ignore these moves, to act as if you can sit out these moves, is the equivalent of saying, "You know what, I don't care if the elephants are about to trample me, I don't care if there is a stampede going on, I am just going to lie here and tough it out in these growth stocks and ignore the pain." How terrific it would be if I could tell you to do the same and you would do it.

Every single investment text I have ever read says you should ignore the thunder and just stay put in growth if not buy more. Every single one! But remember, I don't put much faith in investment conventions. I know better. I know human behavior. I know what happens in real life when you ignore the playbook, when you stick with the so-called secular growth stocks while the elephants are dancing to the cyclical tune. What happens is that you panic. You sell at the worst time, the bottom. You bail. You say, I can't take the pain. I have seen this so many times that it bugs the heck out of me to hear the arid, bloodless graybeards say, "Oh, just ride it out," knowing full well that they aren't! Riding it out is for masochists, and I don't know a lot of masochists when it comes to money. I know that back in 1987, I switched then and there to the stocks that were working and I saved my company. I never again listened to those who advocated riding out the storm in so-called high-quality stocks. Oh, and for the record, my faves never came back; many are still priced at roughly where I sold them almost twenty years ago.

Let me give you another real-life example. A caller rang me up last year during one of my radio sessions where I play "Am I Diversified?" He owned a ton of bank stocks ahead of an imminent series of tightenings. He said he had heard me preach that he should step aside, avoid the pain, that the pain doesn't always produce gain. But he couldn't because he needed the yield that the financials offered, many of which were in excess of 3.5 percent at the time. I laughed. I said, The market works in strange and positive ways. For every major bank stock yielding 3.5 percent, I know an oil stock that yields 3.5 percent. The difference is that the banks are soon going to be yielding 4 percent because those stocks are going down (remember, the dividend stays constant, but you divide it into the stock price to get the yield, and the yield goes up when the denominator—the stock price—goes down) while the oils are going to be yielding 2 percent because they are going higher! My point was that the idea of staying in the financials for the dividends is pointless given the capital depreciation ahead, but if you insisted on yield I know I could find you a like group with a like yield that will go up, not down, ahead of rates.

The Importance of the Fed

We on TV are often accused of spending too much time trying to guess and anticipate the Federal Reserve. Lots of the criticism of the press is on the mark, but the "too-much-Fed-watching" rap sure isn't. Under all the methods I care about—the GDP method, the sector earnings cycle method—the Fed can play a role, either to screw it all up or make it work.

You need to know when the Fed is going to act and which way it is going to move not only because it directly affects what the big boys are going to do, but also because interest rates can be just as important as earnings streams in trying to predict the next big gob of points on a stock.

Interest rates matter intensely when you are trying to anticipate big moves in stocks. They also matter as competition to stocks. When interest rates are high, people prefer bonds to stocks. When the cash rate, or the amount that you get to keep your money in a bank account, skyrockets because the Federal Reserve is tightening rates severely, that can kill even the best stocks. Think about what happened in 2001, when cash gave you a 6.5 percent return. That interest rate helped cause the great turn-of-the-century bear market. Rates matter as a cost of buying stocks; the lower the rates, the more speculative people tend to be because you can borrow money cheaply to buy stocks. Margin buying, using cheap money, fueled the destructive 1999 rally that led to the bear market. I can't stress how important "easy money" from the Fed was in creating the bubble that has since been pricked by none other than much higher Fed rates.

Interest rates are also a major component of what we will pay for future earnings, for the "growth" of the enterprise we are investing in. Remember the process we use to find out what a stock *should* sell for in the future, as opposed to what it sells for now? First we figure out what a company can earn. That's the estimate portion of the price. Then we need to figure out what we will pay for those estimates—the price-to-earnings multiple. To calculate the multiple we take into account all sorts of considerations for the management, the earnings cycle, the macro economy, any political or economic risk. But what often tends to matter more than anything else is calculating the "discount" rate that we will pay for those earnings, something that is entirely dependent upon prevailing longer-term interest rates. I don't want to bore you with difficult nonarithmetic concerns here, but after we arrive at what we think the earnings will be in the future, and after we consider all the sector, macro, and micro issues that could affect those earnings, we then have to figure out what they are worth in the present to figure out what the price of the equity should be now. It is not enough to know what's in the future, we need to know how to relate that to a current value. We need to know what is called the "present value" of those earnings.

Present value analysis mystifies most people. They don't understand the discount mechanism of rates, and how rates help set the current value of assets. Yet we accept the discount premise intrinsically when it comes to our bank account. Let's use that example to drive home how interest rates help set the prices now for what we will pay in the future. If you are going to put $1 in the bank at a 2 percent rate per annum, you are going to get $1.02 a year later. That $1.02 a year later is worth only $1.00 now. That's another way of saying that the present value of $1.02 a year from now is $1.00. Same with earnings. Let's say we think Maytag could earn $5 in 2010. What's that worth now? How do we discount it back to the present? By using the same prevailing rate we would use for a bond. Stocks are considered "long-dated assets," meaning they are discounting the long-term earnings power of the companies underneath them. Just as we calculate how much $1.02 in the bank is worth today by using 2 percent per annum as a rate, we would look at comparable longer-term bond yields to assess what to pay now for those future earnings.

Normally, in a stable environment where there is low inflation, we would tend to want to pay a lot for those earnings. But at times when inflation is raging and bond prices are going down—yields going higher—we want to pay much less; we want to discount those future earnings at a higher rate. Again, consider how much you would pay for Maytag this year if it were going to earn $5 a share next year, versus how much you would pay for Maytag this year if it weren't going to earn that $5 until 2010. This is the market's equivalent of a bird in the hand being worth two in the bush!

I don't want to get too technical. I don't want to slide into "Genuine Wall Street Gibberish," as I say on my radio show. For the purposes of trying to catch big moves off of changes in earnings estimates, what you need to know is that when interest rates are moving higher, the multiple you will pay for earnings shrinks. When rates are moving lower, the multiple you pay for earnings expands. Or expressed another way, when rates are going higher we will pay *less* for the future earnings and when rates are going lower we will pay *more* for future earnings. The economy ultimately determines the long-term interest rates, but the Fed controls the short rates *and* can help control inflation. When inflation runs unchecked, rates go higher, and we pay less for those earnings; we "discount" them more. When inflation runs lower, we pay more for the earnings because the discount rate will be lower.

So because of that present value factor we need to assess any signal that gives us the direction of future interest rates. How does this play out in the real market? When interest rates spiked dramatically in 2004, 1994, and 1990, the price-to-earnings multiple shrank for all stocks because that discount rate went up. When interest rates fell in 2003 we paid more for the earnings than we were willing to pay in 2004. We won't pay a lot for future earnings in a high-rate/high-inflation environment, no matter how good those near-term earnings are. In the beginning of 2004 the story was the incredible shrinking M, because the E didn't go down, but the prices did (M = P/E). People new to the game, people who didn't understand the relationship between stocks and interest rates, misinterpreted the price decline of stocks to mean that perhaps a recession was coming and that the E in the equation, the earnings estimates, wouldn't be made. That was nonsense. It was just the discounting mechanism bringing down prices and chiseling away at the multiple. I call such a contraction in the multiple the silent stock killer because so many people can't see the cause of it—higher rates—until it is too late and stock prices are obliterated. The vast majority of individuals I speak to each week on my radio show pay no attention to rates; the homicidal effect rates can have on prices continually surprises neophytes and even relatively sea- soned investors. You have to focus on interest rates if you are going to buy stocks. Or, to put it another way, rates are like the oil in a car. You don't want to bother with it, but if you don't, you know the engine goes bad. If you don't focus on interest rates as the lubricant to your portfolio, your portfolio will most surely go bad, too.

Remember, I am trying with every fiber and sinew to winnow out the stocks that have the greatest chances of losing a ton of points and focus on the stocks that have the greatest chances of gaining big. Knowing when and how aggressively the Fed will move can often be the key determinant, particularly with cyclical stocks, in assessing which equities will make you the most money in the shortest time (and keep you from losing the most money). I wish I could give you a series of indicators that would tell you when the Fed is going to move. The Fed assesses many things: the real interest rates that the market sets, the CPI (Consumer Price Index), the PPI (Producer Price Index), the price of gold, employment growth, wages. What matters if you are going to be picking stocks is that you recognize when inflation is pick- ing up. I don't like to outthink this process, but when the CPI registers four straight upward moves, I think you should expect that the Fed will have to tighten. Remember, the essence of investing is anticipa- tion. You can't wait until the Fed actually moves. You have to move ahead of the Fed if you are going to capture the maximum points. The reason is that the big mutual funds, which buy and sell stocks fairly emphatically if not recklessly, all know this stuff and own so much of each stock that they have to move well in advance of the actual deed. That's fine. We know it; we adjust accordingly.

Think of the Fed as some sort of bizarre schoolteacher who re- wards the most stupid and uncooperative students and punishes those who do the best, or, in the case of the economy, grow the fastest. Most of the time the economy, like students, is average, call it a B or a C. The Fed does nothing when things are average, virtually sits on its hands. When the economy is roaring, an A economy, the Fed gets all furious and starts using its only real instrument to slow things down, its ability to raise short rates. But the Fed rewards a D economy with joyous rate cuts, and if the economy's flunking, as ours was in 2002 after 9/11, the Fed takes rates as low as possible to get the economy moving again.

The effect on the companies is obvious. With cheaper credit companies can refinance, paying off high-interest debt, just as you might refinance your mortgage when rates decline. With cheaper debt companies can expand and hire and take down more inventory to sell at cheaper prices because it doesn't cost as much to borrow to hold inventory. That's how business gets going again. Of course, the companies are hurt when rates go higher as it may become too costly to build inventory or expand. So the Fed slows the economy when it's A rated and speeds it up when the economy's failing. But remember we aren't as interested in the specific impact of interest rates on individual companies as we are in the effect the Fed's moves have on the methods we use to predict outsized stock price moves. We care more about the perception of rising and falling of rates on future earnings than we care about what occurs to the companies, because the perception dictates the price movements.

I emphasize the Fed's actions here because if the economy were always strong, we would need to own only the stocks of the companies that were producing shoot-the-lights-out numbers. But because the Fed gets in the way all the time to slow down the economy or to speed it up when it is lagging, that shoot-the-lights-out method is a dangerous course of action. If you ignored the Fed, for example, you may have stayed fully invested well into 2001, which would have been a disaster for just about every kind of stock, but particularly for those caught in tech spending cycles, even if the textbooks said that you could still make good money in them.

If you want to minimize the Fed as a force—something you do at your own peril—you could lose unfathomable amounts of money in bad times or get blown out of the game entirely. That's why I emphasize both the Fed and these money-making cycles so much. Ignorance—and the buy-and-hold pattern it instills—is *not* bliss. It is why paying attention to your money makes it grow much faster than when you ignore it, and why you can, with some work, consistently beat the market over time.

A third method of divining big moves, an untraditional one I would like to think I have helped pioneer myself, comes from examining a different, unexploited cohort, which I call the undiscovered stocks of unknown companies. Most of the time individuals and institutions are simply trying to gauge and catch the moves of well-known companies with fully valued stocks—solving for M or solving for E, so to speak, trying to figure out the earnings or the multiple to those earnings that investors will pay—in order to gauge the ultimate objective, the price.

But what if there is no E? What if the companies are so new or so down on their luck that there are no earnings to be found, let alone earnings estimates? What if solving for E or M is impossible because E is too far away in the future? That's the case for many, many companies. Does that mean we have to give up and stay with the tried-and-true where the E and M are predictable and therefore the price somewhat logical if not perfect? Hardly. In fact, while these moves can be rewarding, as we have demonstrated above, they are dwarfed by the gains that can be had by newer companies without an E to game or an M to solve for. In fact, even after companies become discovered, their stocks can still be undervalued. We can make fabulous wine from these ignored and scorned vineyards, but we must also accept the fact that when we labor in the out-of-the-way fields we must be much more careful. We need both a buy and a sell price; we can't simply buy and forget about them. Many of these unseasoned stocks will poison our portfolios if they stay there too long.

Yet, if we don't toil in the unknown/undervalued company cohort, we are going to leave too much money on the table. Remember, they don't asterisk how fast you make the money—months, weeks, days, even hours—and they take it at the bank regardless of the velocity with which you minted it.

If my unknown company/undervalued stock terminology confuses you, it's because I don't like to use the term that Wall Street usually puts on these stocks: small capitalization stocks. I don't like to focus on small capitalization stocks; I like to focus on stocks that have a small capitalization that shouldn't be small because the companies underneath them have too much potential to be stuck with such an appellation.

My method puts a premium on identifying small capitalization stocks before they begin their journey to mid and large cap. As Willie Sutton said about robbing banks, that's where the money is.

It always amazes me that so many people accept the fact that investing in solid, well-known companies, even with the two ways we described before, produces the greatest return. It's simply counter-intuitive. The well-known companies tend to be companies with billions of dollars in market capitalization, sometimes hundreds of billions. On a percentage basis, the shuffling back and forth of stocks that are already in the S&P 500 can certainly yield rewards. However, the biggest rewards come from identifying stocks of unknown companies at the beginning of their journey, when they might be worth no more than a hundred million dollars and are undiscovered, unknown, unloved, and, most important, *uncovered* by Wall Street. These situations have the least information, the most ignorance, and the greatest potential.

This method understands and anticipates that the real value of Wall Street is its ability to promote themes and companies that need money once they catch fire. This method tries to anticipate which of the themes and sectors will be the next Game Breakers. Wall Street is fabulous at taking the seemingly mundane and making it exciting and investible. It loves new concepts that need money to grow: teen fashion, arts and crafts, big and tall, low-carb food, Mexican food, Asian food, down-home food, Indian gaming, nanotechnology, video on demand, homeland security devices, alternative energy ideas, you name it. All of these trends took many low-dollar, low-capitalization stocks on the journey from small to mid cap and, in some cases, large cap. Yet, for the most part investment professionals and amateurs alike shun this cohort as too dangerous and too speculative. Again, they consider it akin to wagering. They prefer to dwell in the vineyard of the perfect, the perfect companies with the perfect information and the perfect values. I like to dwell in the unexplored wilderness where much less is known about stocks and the information—and therefore the prices—can be wildly off the mark. They irrationally fear the losses that could come from the single-digit stocks that don't make it; they act as if stocks can go to minus something.

For the longest time, academics claimed that all stocks are priced perfectly, that there is no information edge available. You can't beat stocks, they say, so you might as well join them, perhaps through investing in an S&P 500 index fund. As you can tell, I have developed some ways to game the big moves from the discovered cohort, but I would be remiss if I told you that most investors can consistently beat the professionals within the vineyard of the known. But in the unknown cohort when the information is available, more money can be made here. Other forces, however, including crowd psychology—behavioral finance—rule this cohort. Given that we know that people inherently judge risk incorrectly, that they inherently buy at the top, that they can't restrain themselves from taking risks, particularly when they are losing, we can begin to predict patterns of behavior that can be anticipated to make you money. We know, for instance, that crowds get euphoric over certain concepts. We know that individuals are tragically overconfident when they should be underconfident, that they are swept away in ways that dwarf the efficient market and make it tremendously inefficient to the academic observer, but not to those who understand the patterns and see them over and over again. Put simply, the academics believe that the "market" will exert rational pricing on all securities, but the "market" is rational only for the thousand or so largest stocks. After that, emotions and psychology play a large role, which you can profit from. When he was explaining why short sellers who bet against the irrationalities of the market often get blown up doing so, John Maynard Keynes wrote, "Markets can remain irrational longer than you can remain solvent." I stand that logic on its head and say that irrational markets can last long enough for you to get in and make hefty profits before you have to get out. Of course, my method will seem like gambling to those who think that all stocks are perfect and all behavior is rational. All I am recommending, though, is speculating prudently—meaning taking into account the behavioral tics of other investors and exploiting those tics to your own profit.

This third method of getting in and out before markets grow rational is perhaps the single best way to make huge sums in the shortest time possible. I am confident that the academics who research behavioral finance will one day exert themselves and trump the rational/efficient folks. When that happens my techniques will be the equivalent of "fundamental" investing. In the meantime, though, let's just make the money and forget about being blessed by the Ivory Tower.

I know that I never cared about such constraints at my hedge fund. I was willing at times to put up to 20 percent of my fund into these potentially gigantic rewarders despite their lack of long-term fundamentals. I had the freedom to do so because no one was watching over me saying, "You can't make that kind of money in a Viant or a Webvan"—to name two bankrupt dot-coms—"knowing that they will eventually burn out." No one was critiquing me or my buys of stocks that were unlikely to amount to anything in the long term, but that in the interim gave you a superb return as long as you didn't overstay your welcome.

At my hedge fund I called this the search for the "red hots," the stocks that were like red-hot potatoes: you could own them for a few days, weeks, or months, but you didn't want to get stuck holding the hot potato unless you had taken your existing capital and a profit out of the situation before letting it ride.

When I started out at my hedge fund, my goal was to try to game the promotional aspects of Wall Street brokerage firms, to try to get into the heads of the analysts who would recommend stocks because they wanted the banking business of the companies underneath them or because they were hoping to attract new companies to come public with their firms. I was excellent at spotting this kind of inherent corruption that existed at all the big firms and was able to game my fair share of upgrades before they happened, a perfectly legal psyching-out of the process. But Eliot Spitzer, the New York State attorney general, ended that game when he determined that the analysts were no more honest than movie critics who are employed by the movie companies themselves. Sure, occasionally they will like movies that are good, but far more often they will push movies that are bombs because that's what they are compensated for. Of course, in the case of a movie, you shell out ten bucks for something you don't like and you can leave, big deal. But when it is your investment money, and stocks are big money, you can shell out hundreds of thousands of dollars listening to corrupt research that was meant only to please the corporate finance client. With the research departments no longer allowed to shill nakedly for their clients, the predictive value of the Wall Street promotion machine is now nil. And believe me, the research game as I knew it has changed for good. You go to jail if you violate these rules. Wall Street analysts have calculated that no amount of bonus money from corporate finance is worth going to jail for.

But that doesn't mean we can't anticipate another kind of promotion that is just as powerful, in fact, more powerful, than the corrupt Wall Street promoters. We can anticipate what the crowd wants, the chattering classes, those people who can't control themselves because they think that every idea is the next Microsoft or Amgen. We can do it because we have enough empirical data about what they like and what sells for them, what piques their interest and gets them hyping things on the Internet, so that we can be ahead of the crowd and ride the wave that they create.

These kinds of stocks are another variety of "Game Breaker." They are like supernovas, stars that shine bright for a short period of time before they explode from their own heat and gas. Game Breakers exist because the most compelling mantra of all investing is "Find the next Home Depot" or "Find the next Genentech" or Yahoo!, etc. Given the fantastic returns those famous stocks have produced, the search is logical even if in its suspension of skepticism it seems, at times, to be lacking in rigor. If we graft a buying discipline on what could look like the next big idea, the next Game Breaker, and tack on a selling discipline that cuts out the losers quickly and lets the winners run, we can make consistently good money simply piggybacking on others who are trying to find the next hot stock. We can limit our downside and, on the upside, take out our stake and then play with the house's money.

Since retiring from the hedge fund I have developed a keen sense of what could look like the next Game Breaker; I have honed the characteristics and systematized the otherwise haphazard process of culling the stocks to separate the potential diamonds from the dirt that surrounds them. This Game Breaker search tries to anticipate crowd psychology. To put it in the language of fashion, which is what this method attempts to exploit, we are trying to figure out which fads are going to sweep Wall Street and take companies' stocks up in wild excess of what would normally be expected. It is important to get into these stocks early, before they receive too much scrutiny from Wall Street, because that's when the best moves can be had.

For a new sector to get the attention necessary to be able to go from a small unknown idea to a mid cap idea with some real heft, the sector has to have what Andy Grove called "10× potential" in his excellent book *Only the Paranoid Survive.* In that book Grove postulates that there are some tremendous ideas out there, like Internet browsers, e-mail, the microprocessor—total game changers. "Technology changes all the time," Grove writes. "Most of this change is gradual: competitors deliver the next improvement, we respond, they respond in turn and so it goes. However, every once in a while, technology changes in a dramatic way. Something can be done that could not be done before, or something can be done 10× better, faster or cheaper than it would have been done before." These "strategic inflection points" don't have to be limited to technology, Grove says. They can revolutionize everything from the movies (silent to talkies) to phone companies (the creation of competitive phone companies through government deregulation being a classic example). The trick for Grove was to recognize that these changes could come from left field and then learn how to anticipate them. The trick for us is to play in left field and see the ball better and earlier than others.

Of course, there are lots of ideas out there that aspire to be 10× ideas that never get there, but my method builds in those losses and accepts them. My method exploits the crowd's inability to distinguish a 10× idea from a lot of ideas that just fizzle and gets you in and out before the fizzling starts.

Let's take one of the more current fixations, nanotechnology, a science of manipulating small particles to make new compounds. Of course, the cynical trader in me says that this is simply the science of manipulating stocks so that more can be formed and bigger underwriting profits can be accrued. As is typical with the stocks of an unknown but exciting new sector, almost anything "nano" will get taken up. The trick is to figure out ahead of time what would have the most credibility if it were rewarded with a market capitalization that might be attractive to Wall Street, which typically doesn't want to touch anything smaller than a billion dollars in market cap.

In the initial stages, I examine which companies have a modicum of revenues, decent bloodlines when it comes to managements, and scientific prospects that sound somewhat legitimate. I do that by reading trade journals, newspaper and magazine articles, and academic studies on what might be working and what isn't. Typically there are a host of these kinds of stocks, many selling below $10. I like to place bets on "the field," meaning that I don't know which stocks will ultimately gain the most credence. To me this process resembles what venture capitalists do, except with odds slightly better for me because there is a ready public exit market whenever I need it for the losers, while the winners can more than make up for the losers. Venture capitalists ride the bad ones to zero; we can bail out whenever we realize they aren't going to fulfill the $10\times$ potential.

If the venture capital analogy loses you, try this one: It's like fishing in a school of bluefish; it's impossible not to catch something when you are in the frenzied field. You've got to get that hook, line, and sinker in the water when a group like nanotechnology bites. You must seize it if you want to rack up big percentage gains in a remarkably short period of time, which is always what I am shooting for when I buy stocks.

Using the example of nanotechnology, to get the players for the field bet, I simply do a Google search for the companies involved, then find out which are public and examine their bona fides as described above. If I am early enough—judged by whether any major Wall Street firm yet covers the group—I pounce. If there is a lot of coverage of the group, particularly by the main firms based in New York, not just the regional firms from the hinterlands, I skip it. Major coverage means I am already too late to the party. The idea's been fully exploited.

Typically, if the science is sexy enough, or the demand strong enough, you can easily anticipate the group gaining steam. You see the trading volume of the stocks pick up, you see the chatter on the stock boards pick up, particularly the Yahoo! boards where my assistants trawl for comments, and you start seeing the more inventive Web sites, like TheStreet.com, writing up the ideas.

As soon as the companies in the cohort get some critical mass, the investment bankers at the regional brokers—not the ones in New York; that happens later—prowl the country and the world for companies that look like nanotechnology companies they can take public or write up with the hopes of getting some of their business down the road.

As stupid and as knee-jerk as this sounds, it is important at this moment to own as many nanotechnology stocks as you can because even the currently hobbled and uncorrupted Wall Street promotion machine can still be effective in moving stocks up when there are compelling technologies and big dollars on the line.

I continue to accumulate the stocks until the analysts at the major firms start their promotion and I stay long the group, that is, I hold these stocks, until the group is fished out, producing some of the best gains imaginable. How do you know when the group is fished out, that is, that the big gains have been made, when you can't trust the multiple process to yield any limits given that the group tends to have no E to put an M on? I let the Street's greed—almost as good a yardstick as its myopia in measuring stocks on earnings growth—tell me when to get out. During the expansion/frenzy process, the merchandise gets created at a fast and furious pace. Underwriting after underwriting occurs as the group goes higher and higher.

I can always tell when the frenzy's about to crash, though, by measuring supply and demand. Right near the absolute top—it's too difficult to call the exact top, and I have done that only once in my life, on March 15, 2000—the underwritings, all of which were fantastic to participate in, begin to fail. Merchandise that was considered "hot," meaning that it went to a premium almost immediately after it was launched, begins to sag. Deals open up and then slip to or below their deal prices. Secondaries—offerings of stocks already public—begin to pop up like mad as insiders, who can sell on those deals but couldn't sell previously because they were locked up on the initial public offerings—dump their shares. The secondaries don't stop despite the hammering they do to the stocks because the insiders know the pieces of paper are incredibly overvalued and want to get out.

At the exact top of the dot-com bubble, for example, every deal, every piece of merchandise, started failing or dropping below the level at which it was priced. None of the deals was working. That was the signal to get out. Supply had overwhelmed demand.

I have gotten into trouble with the intelligentsia and the pundits of the stock world because I tend to press the envelope of these stocks as aggressively as possible right to the very end of when you can still make money. I do that because that's when the gains are most mighty, as short sellers, who are always too eager to sell overvalued merchandise, short and then cover the stocks higher because the pain of short-ing them is too great.

I take heat because it looks like I am recommending and buying the most overvalued stocks in the world relative to the companies un-derneath. But as I have stated over and over again, there is a world of difference between the companies and the pieces of paper that trade on behalf of them, and the biggest money is made exploiting those differences at crucial times. In fact, the rate of return of playing this promotion game, particularly if you can catch it *before* it starts, when you have undervalued stocks of unknown companies, is the single most lucrative game that can be played with the market. The purists hate this and hate to admit that the percentage gains from these levels dwarf any other in the investment process; heck, they think it is pure gambling! Again, I point out that if you are willing to speculate pru-dently, with rules, and obey the sell discipline, you should not care if the companies of the stock you buy ultimately ever amount to a hill of beans. They probably won't. Who cares? You will have made so much money exploiting potentially worthless pieces of paper that what hap-pens to the companies is irrelevant. You simply need to be able to see the world through the eyes of the optimists and recognize what they are willing to embrace without any skepticism. At the same time you must combine that rose-colored-glasses approach with the cunning and rigor that will allow you to anticipate when the jig is up, and many—but not all—of the companies are exposed as frauds or jokes. You can ride the 10× wave as long as you get out before it crashes, or before it is clear that only a handful of real companies is going to ben-efit. That's right—some companies actually do turn out to be the next Microsofts and Home Depots, and with my buy-sell discipline de-scribed later, you should still be able to hold on to some stock after taking profits off the table. You could end up with a portfolio of Yahoo!, eBay, and Amazon, as I did at my hedge fund, playing with the house's money while I shorted the junk mercilessly into the single digits.

It is at the moment when these kinds of stocks with no earnings look like they are going to infinity that the merchandise from all of the crummy and ersatz companies bulges from the woodwork and you have to scram as fast as you can. You have to be prepared to love the stocks at one moment and leave them unmercifully the next. You may have to flip on a dime; flexibility is everything when you trade these kinds of names.

How spectacular can the gains be if you initially suspend the skepticism and accept the possibilities out there? How fantastic can the gains be if you find the unknown and undervalued stocks ahead of others, simply because you are willing to accept that there might be a 10× idea out there? How much money can you make anticipating that something will be adopted by the masses as a potential 10×er? Remember, potential is all you need because with my sell discipline, I promise you will get out ahead of when the cataclysm strikes, or at least be playing with the house's money.

Consider the two charts on pages 141 and 142. The first one shows some spectacular moves I was able to anticipate at my hedge fund and in my writings over the course of the last decade, along with the duration of those moves and the gains that could have been had by the nimble in an amazingly short time. The second chart is the original list of companies I put together at the dawn of the dot-com period simply by reading the prospectuses at the time and trying to figure out who would be regarded as the providers of the picks and axes for the Internet gold rush. In that case, I and a partner, Matt Jacobs, who ran my research department at Cramer, actually created a rotisserie league—yep, like in baseball or football—where we had a mythical pool of money and had to draft players for the team. While we were drafting, the stocks were going up so fast that we quickly changed it to real dollars and were able to make a fantastic rate of return in an incredibly short period.

You can see how you would have done in like periods investing in the S&P 500, the perfect proxy for the stocks out there. The S&P doesn't come near these stocks. The gains on these speculative stocks

The Original Red Hots and the Gains They Made

Stock Symbol	8/30 1999	Share Price on Date 11/30 1999	2/29 2000	5/31 2000	Increase or Decrease in Share Price After 3 Months	6 Months	9 Months
ARBA	267.5	361.1248	1058	417	35%	296%	56%
BRCD	179.5	289.9376	578.2504	471.7504	62%	222%	163%
BRCM	125.3126	179.0626	394.75	260.125	43%	215%	108%
CMTN	3015.625	2085.9375	4346.875	4178.125	−31%	44%	39%
CNXT	371.9604	607.4418	1007.278	385.7364	63%	171%	4%
EXDSQ	19.0313	26.9531	71.1875	35.2813	42%	274%	85%
EXTR	65.625	66.375	111.25	48.875	1%	70%	−26%
JDSU	211.4376	457.5	1054.5	704	116%	399%	233%
JNPR	210.0624	277.125	822.9378	525.5628	32%	292%	150%
NTOP	72.625	58	57.875	29.5	−20%	−20%	−59%
OPWV	1072.125	2610	2513.25	1258.875	143%	134%	17%
PMCS	94.5	103.0626	386.125	306.5	9%	309%	224%
QCOM	183	362.3124	569.75	265.5	98%	211%	45%
QLGC	174	226.25	624	196.5	30%	259%	13%
RBAKQ	56.25	69.9688	149.25	83.875	24%	165%	49%
RHAT	75.5626	210	121.375	32.125	178%	61%	−57%
SPX	1324	1388	1366	1420	5%	3%	7%
VRSN	105.375	185.8126	506	270.75	76%	380%	157%
ZOOXQ	89.75	79	66.25	26.625	−12%	−26%	−70%

are so magnificent that you would have to be crazy not to want to try to get some and lock them in. You get in, you get out, and you sit in cash until the next wave appears. Mind you, this is not backdated stuff like so many huge gains that advisers brag to you that you *could* have had if you had used their service. These are gains that were had! I actually owned and recommended these stocks to others in the electronic pages of RealMoney.com. I simply got out in time, although at the moment I pulled the sell trigger, the move looked incredibly foolish if not actually traitorous to the cause. I took tremendous heat

The New Crop of Red Hots

Stock Symbol	Start Date	Start Price	Finish Date	Finish Price	% Gain	S&P Gain Same Period
BLTI	12/02	$5.00	1/04	$21.29	326%	31.58%
CHINA	10/02	$2.00	7/03	$14.46	623%	30.58%
CPHD	11/03	$5.00	1/04	$13.21	164%	7.42%
DNA	11/99	$160.00	3/00	$469.00	193%	−0.40%
EGHT	10/03	$2.50	11/03	$7.52	201%	4.24%
FARO	1/03	$2.00	1/04	$33.23	1562%	25.70%
FWHT	10/02	$3.50	9/03	$27.27	679%	30.69%
HLYW	4/01	$1.80	6/02	$20.68	1049%	−8.74%
ICOS	3/03	$15.00	6/03	$45.17	201%	24.69%
IOM	1/95	$6.00	5/96	$324.00	5300%	45.92%
MACE	4/04	$2.20	4/04	$10.15	361%	−1.79%
MAMA	2/04	$4.00	4/04	$15.90	298%	−0.25%
MICC	3/03	$1.25	4/04	$27.80	2124%	2.92%
SCHN	12/02	$15.00	1/04	$124.56	730%	24.79%
SINA	10/02	$3.00	9/03	$43.57	1352%	28.58%
SIRI	12/99	$26.00	3/00	$65.06	150%	−3.49%
SOHU	10/02	$2.00	7/03	$42.68	2034%	27.40%
SSTI	6/99	$1.75	6/00	$36.25	1971%	10.19%
SWIR	5/03	$4.00	4/04	$45.03	1026%	21.79%
TASR	7/03	$15.00	4/04	$356.10	2274%	17.20%
TBUS	3/04	$2.00	4/04	$14.27	614%	3.43%
UTSI	9/02	$12.50	8/03	$45.36	263%	15.15%
XMSR	11/02	$2.50	1/04	$30.96	1138%	23.12%

when I said in March 2000 that the jig is up, you have to sell; the heat from those last gains was just plain scorching. But if you understand my style and recognize that you are being a pig if you overstay those huge gains, you will recognize that the gains are so outsized as to be well worth the risk that some stocks won't appreciate at all.

As you can see, if you bought the red hots or the Game Breakers and then sold them and invested in T-bills after each one until the next one bubbled up, you absolutely clobbered the averages. Empirically, the outsized returns simply can't be denied. So then why don't more people seek out these stocks? Why is the investing intelligentsia so unwilling to embrace a Game Breaker strategy? I think it's because such a strategy requires two decisions, a buy and a sell. The traditional buy-and-hold approach to investing, which I scorn, simply doesn't consider any purchase of a stock that requires a later sell as part of the investment process. That's considered wagering and therefore beneath the strictures and gospel of traditional investing *even though it slaughters traditional investing when it comes to returns,* which is and will always be the *only* way to measure performance.

To those who still insist that it is impossible to identify and isolate the Game Breakers before they happen, consider the stories we highlight on my CNBC show. Anyone who watches knows we frequently vet these small caps before they take off on their trajectory. Take the stock of Taser, which I discovered on national TV when it was less than a $100 million company after I had the company's management on my CNBC show.

After studying the company's fundamentals and its technicals—including the small number of shares outstanding—I said it could easily go to $1 billion in a short time. It was not hard to see that Taser could put on a lot of capitalization. It had a unique product, a good buzz—remember we are anticipating fashion—and, best of all, an extremely limited float (number of shares outstanding), so if some institutions tried to buy it they would have to take the stock up beyond what most thought was possible. Six weeks later the stock became a $1 billion market capitalization stock as the frenzy took over. When it got to $1 billion, I said enough was enough and suggested people take profits, that the frenzy had grown out of control. It peaked shortly thereafter and declined precipitously, as these stocks often do when they reach the $1 billion level and the volume expands, signaling that there is, at last, too much float and the stock has finished its upward trajectory.

Getting in and getting out in time is possible and doable if you follow my buy and sell disciplines.

For two years people have been buying Sun Microsystems because it is a nice low-dollar stock. For two years it has been among the most active stocks on the NASDAQ. And for two years it has done nothing. That's because we are late to the game of Sun. It's an old stock, one that has already had its day. Same with Gateway. Or EMC. I am looking for stocks with velocity, stocks that can move, and move quickly, not quagmire stocks that sit and move in small increments. Low price alone does not make a stock a good investment.

What are the ingredients for the recipe of a mass-psychology-driven move upward? What should you be looking for in order to spot these huge gainers ahead of the monster leaps? I break it down like this:

40 percent management. This includes speaking with the company and evaluating management ownership and recent changes in ownership, ability to sell the story, and accessibility of information on the company. The salability of the story and the credibility of management are subjectives that can't truly be measured. They provide the springboard for all other work on the topic. I talk to the management of almost every company I can get on the phone; firsthand knowledge is important when you are riding these rockets.

30 percent fundamentals. That means cash-flow growth, earnings growth/potential, balance sheet, liquidity. The stocks that could turn into Game Breakers tend to have real financials; they are not shell companies. At times they have real profits; they always have revenues and rapid revenue growth. They are not just penny stocks thrust upon the market by the fraudsters in the boiler room.

15 percent technical analysis. This includes stock momentum, support levels, simple chart reading. I am not a chartist, but I am looking for stocks that have been basing for a long time. I want to see stocks that could break out or are about to soar if the crowd lights a match under them. Consider the chart work the search for a bag of Kingsford Match Light charcoal before the match gets struck.

15 percent what I call "TheStreet.com alpha factor." That's a proprietary measure I have created based on the stock's float, low volume relative to the float, how the stock has reacted to strong news in the past, and the short interest ratio. It is a measurement of the potential "short" pressure on the name, meaning whether there is enough stock out there, physically enough stock, to absorb the buyers' demands without it flying through the roof. This factor is a precursor to a stock's velocity, a tell that allows you to approximate how fast a stock can go from zero to sixty, if you will, without gravity or stock supply interrupting. These stocks work only when the size of the stock is "too small" for the concept and has to be supersized quickly by the crowd. That's one of the reasons I like to work off a screen that yields stocks that have a minimum of 100,000 shares, $100 million in market cap, and a price between $1 and $15. That's where most of these stocks live. Supply—merchandise for sale—has to be hard to come by, and when it isn't hard to come by, the move is probably already over. Supply must be so tight that when a buyer of 5,000 shares comes in, the stock is tough to find without moving it up to where sellers are. That's the Match Light scenario in action.

Consider the gauntlet we put Taser through. First, the company had seasoned management that had been in the business of developing stun guns for years but had not been able to crack any major police market. The balance sheet and the cash flow were superb. The stock had been basing for ages and most of it was held by just a few people, including insiders. Given the incredible news backdrop—that police departments all over the country were suddenly united in adopting Tasers because the number of fatal police shootings is a politically charged issue that hurts the overall functioning of the police and the elected officials—once one or two major police departments went to

Taser, it wasn't much of a leap of faith to think that there would be many others behind them. The Miami force, known as both progressive and reformist, gave the signal when it picked Taser over the standard handgun for its manslaughter-plagued officers. Given the "tight" float (there were barely 1.5 million shares outstanding) and the demands on that float, it was, in essence, a predictable short squeeze that created instant wealth as the stock galloped from $100 million to $1 billion. It ramped and kept ramping until the market was overwhelmed with supply and the move was over, even though the news background stayed positive. How could we measure when the supply had caught up with demand? The explosion in volume told us that the stock had at last found a level where more wanted out than before; that changed the balance and left the stock hanging too limply. If we had waited until the fundamentals turned (the company would soon begin to lose business because of fears that Taser might be thought of as an instrument of torture and because the stock's capitalization gave it no room to lose any contract in any major metro area) we would have given back much of the easy gain.

What's working right now at this very minute, you ask? Tough question, because this is a moment-to-moment cohort with no room for buying and holding. That doesn't mean, though, that I can't be toiling in this vineyard for you anyway. For those of you who are Web savvy, because you have bought this book I will give you this URL: www.thestreet.com/stocksunderten. It allows you to participate for free in a service that isolates the potential next 10×ers before they occur and while they are still under $10. It is called the "StocksUnder$10" electronic newsletter, and while I would love to give you a list right here of what fits, the short time frame for selecting such winners makes it impossible to do anything other than send you to the site with my compliments. What's working is too fluid, changes too often. Try it out. You will see that this type of investing—gambling, if you like—is actually far more predictable and gameable than the Wall Street experts think. The next Game Breakers are out there. Like a good venture capitalist, you can own a bunch of them with this service, and you can get out of the losers before they crash and stay with the winners as they produce ever bigger gains.

As is so often the case, the process seems counterintuitive to many investors, who are often caught at the top when playing these stocks without strict rules regarding losses and without regard to the fundamentals, which, as always, do matter. That's why I have taken to using the metaphor of the Holland Tunnel Diner to explain this kind of investing to the public. After a brutal night in the city where we'd drunk too much, my wife and I used to like to stop at the Holland Tunnel Diner, a grungy place with a red-hot griddle, for a couple of egg sandwiches to sop up the inebriation. I used to marvel at that griddle man because that griddle was so hot it could fry an egg to perfection in what I measured to be nine seconds. But if the egg was left on for a tenth second, the griddle man would burn the bejesus out of it.

When you are playing the crowd promotion game, when you are solving for M without an E, you've got to be that griddle man at the Holland Tunnel Diner. You have to play it until the heat gets so hot that it makes a perfect egg sandwich, but you must bolt from the griddle before you overstay for even one second. Otherwise you could wreck your whole portfolio.

Fortunately, unlike the Holland Tunnel Diner, our griddle emits warnings. For individual Game Breaker stocks we see the volume expand; we see the secondaries get filed; we notice the insiders bailing. For the group moves, we see new underwritings and we see those fail as the IPOs go to a discount to price almost immediately. These pitfalls are obvious to anyone paying attention not to the companies themselves, but to the supply and demand in the marketplace. When the secondaries break down at inception and the primaries, or IPOs, retreat to a discount immediately, those are signs that things have overheated and you have to go elsewhere pronto. Don't worry, it is incredibly easy to spot these warning signs. With sector moves it's the moment when underwritings are coming through the chute like torrential rain only to sink in the muddy discount almost immediately. Every single group move of consequence has experienced this pattern, where you still have time to get out before dreadful financial consequences occur. It is usually at this moment that the press discovers the trend and there are dozens of articles everywhere about the "craze" that is no longer a craze but is a solid idea that is going to produce the next Home Depot or Genentech or Microsoft. That's the moment when the skeptics seem silly and the "new era" folks seem most wise. That's the moment when it looks like money grows on low-hanging branches and you don't need a ladder to pick it off.

When you hear that kind of talk, when you read that kind of gibberish, be prepared to get the hell out of the diner or pay the price for the burned egg sandwich.

6

STOCK-PICKING RULES
to
LIVE BY

You now know all the strategies I know about finding the biggest gains in stocks. Now, what tactics do you use to keep those gains and to sell before your gains turn to losses.

When I started writing for TheStreet.com eight years ago, I entitled my column "Wrong" because I believed fervently that if you lost money, even if only for a day, it would be "wrong." As a hedge fund manager I thought there was no excuse to lose money on trading. None. Although of course it happened all the time. That didn't make it forgivable, though.

As a hedge fund manager, managing impatient wealthy money (and, by the way, all wealthy money is impatient), I had little tolerance for losses. I could say only so many times, "Look, I really believe if we wait long enough we can have a home run here." At times the speed of the gains was more important than the size of the gains. The preoccupation with near-term performance was amazing to me and gripped me as soon as I started my fund in 1987. What rich people cared about was being with the "hot hand," with who was making money now, hand over fist, who was beating everyone else *now*. It was so NFL-like, you were either the champion or "they," the investors, went home with someone else.

When I started running other people's money I thought I could report yearly. But no one would give me money unless I agreed to report quarterly. Heck, it was their money, so naturally I agreed. A couple of years into the process and the next thing I know, they want reports monthly. A few years later and they want weekly. In my last few years many of the partners wanted daily performance. They didn't want to wake up one day and find they had lost money, so they grilled me endlessly about how we were doing. As someone who could go long or short, I knew that meant that when the market was up they expected me to make money and when the market was down they expected me to make money. If I could short and the market dropped 2 percent, they expected me to make 2 or 3 percent. If the market rallied 2 or 3 percent they expected to hear that they made 4 percent.

I used to complain to my wife that I had become a dancing bear *and* a dancing bull, a circus animal. I had to deliver results constantly. With that kind of partner-fueled obsession you are driven to trade. You can't let positions run against you, even for a minute, or you risk remonstration at the close of the market (I wouldn't let the partners speak to me when the market was open). You have to stop out all losses before they become consequential, even if it is for positions that you believe in. You can't sit in a good position, an AT&T Wireless, for example, while it goes down and you build it up, because the partner critics won't tolerate the short-term unrealized loss. They think that any loss on the way to riches is "wrong." You have to book every gain as quickly as it can be taken, lest it be taken away. I had to expand my trading day to between 4:00 a.m. and 11:00 p.m., trading in any market that was open—Finland, Japan, Hong Kong—just to be able to rack up enough short-term gains to please the partners.

There is no doubt that the model I adopted, quick trading gains whenever possible, is a good one that led to immense riches. But it isn't at all replicable for you, unless you want to give up every aspect of

your life—including your family, as I did—to succeed. The price is
just too high for a model of extreme short-term performance, even
if it delivers above-average returns. When I quit my hedge fund at
the end of 2000, I vowed that I would never again put myself in that
position. I knew that such a short-term trading style was not sustainable and would not even necessarily beat a longer-term, more tax-
advantaged style of investing. I had an opportunity, not long after I
retired from the hedge fund, to manage money in a slower fashion, at
a mutual fund. There I wouldn't be taking 20 percent of the gains,
both realized and unrealized, as I was at my hedge fund. I would be
taking only 1 percent of the entire asset base as a fee. That intrigued
me, until I recognized two terrible aspects of the mutual fund business: One, I would have to be selling my fund constantly, and two, I
would have to be accepting money all of the time, regardless of
whether I needed it or could use it.

As difficult as it was as a hedge fund manager with daily demands
on performance, I could see where these two demands, the selling demand and the imperative to take in more money all of the time, could
be disastrous to performance. I rarely, if ever, opened my hedge fund
to new money. I insisted that you be nominated by a partner in the
fund already, as a way to be able to keep the asset base from growing
too quickly. Nothing's worse than taking in too much money when
you can't handle it. Almost all my temporary bouts with underperformance came when I took in new chunks of money and couldn't adjust
to the new position size. My goal as a hedge fund manager was to make
24 percent after all fees, year after year. That was what I had done initially and I thought it was a great goal to maintain. But making 24 percent when you are running $10 million or $100 million is quite
different from when you are running $250 million or $500 million, let
alone the billions that all of the successful mutual funds have under
management. At my hedge fund initially I could make $20,000 a day
and hit my benchmark. By the time I quit I needed to make $423,000
every day to make my "quota." I did it, but it was incredibly hard.

Given the incentive of the mutual fund model, though, which pays you for asset growth through sales more than for performance, you are setting yourself up to underperform the averages. If I kept growing I would have had to be making a million dollars a day just to stay even with my record. The biggest enemy of great returns is the law of large numbers; it's simply too hard for most mortals to beat the market when they are running gigantic sums, particularly when those sums are coming in over the transom every day. Especially when you are out there glad-handing to raise more money when you should be inside analyzing companies.

So, I decided to heck with it. I'm not running other people's money in a hedge fund manner; too stressful. And I am not going to run other people's money in a mutual fund manner; too prone to underperformance. What's the point of playing the game if you aren't going to make big money, bigger than the next guy?

Instead, what I decided to do was free myself of the constraints of both business models. I would run money myself, my money, and I would do all of the things that I couldn't do that constrained my performance at the hedge fund. I would build big positions in companies I loved and own them over time regardless of the short-term vicissitudes. I would stop worrying about the day-to-day performance and concentrate on long-term performance. I would no longer blast as "wrong" short-term glitches on the road to long-term wins. I would have a trading discipline and an investing discipline commensurate with this new, commonsensical view, and I would make money both short- and long-term when I thought it was right, not when they, the investors, thought it was right.

In short, I became, in a word, *you*. And you know what I discovered? Being a private investor like you beats both models. You can easily outperform the short-term-obsessed hedge fund manager who is always looking over his shoulder trying to please the partners. And you can totally trump the mutual fund model with its endless obsession with growing assets under management and salesmanship.

Strangely, many of you have no idea how good you have it. I take calls from people on my radio show who complain that such and such a stock is going against them or that it is dropping when it should be rallying. I will say, "Don't you believe, don't you have conviction?" If they say no, I say, "Well, by all means sell it." But if you are on your own, and you like the company underneath, and the stock is being marked down because of the occasional craziness of the market, that's an opportunity, a blessing, a gift! Most people just can't run their own money well, though. They just don't have the qualities or the rules they need—the discipline to see it through and to beat all of the others out there, including the high-priced managers that they are willing to throw their money at for no reason at all.

The following sections of this book are about the discipline you need to trade and invest like a pro without the inherent bias against performance that pros in the hedge fund and mutual fund camps have. This chapter will help you to get all the advantages the pros have in handling money with none of the disadvantages. You already have all the basics: the skills to analyze price-to-earnings multiples, the ability to understand the cycles that drive stocks, the knowledge of the best places to look for big gains. Now you need the tools—the real tools, not the silly stuff that passes for tools advertised by brokers desperate for your business—to trade and invest your portfolio to riches.

The Ten Commandments of Trading

1. Never turn a trade into an investment. If there is one concept you must take away from this book, it's that you must never, ever turn a trade into an investment. First, let's talk about the process of buying a stock. When I decide I am going to buy Kmart, the reconstituted real estate and retail play, I have to declare right up front whether I am buying it for a trade or an investment. A trade means that I am buying it because of a specific catalyst, a reason that will drive it higher. That catalyst is a data point, a recommendation, a belief that things are better than expected when the earnings come out, some news about a restructuring, or something material that could occur. There is a moment to buy and a moment to sell. But you must declare first before you buy. Here's why. The vast majority of you will buy a stock for a reason and then either the reason occurs and nothing happens, so you then decide, darn, I'll just call it an investment and I will buy more as it goes down, or else the reason doesn't occur—the reason may never occur—and you decide to hold on to it because, well, what's the worst thing that can happen? The answer of course is plenty, and almost all of it bad. The answer is that you would never have bought it in the first place if you didn't think the reason was going to occur, so there is no reason for you to own it now. I have seen myriad investors turn trades into investments, developing a rationale or an alibi to fool themselves that they are doing the right thing. That's because they don't make the distinction between a trade and an investment. When I want to "invest" in a company I buy a small amount of it to start and then hope the market will knock the stock down so I can buy more. When I want to trade, I put the maximum on at the beginning because I believe the data point is about to occur. I never buy anything for a trade without that catalyst. I never buy anything for a trade just hoping it will go higher; there can be no hope in the equation. I buy down when I am investing. I cut my losses immediately when I am trading if the reason I am trading the stock doesn't pan out.

2. **Your first loss is your best loss**. People know when trades have gone awry. They know the stock doesn't act well. On my radio show I talk about how stocks talk to me; they tell me things. Actually, of course, they tell everybody everything, but most people don't know how to listen. If you buy a stock for a trade and it starts going against you in a meaningful way, perhaps a decline of 50¢ or more, you may have a real problem on your hands. I am not kidding. When it comes to trading I am an extremely disciplined person. I like to cut my losses quickly and get over them quickly. That's why I say that my first loss is my best loss. All other losses tend to be from lower levels and at bigger cost to me. Again, people instinctively can feel the trade going awry

but because of ego or pigheadedness, they don't want to heed the thunder and they stay in only to have to panic out at lower levels.

3. **It's okay to take a loss when you already have one.** One of the silliest things individual investors do is to pretend that they aren't losing money simply because they haven't realized the loss. I talk to investors all the time who rationalize that they are in the money until they take it off the table—regardless of whether they are profitable or not. Nonsense. A loss is a loss, realized or unrealized, and most of the time it is better just to take it than to act as though you don't have one. My goal is to get you to realize the loss before it does so much damage that it cuts into your gains. No one can come back from the chronic loss position; no one is good enough or has enough ammo to stay in the game. Cut your losses now; let your winners do the running.

4. **Never turn a trading gain into an investment loss.** You've just made a terrific trade, you bought Philip Morris (now Altria) before a great quarter and watched it go up 4 points on the good earnings news. Do you take the trade? Or do you begin to wonder, "Hmm, this MO is better than I think; I should hold on to this." I did that once, that exact trade. I bragged to the Trading Goddess as I was driving her to the airport for a flight to Paris. I told her I had a big gain on a couple of hundred thousand shares. She reminded me immediately never to use the word "gain" unless it was taken, because as far as she was concerned, there was nothing booked so nothing had been done. A week later I picked her up at the airport, back from France and gay as I have ever seen her. She could see through my sullen look immediately. "What did you screw up on?" she asked, knowing full well that the only thing that could have made me unhappy at that juncture was a big loss in the market. I then had to describe to her that a day after she left a court had ordered Morris to pay billions in tobacco medical damages to everyone who had ever smoked a cigarette, or something like that. The stock had dropped 15 points. She reminded me of the cardinal rule, that a trade is just a trade, and when you turn it into an investment

you have overstayed your welcome. I had turned my solid six-figure gain into a multi-million-dollar loss. Let my loss be the lesson to you, so you don't have to learn it yourself.

5. Tips are for waiters. At one point in both our lives, my wife and I were waiters. To be more accurate, I was a busboy, because you had to be twenty-one to serve alcohol in the state of Pennsylvania. She was a waitress. Later, when we worked together, my wife would handle all the incoming calls from brokers. That meant that at least four times a week I had to hear her lecture someone about the tip they were giving us, telling the poor shmoe on the other end of the line that we were both waiters once and that they should save the tips for those in that profession and not hit us with them. Why was she so adamant? Because the logic of a tip, or really, the illogic, is so palpable. If you really "know something," then you are per se an insider and aren't supposed to tell anyone without running afoul of the securities laws. And if you don't know something, you should shut the hell up because you don't know what you are talking about. So, any tip is, per se, a bum steer—unless it is left at a restaurant. This no-tip rule is a very hard lesson, because invariably the people offering tips are experts at making them sound like genuine insight. But believe me, the only reason someone really gives a tip is so he can get out of what would otherwise be a terrible position that he's stuck in and will definitely lose money on if he doesn't get you to take him out of it.

6. You don't have a profit until you sell. This commandment is a variation of the rule of not turning a trade into an investment. People constantly confuse booked gains, real gains that you can take to the bank, with phony paper gains that are meaningless because they can be taken away. Most people are also reluctant ever to take a profit because they don't want to pay taxes. I always tell people that if we could just rewind the videotape to January 2000, when people were sitting on trillions of dollars of unrealized gains, we would be able to drill this point home well enough that people would respect it. Gains not taken can be losses. Gains taken can never be losses. It's that simple. I stress this point because we have all been brainwashed not to sell; we think it is sinful. It is commonsensical. It is logical. And it is the only way to be sure you get rich in this business.

7. Control losses; winners take care of themselves. One of the amazing things about this business is how often I hear people say, "If it weren't for that Nortel position, I would have been up big," or, "I would be making a huge amount of money in the market if only I hadn't let Lucent run against me." It takes only one or two losers to wreck a portfolio. I try to devote far more of my time toward my losing stocks than my winners, and not because of some sort of masochistic streak. Rather, I recognize that stocks often telegraph declines. I recently bumped into a policeman in town who owned a couple hundred shares of Enron. He was thanking me profusely because I told him at $20 he had to bail. Of course he was reluctant to do so; the stock had been at $80 not long before. I told him that loss control is the paramount concern for all of those in the market, because the winners, the good stocks, tend to take care of themselves. He sold the Enron. He told me that if he hadn't he would have wiped out all of the gains he had had in all the other stocks in his portfolio. I tell the story because it is typical; one bad apple in this business truly does destroy the whole barrel. Take the loss before it gets hideous. Don't buy into the notion that you can't sell until it comes back and then you promise not to do it again. That's how losers think. You need to think like a winner.

8. Don't fear missing anything. I can't tell you how many times I have had my heart in my throat, pounding, pounding, because I didn't have enough in the market. I can't tell you how often I felt that I had to "play," I had to be in because the market was going higher and higher and higher without me. Do you know that almost every time I had that feeling, almost every time I had that "I can't miss this action" drama playing around in my head, I lost money? Discipline is the most important rule in winning investing, and sometimes that discipline means admitting that you missed the opportunity and it is too late. I almost always feel like I have missed something right near the top of the move. When I was in the Bigs, I used to turn that sentiment into a profit in my final years by actually betting against the market when I thought I was missing something, because that heart-stuck-in-throat feeling correlates with the tops of moves, not the bottoms. Always remember that the best time to buy is when it feels most awful, not when it would relieve the incessant pain of fearing the next big rally, especially given that that rally invariably has already occurred.

9. Don't trade headlines. The press is almost always wrong in its quick takeaways of what business news is about. Some of it is the rush; Reuters wants to beat Dow; Dow wants to beat Bloomberg. Some of it is the lack of grounding of most journalists in business news. And some of it is complexity: The headline can't capture the reality because the reality is a jumble. Headlines that present stories about such and such a number being "better than expected" are the types of headlines that punish traders constantly. They can't understand how they could be wrong because the "tape" just said that the quarter was better. Typically, the reality is that there is something else, some other metric that might be important, or that the quarter is finagled with one-time gains. I think that you have to wait to read the whole story and you can never be sure of what that story is going to be from the headline. This point is very important because with electronic trading you can move too fast, and often many of you do. Learn the whole story. If this really is a great opportunity, you will not miss it by taking time to iniform yourself.

10. Don't trade flow. You are watching CNBC, you see multiple "takes" or trades to the upside in IPIX or MACE or some other four-lettered hot stock. Do you want to go buy it? That's called trading flow. People always want to trade flow. I used to get calls from dozens of brokers saying that they had big buyers of Microsoft or big sellers of EMC, and my instincts were to go along with the trades, to buy because they were buying. Wrong! When you have no idea why people are buying, when you are just operating on the buys and sells of others, you are trading on ignorance. Ignorant traders never ever win. I promise you that by trading flow you will lose far more often than you will make money, even though it seems so easy. Why would they buy if they weren't right? The answer, of course, is that many investments made by others are ill-considered and attempting to piggyback off them is nonsensical even if it feels great. No matter how many times I stress this point, people still see large buyers on the bottom of the TV screen and they go nuts imitating them. That's just plain stupid. Do you think they will tell you when to sell, too?

Twenty-Five Investment Rules to Live By

1. **Bulls and bears make money; pigs get slaughtered**. My favorite expression of all when it comes to the market is that bulls make money, bears make money, and pigs get slaughtered. In fact I have a tape of pigs snorting that I play on *Jim Cramer's RealMoney* when I think that someone's been too greedy. I am all about common sense, which, unfortunately, seems rarely to be interjected into the investing dialogue. It makes sense that a bull can make money when the market moves up, and it makes sense that a bear can make money when the market moves down; both going long and shorting are noble endeavors. It's when you act piggish, when you refuse to take anything off the table after a huge run, that you get hurt. My style of investing is to buy down, simply because I believe, when I am *investing*, that I am buying shares in an enterprise, and unless that enterprise has faltered in the interim between my decision to buy and my buying, I stick with it. I use the market's irrationality and randomness in my favor to accumulate more stock, to the point where I am perfectly willing to have up to 25 percent of my portfolio in one name if I think it is absurdly valued. Just as a market can take a stock down irrationally, it can also take a stock up irrationally, although far too few individual investors think this way. The difference is that when a stock goes down irrationally it is getting cheaper and cheaper, but when a stock goes up irrationally it

is getting more and more expensive. In any walk of life other than investing in stocks there comes a price that we are not willing to pay and a price where we would be a seller of goods. Only in stocks do we feel we should hang on regardless. That's just plain against common sense. When you are a pig, therefore, I expect you will be slaughtered. Many people have asked me how in March 2000, within ten days of the top of the market, I knew to take money off the table and begin to short (arguably my best call since the cash for the crash call in 1987 that my wife steered me to). The answer, in a rather unrigorous and noneloquent moment, is that I was not willing to be a pig. I had made a ton of money virtually in a straight line and had watched many of my stocks go to absurd valuations. Of course, at the time, people had plenty of justifications, intelligent, rational-sounding justifications for staying in the market. But my "bulls make money, bears make money, pigs get slaughtered" philosophy got me out right on time.

2. It's okay to pay the taxes. At the time when I said to take money off the table in March 2000, I received close to a thousand e-mails from people saying that if they took the profits that I was advising them to do, they would have to pay a tremendous amount of tax, much of it short-term, which, of course, carries with it much higher rates than long-term gains. I wrote back to each person individually saying that if you don't take profits, you won't have profits, that the least of your worries is the tax man. Not one agreed with me. The abhorrence of taxes transcended good judgment. Years later, I am still getting e-mails of apology from people bemoaning the fact that they cared more about paying taxes than taking profits and that their portfolios subsequently shifted from being well into the black to dripping with red. *Never* consider taxes as a reason to hold a stock if the stock has gone up too far too fast and can head back down hard. *Never* hold on to something not worth holding on to or something that has gotten dangerously overvalued simply so you can wait until the gain goes long-term. This is the single biggest investment mistake people have made in our generation, and despite the trillions lost in the bear market of the turn of this century, I still see people making this error. Shameful, just shameful. Taxes do not trump fundamentals; dangerous stocks are dangerous whether they are owned long- or short-term. You can't base investment decisions on the tax man.

3. Don't buy all at once; arrogance is a sin. I consider myself one of the greatest market timers of my era. I was able to accumulate wealth as quickly as I did because I timed lots of big moves, getting in right and exiting right. Yet, when it comes to buying stocks, to the way of buying stocks, I never buy all at once. I buy increments on the way down, spaced out gingerly to avoid emotion. Similarly, I never commit a lot of capital at one level, and I space out my capital commitments. Let me give you some examples. For my retirement account, my 401(k), I like to put aside a twelfth of my commitment every month. But if I catch a market break, a substantial market break of 10 percent, I speed up the next month's contribution. If I catch a break in excess of 15 percent I put in the next quarter's contribution. And twice in the last ten years, when there was a 20 percent decline, I invested all that I had left to contribute. That way I was able to take advantage of the declines and average in at great prices. I did it this way because I know I am fallible. I also know behavior and common sense. I know that if I commit all my money at one level and then the market takes a huge tumble, I will be so angry and sullen that I'll believe that the market itself is rigged or that it can't be tamed or that it is just too hard. I hear those sentiments from callers every day on my radio show, and I know that they can only be combatted by humility and a recognition that the market can be an unpredictable morass at times, but over the long term it makes plenty of sense.

Similarly, when I wanted to build a position, a sizable position in a stock, I never bought it all at once. I recognized that there was inherent fallibility in my moment of buying. Perhaps the market was about to take a huge tumble. Perhaps some negative event would occur that would make the buy seem ludicrous a few minutes later. So space them out. That's always been the way with me, even though it often drove my brokers up the wall. They hated the fact that instead of going in and buying 50,000 shares of Caterpillar in one fell swoop, I bought 5,000 every hour, or 5,000 at one level and then waited for a 25¢ drop to buy the next 5,000. They wanted to get my order done; I wanted to get my order done right. You are the client; you are in command of your money. Don't let anyone rush you or make you put it all to work at one level. How do you know that tomorrow the market won't crash? How do you know that tomorrow there might not be an unbelievable opportunity to buy one of your favorite stocks at a much better level, but you have just committed all the money you had? Accept the fallibility of man's judgment and use it to your advantage. The worst that happens with my method? Simple: You don't get enough stock on before a very big move. You don't have as big a profit as you would like. Now that's what I call a high-quality problem!

4. Look for broken stocks, not broken companies. Most people so closely affiliate the stock with the company in their minds that they can't tell the difference between the two. That's nonsense. There are lots of very bad companies with very bad stocks. But there are also lots of good companies with very bad stocks. Your job is to know the difference, because the former is no bargain and the latter defines a bargain. After every sell-off of any magnitude, and we will surely get a dozen of them every year, there will be stocks that have been crushed unfairly. Most people gravitate toward the broken stocks of broken companies, the Suns, the Gateways, the CMGIs. Instead, they should focus on the companies that have been unfairly beaten up. On my radio show, I say, Don't buy damaged goods, buy damaged stocks of companies that are on the mend or improving. How can you spot the disparity? Simple homework. I can't tell you how many conference calls I go on with companies where they say, in plain English, even though our stock is down, our business is particularly strong. A year ago, Yellow Roadway, the best trucking company on earth, reported a shortfall because of some execution problems involving the merger. The CEO, Bill Zollars, came on my CNBC show and said the model

wasn't broken; the business suffered a hiccup, but the stock was refusing to recognize what the business knows: the hiccup's over. Sure enough, the stock subsequently moved up 50 percent when the company reported its next quarter. It was the classic example of the broken stock masking the healthy company.

During sell-offs I always tell people to build a shopping list of what they want to buy while it is happening and stay current about those companies so they can buy them at markdown prices. Remember, in the end, the stock market is just a big store where inventory at times has to be moved. Sometimes the marked-down merchandise at a department store or a supermarket is broken. Don't waste your time speculating on broken companies—those are the spoiled fruit on sale at the supermarket. There are enough healthy companies out there whose stocks have been knocked down for unfair reasons that you don't need to buy spoiled rotted companies that are crummy at any price. Chances are that most companies deserve those low prices and won't go up unless you get real lucky. You don't want luck, or hope, to be part of the equation.

5. Diversification is the only free lunch. Nonetheless, nobody wants to be diversified in real life. They want 100 percent of the next Microsoft; they want to put it all in a couple of stocks that could rally off the next big tech thing. But life's not like that. You have to be diversified to spread the risk. I always explain this in the commonsense way that takes you back to the supermarket: Would you put all of your eggs in one basket? Would you be willing to let all your chips ride on one number at roulette? Of course not. Then how can you have all of your money on tech or health care? How can you make such a big bet on one sector? It's just plain foolhardy.

Why don't people realize it? Because most people process the downside ineffectively. They don't understand that you can lose everything if you are concentrated. You know, though, that the same people who would buy nothing but tech would quickly realize that a dinner made up of four beef dishes is just plain unhealthy. These same people who would put all of their money in Enron would recognize that betting the farm on a lottery ticket is the height of folly. These are pieces of paper, for heaven's sake. Some of the pieces of paper are going to turn out to be worthless, even ones you think are worth a lot. Some are going to zero. The only way to ensure that you are not destroying your nest eggs is to diversify the cartons you place them in.

The toughest thing about diversification is that it is a real party spoiler. When I started my radio show the NASDAQ was much higher than it would be a year later. I wanted people to sell some tech and buy some dividend-producing stocks. I got so despondent about how unwilling they were to do so that I started the game "Am I Diversified?" I believe I have personally helped tens of thousands of people fight off the unmitigated assault on their wealth that was the bear market of 2000. But there's plenty more work to be done. Not one year after the bottom, I started getting those "I own EMC, Oracle, Microsoft, Hewlett-Packard, and Intel" calls all over again. I had to painstakingly remind them how all of these stocks trade together, and if you catch a squall in the market, you are liable to drown in tech stocks. If the goal is to stay in the game, there is no worse way to try to accomplish that goal than to stay in one sector. You will hate me when the market is straight up, but you will love me when the market goes down and the sector you would have otherwise owned is swamped by sellers.

6. Buy and homework, not buy and hold. When I started *Jim Cramer's RealMoney* I had a ton of people who didn't want to part with their failing tech or biotech stocks. I always told them, fine, they could continue to own them if they could just answer a few simple questions in English: What does the company do, what price-to-earnings multiple does it sell for, and whom does it compete against? No one could tell me. They just said that they were taught to buy and hold and that anything else was just speculation. I thought long and hard about this misapprehension and decided that the key issue was that they were buying and holding when they should be buying and doing homework about what they bought. Homework is analyzing the Web page, conference call, articles, research, and the like that I discussed earlier. If an investor didn't do those things after he bought, one hour per week per position, I thought he was being reckless, and I said it out loud. I told people that they had no business being their own portfolio managers. They either had to give it up to an index fund, if they had no time, or they should just put it with a couple of funds or managers and review them regularly. But the idea of buy and hold after the tragedy we went through in 2000–2003, one that is on bad days still very much with us, is just preposterous.

If there were truly an arbiter, if there were really an organization or an entity that regulated who had a right to come public, with some standards about how much money they are making and how good their balance sheets are, then you could buy and hold. But the one thing we have learned in the last five years is that anybody can bring anything public and we can't let the low barriers to entry into the stock market hurt us. So the mantra is buy and homework, not buy and hold. Always remember that no asset class over the long term—defined as twenty years—has ever beaten high-quality stocks that pay dividends. But unless you keep up and do the homework, how do you know if your stocks are high quality enough to pay a dividend one day? Without the homework you shouldn't own individual stocks. It is too likely that you will stumble and too likely that the long-term payoff of stocks will elude you. I can't tell you how many times I have bought the stocks of good companies that subsequently went bad. That's what the homework should tell you. It is a check on when to bail because a company's not coming back. It is not designed to find a hot stock so much as it ensures that you don't have your portfolio wrecked by an ice-cold one.

7. No one ever made a dime by panicking. No matter how many times I tell people that panic is not an investment strategy, I see people cut and run at the very worst time. When you sell into the maw, when you join the rout, you *never* get a good price. You feel good momentarily, you feel relieved that the pain is "gone," but it's always wrong.

When I ran my hedge fund I made millions of trades. I dutifully saved all the trading records in giant boxes and then at year end went over every single trade to look for the biggest panicked losses—you know which ones you panicked on—and then I would look at a chart of the stocks the day before I sold them, the day after I sold them, and a week after I sold them. Do you know in almost every single case—and I am talking millions of trades—the stocks were up the next day and up appreciably a week later. That doesn't mean they weren't substantially lower a month, a quarter, or even a year later. It does mean that it was the wrong time to execute the sell strategy. A patient, less panicked style always generates a higher return. Always. That's a certainty in a world where there is very little certainty.

In the mid-1990s I let a film crew into my office as part of a *Frontline* documentary on the markets. It happened to be a day where I panicked and sold half of my portfolio to Goldman Sachs at a price about 5 percent lower than the previous day because I thought the market was going to be down 10 to 15 percent. I kept a copy of the tape and I watched it every time I felt a panic attack coming on, because on that day, the very day where I felt that things were coming unglued, the market actually rallied. I wish I could say that it was just irony, but it was rationality. Typically the panic comes at the *end* of the sell-off, not the beginning or even the middle. The panic marks the capitulation of all of those who tried to stay the course. That's why the panic tends to be the bottom. In October 1998 I forgot about *Frontline* and panicked into a gawdawful tape, the second time in three years that I went against my discipline. Then, too, the market looked like it was going to crash. Instead it rallied steadily after I made my sales.

If you are one of those people who simply refuse to believe me and my empirical work on this, do me a favor. Next time you feel a panic attack coming on that tricks you into wanting to sell, adopt the approach of the Trading Goddess and "throw a maiden into a volcano." That's where you take one stock and sacrifice it in order to forestall taking a more drastic action. Remember my goal: to keep you in the game. Nothing drives people out of the game faster than waiting and holding and then selling at the panic bottom. Don't let it happen to you.

8. Own the best of breed; it is worth it. Here's a principle that is followed strictly among professionals, yet is studiously ignored among the hobbyists and amateurs. So many people are suckers for cheap. So many people look at the $E \times M = P$ and say, "Wait a second, that's too high a multiple to pay; Intel's not that much better than AMD." Or, "There's no way that I will pay that much of a premium for Procter over Colgate." Shame on you. The biggest bargains tend to be the best of breed. The amateur loves a "cheaper" alternative, whether it is cheaper in stock price or cheaper in multiple. The professional says the reason why Walgreens has a more expensive multiple than Rite Aid is that it is much better, and when things get difficult, management is more likely to figure out their problems than to get buried by them. When the choice is among two or three companies in an industry, always go for the one that's the best of breed regardless of the price. Far too often the market simply misprices the weaker of the two, giving it too much credit. The underdog hardly ever wins in this game.

9. He who defends everything defends nothing, or why discipline trumps conviction. One question I am asked repeatedly in my business is, "Don't you worry about your stocks?" The answer is that I am always worried about my stocks, always, but I am particularly worried when they go *down*! I am doubly worried when they go down when the market as a whole is going up. That's a sign to me that something's wrong, that someone knows something I don't know and that I'd better find out or I won't be able to take advantage of the weakness to buy more—I will have to sell instead. That's why I demand that if you are going to have your own portfolio you have the time and inclination to make the calls, or read the homework or listen to the conference calls or check the Web sites and articles that will determine whether it is a buying opportunity or a selling opportunity. Of course, there are plenty of times when stocks go down and the homework shows you nothing. There are plenty of times when there is chicanery in the numbers, or there is puffing by the management, and we don't really know the truth. Or, worse, someone does know the truth, and it was found out at the seventeenth hole at Baltusrol and is known only to a select—and illegal—bunch of insiders. There are also tons of times where you simply have too much stock in the market versus what the market's going to do; you are too "long," as we say in the vernacular. So, what do you do? How do you manage a portfolio under conditions where things go wrong with the stocks you own and things go wrong in the market? There are no magic bullets, but I believe that when in doubt, discipline trumps conviction. You have to have a discipline, a discipline that ranks all of your stocks so that you know which ones you are willing to buy right now and which ones you are willing to sell if you need the capital to sell. You need to rank stocks because not all stocks are created equal and when things go awry you have to be willing to "circle the wagons" around a few good stocks and buy them down so you get a better basis.

I can't tell you how many times, either because of overconfidence or because of an excessively benign period of market rallying, I was lulled into being too long. That's why I developed a four-step system of ranking every stock I own: 1 is a stock I want to buy more of right now, 2 is a stock I want to buy more of if it goes lower, 3 is a stock I want to sell if it goes higher, and 4 is a stock I want to sell now. I actually used to get off the trading desk at my hedge fund every two hours and rank the stocks I owned, forcing my portfolio managers to have only one or two 1s and making them choose what they really liked. The rankings force discipline and make discipline trump conviction. A wise soldier once said, "He who defends everything defends nothing." In war that means don't defend every beachhead and valley. In investing, that means trying to buy all of the stocks that you "like," because no one, not even Bill Gates, has that kind of money. That's how I run my money. I know that I can't protect every stock, so I choose the ones I believe in the most and I buy them down, I "defend" them and let the others go. In a serious sell-off, the 1s become the only stocks I will own, and I will sell off all the others. This method keeps you from being a kid in a candy store at the worst possible time—when you are about to get your fingers cut off. It requires you to examine every decline as a potential point of action. It also is proactive. *You* are determining what you are selling, not the market. Most people sell because they can't take the pain; this method builds in the pain and turns a decline into an asset. Almost all my great investments since I started ranking stocks ten years ago came from buying my 1s at the time when everyone else was selling them.

10. The fundamentals must be good in takeovers. You want to speculate in takeovers; who can blame you? You want to catch the next Mandalay Bay or the next Nextel Communications. You think that you can wait it out because the payoff will be big. Let me tell you what I think of that: You are a fool if you speculate on takeovers. What you must do is buy undervalued good companies that are doing well. If you go and buy stocks with poor fundamentals betting that someone will take you out with a high bid, you are going to be wrong far more often than you will be right. In my last year at my hedge fund I decided that after Best Foods got a takeover bid it was inconceivable that Campbell would stay independent. Just inconceivable. Too good a brand, too easily acquired. I knew that the family behind the brand was getting restless, and in the meantime the stock had a 4 percent yield. My associate Matt Jacobs, who later became my research director, asked me how the fundamentals were. I told him that the takeover story was "too good to check out," and that if I really drilled down on the fundamentals I would probably not buy it. A year later, after a slash in the dividend and several shortfalls of a gigantic magnitude, I had lost more than 10 points on Campbell. Funny thing about the fundamentals: If the market doesn't like them, the potential acquirers won't, either. When you buy crummy companies and they go down, you can try to console yourself by saying that "maybe I will get a bid." It is far more likely, though, that you will have a Campbell on your hands. Remember the premise of this book: Let me be your lab; I have made every mistake in the book. You can't speculate on bad companies betting that they will get bids. They don't. Nobody wants them, least of all other companies.

11. Don't own too many stocks. You can overdo the virtues of diversification and become your own mutual fund. Given my constraints about time and inclination—you need one hour per week per stock to stay on top of the fundamentals—it is impossible to own more than twenty stocks unless you are a full-time stock junkie. The right-sized diversified portfolio where you can do it yourself is a five-stock portfolio. Too few and you lack diversification; too many, and you can't stay on top of them. Try to come up with a "just right" formula that allows you the comfort of staying on top of every position.

12. Cash and sitting on the sidelines are fine alternatives. Lots of people believe in being fully invested at all times. Lots of managers think they are supposed to be fully invested at all times. This is total nonsense. Lots of times the market just stinks and you want to have cash. Lots of times there is nothing to do except sit in cash. One of the reasons why I outperformed every manager in the business in my fourteen years at my hedge fund is that there were substantial blocks of time when I was largely in cash, including the 1987 crash. Cash is a great investment at times. It is a perfect hedge, as opposed to shorting the market, because if the market keeps going higher as it did, say in 1999, far longer than anyone thought, you could face devastating losses. I think that cash is the most underrated of investments because nothing feels as good as cash when that market comes down. It is one of the reasons why if you follow my method of how to trade around a stock, you will know that as the market spikes I take stock off, raise cash, and reposition myself for the next decline. Some people confuse this with buying on dips. I don't buy on dips; I sell strength and buy weakness in the stocks of the companies I love. When the time is right I almost always have the cash to put to work because I believe so strongly in cash as an option.

13. No woulda shoulda coulda. One of the most despicable traits of amateurs, and even some professionals, is second-guessing. You make a call, you go to buy Newell Rubbermaid, and then it has a short-fall. You sit there and stew about what should have happened. Or you sell Cyberonics the day before it doubles and you ruminate all the next day about what might have been. That's all nonsense. The market requires you to have the right head on at all times. You have to be ready to see the ball right for the next pitch. There is no time to re-monstrate. You clear your head and go right back out there. If you want to be introspective and constructive, bracket some time at the end of each month, or maybe the end of each quarter, to assess your strategy. But to second-guess decisions is to put yourself in a loser mind-set. Mind you, I want the pain felt. When I thought one of the younger people in my office made a mistake that was costly, I made them wear the symbol of the stock that they screwed up on as a Post-it on their forehead for the day. But I insist that any time spent saying, "If only I . . ." is time that keeps you from getting the next big stock. My wife, by the way, believes that women are such good traders because they lack the second-guessing instinct that men have. Whatever, but she taught me to steel myself and to come in the next day without the mental baggage of a screw-up so I could be ready to swing at the next fat pitch.

14. Expect corrections; don't be afraid of them. When a correction happens, investors sometimes decide that they want nothing to do with the market, that the correction signifies that something is wrong and the market can't be touched. That's another very big mistake. Corrections happen all the time after big runs and they are to be ex-pected, but you can't write off the market when they happen. I always tell the story of Joe DiMaggio after his fifty-six-game hitting streak— still the most amazing baseball feat of all time. When he failed to hit in game fifty-seven, should you have traded DiMaggio? Was he finished? Is that smart thinking? Same with the market. Corrections are to be expected; when they happen they are not a reason to panic. They can be great opportunities even as people insist that they've wrecked the charts, taken out the two-hundred-day moving average, or made the market unpalatable, claptrap that I hear every time the market snaps a winning streak with a couple of big losses.

15. Don't forget bonds. We always look at the stock market as a hermetically sealed operation. We don't think of it in the broader context of all markets. Big, big mistake. You have to be aware at all times that there is an intense competition going on among assets. The most important rivalry is stocks versus bonds. When interest rates are high, particularly for risk-free investments like U.S. treasuries, that's formidable competition for stocks, where there is a ton of risk. The tug of war between the two goes on at all times. When interest rates go higher there will *always* be someone who says "I like these more than stocks" and stocks get sold off. That always happens. But many of the people who got in the market in the last decade don't even think of bonds. That's financial suicide. It was no coincidence that the Fed had the overnight cash rates as high as 6.5 percent at about the time that the bear market of 2000–2003 began. The ratcheting of rates that the Fed did in 1999–2000 and back in 1994 crushed the market, just crushed it. And that will always be the case. Pay attention to interest rates and bonds; ignore them at your own peril.

16. Never subsidize losers with winners. So many bad portfolio managers and so many terrible individual investors always sell their best stocks so they can hold on to their worst stocks. You can always tell when you see this pattern. You will be reviewing someone's portfolio and it will be the biggest pile of junk, and you will say, "What happened to your blue chips?" They will say, "I had to sell them to buy more of these stocks because these stocks kept going down." Everyone has this problem. I have counseled enough hedge funds that were in trouble to know that the first thing that gets sold are the best ones because "they can be sold." There's always a bid for the good stocks. But when you have a handful of good and awful stocks, you don't sell the awful ones because "they are down too much," or because you "will knock them down" if they are small stocks and you have a lot of them. I understand that problem for institutional readers, but individuals, please, do not subsidize losers with winners. If you own companies with deteriorating fundamentals—as opposed to good companies with deteriorating stock prices—please sell the bad ones, take the loss, reapply the proceeds to the good ones, and move on.

17. Hope is not a part of the equation. Emotions have to be checked at the door in this business. I often hear people say "I hope" that a stock goes up. This is not a sporting event; this is money. We have no room for rooting or hoping. We are buying stocks that we believe should go higher because of the fundamentals and avoiding stocks where the underlying business is bad and getting worse. Where should hope fit in? Nowhere. People treat this business at times like a religion. They believe that if they pray that things will work out, maybe they will. Or they fall in love with these miserable pieces of paper with the idea that the love will be requited. Be realistic. Hope, pray, love, rooting—these are all the enemies of good stock picking. Hard work, research, being realistic about the prospects is the stuff of good stock picking. I can still recall the ringing in my ears when I would get off the trading desk with my wife and she would say, "What's the deal with this Memorex," and I would say, "I am hoping it gets a big contract." She would scream, "Hope? *Hope?* We need *hope* to make this work? Sell it and get me something where we have more in our favor than just hope." Many times she didn't even ask, she just sold it after I used the word "hope" to see if I would buy it back. Invariably I didn't buy back the stocks I was hoping something good would happen to.

18. Be flexible. Readers of TheStreet.com hated me in the spring of 2000 when I turned bearish. They despised the fact that I could turn on a dime, hate the very stocks that I had liked, suddenly shorting what I was going long just a month before. They thought I was lacking in rigor, a joker even. I even got plenty of death threats and was worried about my personal safety because the change I made was so stark. But you know who agreed with me? The insiders. All of my views that changed had to do with hearing the companies at conferences—all available on the Web—saying "something's not as good as it was before." This was granular stuff, like being at the Nortel meeting when former CEO John Roth said, "Business has gotten softer in the last few weeks," or being with Cisco when the company said, "The quarter is not yet in the bag," when the quarter was always in the bag by this time in previous years. You see the situations change, the business conditions change. Something that might be good one month can turn bad.

Maybe you don't care and you are only in it for the long term, but if you are playing fireflies, Game Breaker stocks, and their business hits a wall, their stocks will soon hit a wall, too. I never took action on a stock, going from buy to short sell, unless I heard from the company first that things had gotten less predictable or that business had softened. That's why the homework and the conference calls and the writings are so important, because if a business is saying that things have gotten soft, it must do so in a public forum, and you have to be listening to that public forum as or soon after it is happening. If you are devoting only fifteen minutes a week to each position you have, you aren't doing enough homework to be there at the inflection point of good to bad and you will be caught, as so many were caught in the great bear market of 2000.

19. When high-level people quit a company, something is wrong. I don't believe in shooting first and asking questions later. I think that there is almost always time to do homework to see what's up with a stock—except when a major executive leaves unexpectedly. One of my cardinal rules—and these are all cardinal rules here—is that I will not own a stock when a CEO or a CFO leaves suddenly. I just sell it. I might buy it back later, even if it is higher, but I don't like to own stocks where either of these two heads suddenly departs. Sometimes I am going to lose money because I will have acted rashly. But then again, for every one of those situations there are ten like that of Enron, where CEO Jeffrey Skilling quit abruptly for the usual "family reasons" in the summer of 2002 when the stock was at $47. The stock went to zero soon after. People don't quit for family reasons when they are needed at companies. They just don't. You can't be sure what the real reason is, but when someone leaves like that, someone is making a statement. You have to make a statement, too. You have to sell.

20. Patience is a virtue—giving up on value is a sin. Sometimes stocks you like do nothing. They can do nothing for ages. If you are a professional investor at a hedge fund, this waiting can be unnerving. You have people calling you daily and asking you how you are doing with their money. If you have lots of stocks that are doing nothing, they will take the money away and you will have to sell those stocks anyway. But individuals have no such pain. Individuals can sit on stocks as long as they want. Unfortunately, when I counsel patience individuals get antsy. "If it were any good it would be going up now, no?" Do you know how patient I was in owning Intel? For eighteen months I watched Intel do nothing in the late 1980s. But I believed. I held on to it because at that time I had only a few partners, and none of them needed to know every minute how much they were worth. Later in my career I could never have held on to an Intel that long. Lots of stories take a long time to develop. Lots of turnarounds take eighteen months to two years. When you buy a stock and you recognize that it could take a long time to turn, mark it as such in your mind so you don't get tired of it and just sell it. Stocks that are stuck in the mud a long time tend to romp like thoroughbreds when they are freed from the gate. Do you have the patience? If you don't, let someone else run your money.

21. Just because someone says it on TV doesn't make it so. This is one of my favorite tenets. So many jokers come on TV. So many clowns, people who know nothing. Sometimes people get on because they are telegenic. Sometimes they get on because they look good. Sometimes they get on because they have great PR people. Sometimes they get on because they are friends or because we owe them a favor. Oh yes, and sometimes they get on because they are good. The last is the exception. I can't tell you how unimportant performance is to the media. They are embarrassed to ask about it. They don't want to be in the business of grading content or making decisions about whether someone is any good or not. That could leave them with no one to come on the show! That's right, they need to book these shows; that's the primary motivation, *not* bringing you people who know the most about stocks. Not all programs are like this, of course, but far more than you would like to believe. Yet I constantly see people who say, "I bought Covad because I heard this really smart guy say he liked it on TV." Well, let me ask you something. Was he selling it to you when he did? Do you know? Here's an odd fact: I am the only person who comes on TV who has to disclose his positions publicly. I volunteered to do this to protect everyone—my listeners and myself—from charges of pumping and dumping. Nobody else has that restriction, even though it is illegal to pump and dump. But if we asked managers to swear that they don't use the networks to sell their stocks, would they come on our programs? Don't they have an obligation to do the right things for their shareholders? If someone recommends a Covad and it goes up 15 percent when they do, do you really think they keep it? If so, think again. Don't trust anything you hear; go do the homework. If you like it, then buy it. But remember you are *never* going to get the sell call from the TV. Ever.

22. Always wait thirty days after an earnings preannouncement before you buy. Nothing seems more tempting than to buy a stock after it's been completely poleaxed by an earnings shortfall preannouncement. Nothing, however, could be more foolhardy. Here's why: A company preannounces a soft quarter not because it is having a soft quarter— that goes without saying—but because there is no way out and things are getting worse, not better. That means you are buying into a situation where things are deteriorating as you are buying. My advice: Wait at least thirty days from the preannouncement if you insist on buying. By that time the bad news, the ongoing bad news, should be factored into the stock price and you can begin to anticipate positives going down the line. Never buy a stock just because it's down on a preannouncement. That never works. You will lose money. I promise you.

23. Never underestimate the Wall Street promotion machine. When Wall Street gets behind a stock, that stock can go much farther than if the fundamentals were doing the driving. There was a time when Wall Street firms would compete with one another to sponsor companies so that when the stocks of the companies got high enough, the managers would hire the brokers to do deals. That stuff still goes on, but it is no longer linked so closely because the analysts who do the shilling can't be paid by the investment bankers, courtesy of the investigatory work of New York attorney general Eliot Spitzer. Still, when a company's stock gets picked up with a buy from a major firm, that stock is going to go higher than it should. That kind of sponsorship is what I like to sell into. Remember, I believe that that stocks are inherently poor, short term, at tracking the fundamentals of the companies. Longer term they are great; shorter term, though, when they ratchet up because of sponsorship, that's the time to bail, not buy. That's one of the reasons why I advocate buying weakness and selling strength at all times. When you get the artificial strength of a buy recommendation—there are very few sell recommendations, so I don't care about those—use it to do the unnatural, counterintuitive thing, and sell.

24. Be able to explain your stock picks to someone else. One of the worst things that ever happened to stock picking was the Internet, because it took away one of the most important brakes on the process: talking to someone about a buy. Buying stocks is a solitary event, too solitary. As I love to say, we are all prone to make mistakes, sometimes big ones. One way to cut down on those mistakes is to force yourself to articulate why you would like to buy something. When I was at my hedge fund I always made every portfolio manager sell me the stock, literally sell it to me like a salesperson, before I would buy it. If you are in a position where you are picking stocks by yourself, get someone to listen to you, let you articulate the reasoning, the philosophy behind the buy, why you like it. The simple selling of the idea, the notion of fleshing it out in a coherent way, often reveals one or more flaws.

When my wife played this role she always asked me questions like a journalist. Here are some samples of questions that she asked me over and over again, some of which often stopped buys in their tracks:

1. What's going to make this stock go up?

2. Why is it going to go up when you think it is?

3. Is this really the best time to buy it?

4. Haven't we already missed a lot of the move?

5. Shouldn't we wait until it comes down a little more?

6. What do you know about this stock that others don't?

7. What's your edge?

8. Do you like this stock any more than any of the others you own and why?

The last question was particularly crucial because my wife never liked to add a stock without subtracting one, in part because she believed it was impossible to have dozens of good ideas at once that you could have an edge on. That's valuable advice. Without a sounding board, you simply aren't being rigorous enough. If you are in a jam, heck, call me on my radio show on Friday and articulate it, and I will give you the straight up or down in the "Lightning Round," the ultimate test of your conviction. Buying a stock should be like buying a car; there's a lot that goes into it. Don't short-circuit the process. Or as my wife would say, "Look for reasons not to do it," because they will certainly surface soon after you buy the stock.

25. There is always a bull market somewhere. At the end of every radio show I sign off with, "This is Jim Cramer reminding you that there is always a bull market somewhere." I say that because I can't stand the bellyaching I hear from professionals and amateurs that there are no good stocks out there. There are always markets and sectors and exchanges that are in bull mode. Even at the height of the just-completed bear market in 2000–2003, you had tremendous outperformance first in the food and beer stocks and then in the silver and gold stocks. These weren't proverbial flash in the pan moves, either. These were real, sustained, and totally catchable. There's a terrible desire among professionals and amateurs not to try something new, not to look at new markets or new stocks. The aversion comes from the amount of work that is required to learn new groups and from the belief that you can't stretch your knowledge. That's nonsense, as I showed you in the metrics section. In every situation, $E \times M = P$, and it can be solved for. More important, the obvious nature of the bull sectors should be self-evident to you by looking at the tables of exchange-traded funds that are readily available online in dozens of places. If you want to read about where the best bull markets are in what sectors, there's a terrific free publication put out twice a year by Fidelity for its investors, *The Fidelity Sector Fund Report,* which is the single best text about which sectors are doing what and why. I devour it as soon as it comes out, as I have for ten years. It's a brilliant document, and it will be obvious to you, as it is obvious to me, that there is always a bull market occurring at any given time somewhere on the planet, and is totally worth nailing, instead of bellyaching about how Cisco and Intel and Microsoft don't move anymore.

7

CREATING YOUR DISCRETIONARY PORTFOLIO

You're a baby boomer who just inherited $50,000. You are a young executive who finally has saved $10,000 from his paycheck. You just got married and you want to make some money in the market, not just watch your retirement index fund grow. You want to build a portfolio of stocks. You want to manage it yourself. How do you begin? Do you just grab a couple of stocks that are top rated from some broker or that score well on some quantitative tracker and let 'er rip? Or is there more to it?

If you are like most people, jammed to the gills with work, not a spare hour of time to be had in a week, let alone a day, and you still want to pick individual stocks, I've got some bad news for you. I won't play. I won't endorse your owning stocks or building a portfolio. You can't do the homework necessary to do it yourself. You don't have the time or inclination. Period. You will lose too much money. Hand over your money to the mutual fund manager.

I have spent the better part of the last five years doing repair work for individuals in your shoes who built their own portfolios during the heyday only to see all their hard-earned work immolated in a pyre of Commerce One, Internet Capital, and Lycos. Money just shredded into cold coals and burned out sparks. Fizzled to nothing, because people didn't know the basics, they didn't do the homework, and they ignored the cardinal rule to diversify to minimize the risks of single-sector annihilation.

I know the pushback. I can read your mind right now: The professionals didn't do it any better, either, most of them lost big, too. So I can do it better and it will cost me less. Here's the problem: Managing money is difficult, time-consuming, draining, and a totally alien experience for almost everyone who has come out of the educational system of the United States, where, if you are lucky, you may have learned the difference between a stock and a bond. You most likely figured out how to balance a checkbook on your own, but beyond that, handling money is tough for you. And now you want me to endorse your setting up a portfolio? Dream on. You'll be like all the other callers I talk to every day on my radio show who have crushed their own nest egg with reckless purchases based on bogus investment tools and advice that made them feel more confident about buying than they should have been.

But you've paid for the book, you've gotten this far through my basic training, you've digested my Miranda warnings against doing it yourself, and you won't take no for an answer. You insist that you can take control of your finances, that you are not going to let some broker churn you or some mutual fund rip you off. Your confidence that you can do better is unshaken. I will help you, but only on the following conditions:

1. You will do the time-consuming, sometimes tedious homework that I described earlier in the book. No shortcuts. You have to do it all. Remember, in my world it's buy and homework, not buy and hold. Take it from me, I speak to dozens of people who bought and held crummy stocks that they never should have purchased, let alone held. You have to listen to the conference calls—they are very time-

consuming and dense—read the articles, get the annual and quarterly statements and reports and understand them. If you don't, I will mentally buzzer you as I had to do to Dorothy from Queens, New York, who called me on my radio show last year claiming she had done all the homework that was necessary to buy International Game Technology and was "ready to pull the trigger." Just one thing, though, she said; she wanted to know why the stock was down 3 points, given that everything was so hunky-dory. I asked her, "Did you listen to the conference call on the quarter?" She said no way. I said had she listened she would have heard management say that contrary to the last few years of great consistent earnings, this year was going to be "lumpy." You pay up for companies with consistent growth, as I have demonstrated. You slaughter consistent growers that suddenly turn lumpy in their earnings generation. Now the stock will have to go from growth to value hands, and that takes many quarters and takes off many points. Dorothy was all set to be fleeced by the process because she thought she had done the homework after reading some articles about the potential of Indian gaming. Turns out she hadn't done anything substantive to merit her opinion. Thank heavens she called; the stock got obliterated shortly thereafter. Most of my callers, when asked if they did even the most basic level of homework, admit that they haven't when I define the homework substantively. Don't be a casualty; do the kind of studying that you would have done for a social studies test in seventh grade. You would do the work if you set out to buy a new car; stocks are even more expensive and don't come with warranty protection. No money-back guarantees here! Caveat emptor still lives in the stock market, despite the attempts by the tort lawyers to change it.

2. Which brings me to the second caveat that you must agree to before you get my blessing to run your own money instead of turning it over to others. You must promise to spend a minimum of one hour per position per week doing the research. I know this commitment sounds onerous. It isn't; it is commonsensical. There's a lot to do to maintain a portfolio, and I find myself routinely spending at least an hour a week staying on top of each of my positions. That's why I arbitrarily cap my positions at twenty-five; I have only about twenty-five hours each week free to do research because of my various commitments. When I have more positions than that, I fall down on the job and can't stay on top of things. And I am a very fast researcher and fact-gatherer about my companies. The difficult thing about this rule is that you can't be diversified to my liking unless you have five stocks in your portfolio, which means that you need to have five hours free a week to run your own money. Don't freak out; it takes five hours to watch an afternoon of football. It takes about five hours to go to a baseball game. You go to the movies, it's about a four-hour experience. Are those activities more important than your money? I didn't think so. If you don't have the time, skip to page 198, because you are not going to be a good enough portfolio manager. You just don't have the time. If you have only four hours, give the money to one of the fund managers I recommend. You can be a great client in four hours.

3. You must be interested in business, in what makes a business tick, to do it yourself. You must be curious about how a business makes its money, what its metric is that has to be beaten—gross margins, revenues, seat miles, average selling price per unit, etc.—and how much growth you think a company may have. If you don't have that inclination to find out these things, you won't know whether a decline in a stock is a buying opportunity or a time to puke up the stock—and if you don't know that, I guarantee you will lose money. If you can't explain to me in thirty seconds what a company does and what you are expecting out of that company, go be a great client; you won't be a great investor. I am not asking you to be a stock junkie, like me; I am asking you to have some authority and curiosity about companies before you buy them.

4. You must have someone, not necessarily a broker, you can bounce an idea off of, someone whom you trust, so you can get a second opinion on the stock before you buy it. I didn't use to believe this, but Byron Wien, the great strategist at Morgan Stanley, put this idea into my head during the beginning of the dot-com period. I was telling him my idea for TheStreet.com. I said that lots of people were going to go "self-directed," industry parlance for doing it yourself. He laughed and said it will never happen because people, in the end, are so fallible, they are going to want to interact with another human being first, as a sounding board, if not talk directly to a human broker, just to get some sense of whether the idea is so stupid and reckless that it shouldn't be done. I told him that millions of people were flocking to online trading. He told me that it was just a matter of time before they lost everything, in part because the idea of having to explain a buy to someone, explaining why you own something and why it is worth owning, requires the scrutiny of another person. The sounding board is worth the commission, he said. Of course, I was right and he was right. Millions went online and bought, and then those millions lost billions in part because they never bounced the zany, wacky ideas off anyone else. They never articulated why they liked something. You remove that embarrassing interchange and you will embarrass your-self a heck of a lot more on the back end. Get a sounding board before you buy. Don't have one? Call me Fridays on the "Lightning Round" at 1-800-862-8686 or during one of my second-opinion shows, where I can help you. Otherwise, again, have someone else run your money.

5. Finally, I can't have you get discouraged and quit. The whole process is a game of endurance. Think long-distance running. There are periods where you want all your discretionary money in cash, and there are periods where you want every dollar on the board wagering for you. Remember, I'm not talking about the retirement account. That's too sacrosanct to play with; you need to keep that with others unless you know already that you can beat the market. As I have said elsewhere, I am a rank conservative when it comes to retirement: I want the money as diversified as possible into high-quality equities as defined by an index fund or a mutual fund that acts as an index fund with a brain. We aren't fooling around here. As you get older, you need to have fewer stocks and more bonds. But that's not the kind of investing we are talking about here. What I am talking about here is the notion of setting up the portfolio and then having the discipline to stay with it, to review it, and to cull it and revise it. I will give you very specific advice later in the chapter how to rank things like a pro. We know that no asset class has beaten high-quality stocks that pay dividends over a twenty-year period. But we also know that many people get fed up during the tough times and blow their stocks out either because they can't take the pain or their stocks aren't of high enough quality to meet the test. Sign on for the long term, not a couple-of-years hitch. That will solve a lot of your problems.

Okay, now you have gone through the warnings and you have checked off on all five preconditions. You are now ready to build a portfolio to augment your paycheck. I am going to assume that you can build up to ten stocks, that you are willing to give it ten hours a week. If you can't do ten, cut it back to five and just take my top five from the Chinese menu I have prepared.

I am not intentionally trying to steer you to any one company. I have come up with a menu that makes it so you can get involved with a portfolio and stay involved, and use your expertise (which you may not even realize you have) to pick stocks. I want you to feel free to deviate from the list, but if you pick from it, I know you will be diversified in areas and types of stocks, and that will keep your risk to a minimum and your rewards to levels you are not used to achieving. I present it in menu form by sector or by risk-reward. You have to choose the stocks because, after all, it is *your* portfolio. This way, with this menu, I know you won't just own five tech stocks. I know you will be diversified and not get clobbered on the down days. I know you will stay involved because you are doing the picking, not me. I can't be your guru; who knows when I won't be there to hold your hand. You need to be your own guru, but I can give you the parameters, the guard rails so to speak, to be sure you don't plunge off the bridge into the sea of red ink that awaits so many who try to do it themselves.

1. Your first pick should be a stock of a company from your neighborhood, something that you know or can relate to, a company that employs people close to you or you can ask around about. Let me give you some examples. My first stock was an aircraft parts manufacturer in my hometown that was desperately searching for employees soon after I got out of college. I knew that in my lifetime the company had periodically been hiring and periodically laying off people, but I had never seen it recruit as aggressively as in 1979. I looked at the financials. It didn't have a lot of debt. I read what was available publicly— not much then, a lot more now. I bought the stock. It doubled in about seven months' time. The next stock I picked was out of a business magazine, a company in a business I knew nothing about, women's clothing, and I lost about 70 percent of my money in about seven weeks' time. That doesn't mean you are immune when you buy locally; it does mean, however, that if the stock goes down at first or if it gets hammered, you can more easily check around with friends and neighbors than if you are buying the stock of something with which you are not familiar. After that, I stuck close to home, or at least to something I would have some firsthand call on.

Please be careful when you work this hometown advantage. I bought the stock of a company once that had a factory that made precision instruments for aircraft dashboards. The local paper kept talking about how the division was hiring like crazy and getting big orders, but it was part of a larger company that at the same time was imploding under a mountain of debt. My method doesn't absolve you of homework; it is just a way to be able to get a feel beyond what you might get by just buying shares in some tech company that you know nothing about that could be slaughtered as you continue to buy down for no good reason.

There used to be a toy and novelty store down the block from where I lived in Brooklyn. I went by it every day to pick up a little trinket for my kids, something my dad used to do for me when I was growing up. Each day I heard the "boys" who ran it talking about what was hot and what wasn't. From them I had a very nice hit in Mattel, a comeback story. But one day I heard them cursing about the stock market. They had no idea who I was. One had bought Seagate, the other Daisy Systems. I told them at the register that I was always interested in stocks and that I was intrigued by what they knew about Seagate and Daisy, both of which I happened to have been shorting for my fund. They freely admitted they knew nothing; they had just heard these were hot stocks from someone on TV. I laughed and told them to get out now. Seagate was cut in half soon after; Daisy filed for bankruptcy. Classic—they were making me money with their inventory and they were buying stocks they knew nothing about.

Having trouble finding a local company or local news about one, like Mattel? Check the business pages of your local paper. They usually have a good read on the companies in and around town. Of course, you need to be able to stay current beyond reading that paper. All of the rules of homework apply, but that is a nice way to start. Many papers have beefed up their business coverage these last few years, and I always found them—still do—to be of tremendous value in finding new ideas. The best papers are the real local papers, the weekly local paper that covers just your area, your suburb, your neck of the woods. That's where the really great ideas come from.

2. Your next pick should be an oil stock. I almost never see a portfolio with an oil stock in it and it drives me crazy. These are some of the most consistent performers, with high-dividend yields, great cash flows, and businesses that do well in times of tension. I am a huge believer that we are going to see continual increases in demand for oil worldwide, and until a better fuel is found you should own shares in one of these companies. Exxon, British Petroleum, ChevronTexaco, ConocoPhillips, and Kerr-McGee all could be great for many, many years. They will be boosting their buybacks and raising their dividends as their cash flows have increased faster than any other sector. Oil is in what we call a "secular bull market," meaning that it has characteristics of longevity that counteract the traditional cyclical nature of so many businesses. Strong or weak economy, it seems, oil's staying

up there as a valued commodity. Can't come up with a stock? What brand of gas do you buy? That will probably be fine. Yeah, it is that simple.

Oil used to be 20 percent of the S&P 500 when I got into the business of stocks. It subsequently went all the way down to 5 percent two years ago. As I write it is only at 7 percent. I think that it belongs at 10 percent. When you see it there, you are free to take a profit if you want to. Not until then, though. These stocks have fallen well behind the price of crude; that will change over time and you will be the beneficiary.

3. You need a brand-name blue chip that currently sells at a 2.5 percent yield or greater. At any given time the market's putting on a sale of one of these and you just need to find which one is right. Why 2.5 percent yield? That's above average for the S&P and it affords you protection if the stock gets hit. I don't find a lot of 2.5 percent yielders getting crushed because they have a floor. The floor will be lower when the Fed finishes raising rates, but I think that it is nice to know that the worst thing that happens is you are getting an even bigger yield as the stock goes down. Consider one of the major chemical companies or conglomerates if you are having a hard time choosing. Try to get one with a history of raising dividends when possible. Please, please, don't buy the stock of a company that is borrowing to fund the dividend. I know I can count on you to spot that, because you agreed to my Miranda warnings earlier in this chapter. Remember to use the weakness in the market to buy a high-quality dividender on your terms.

4. You need to own shares in a financial, one of the largest portions of the S&P 500. I like to own local. I have had phenomenal success over a twenty-year period owning a local bank or a savings and loan. One of my biggest hits came from Commerce Bancorp. When it opened near me I was attracted to its seven-day-a-week service, and we decided to bank there. About three months after we put our money in CBH, I told my wife that I was going to be attending a conference where the CEO of CBH was going to be speaking. She told me that I should give him a piece of her mind because the sun glare in the afternoon made it impossible for her to read the screen at the automated teller. Sure enough, I got a moment with Vernon Hill and I told him that we were Commerce Bancorp users but that my wife didn't like the glare at her branch. He asked which branch, I gave him the location. It was a Saturday. On Monday my wife went to the branch and a glare shield had been added. That's my kind of service. And that's my kind of stock. I had a similarly positive experience with a Third Federal Savings when I used to live in Doylestown, Pennsylvania. I needed a mortgage; they came to my house, at night. Didn't even have to ask them to. I checked out their branch, looked at their financials, and ended up taking down a big chunk and getting a nice payback within a couple of years, with a good dividend, too. Every town has some publicly traded banks. If you have a good experience, go buy shares in it, provided that it has a good history of earnings and dividends, something that you know how to find out because you have agreed to do the homework in advance. Your visits to your bank are your gut checks that are so necessary to know whether you should buy more or not when the stock gets hit. And the stock will get hit and hit hard at some point while it is in your custody, as Commerce Bancorp did. I don't care whether you buy a savings and loan or a bank; I do care that there be insider buying in the institution—just some because I need to see conviction—and it sure helps if there is a nice-sized dividend relative to the rest of the market. I especially like situations where you can get in on shares in an IPO of a new savings and loan because you are a depositor. That's been the single biggest source of wins for thousands of investors who pay attention to where they bank.

5. No other financial writer in America is going to tell you what I am about to tell you next and frankly, I could not care less. I know you crave speculation and I know that some speculative investments can be rewarding. I am not willing, like so many others who write and talk about the market, to deny you that feeling. It is too ascetic and unnat-

ural. I know you will speculate anyway. It's human nature, in the same way that gambling and lottery tickets attract so many takers, no matter how many times you tell people it is a sucker's game. That's why to round out your top five investments I am blessing an investment in some risky, on the come, next Microsoft, Home Depot situation. You can choose something that is being recommended by the *Stocks Under $10* newsletter, perhaps, which I have a hand in. Or you can choose a tech or a biotech company that has some potential to be a huge company. I am blessing this because I have found that investing is a lot like parenting; if you don't give your kids a little room to do something daring, to break a few rules, then they will break all of the rules and cause tremendous heartache. I am telling you, go, with 20 percent of your money, and buy something that you think could be a terrific investment, a hunch, a potential home run. But if you do, please, I don't want you to put one penny more into speculation than that. You are taking a pledge. You must swear to me you won't put more into the speculative portion of your portfolio even if it is crushed and you want to average down. This is the portion of the portfolio where you can expect to lose your investment, and you should accept that. I don't want you losing more than your 20 percent, though, because you can't make it back with the consistent growers you own elsewhere in your portfolio. The math's just too brutal.

Mind you, if you have the time and the inclination, you might use this slot, again keeping in mind it is only 20 percent of your investment, in a pooled fashion. Some of the best investments I have ever made are in baskets of down-and-out stocks that can either go to zero or make you a fortune. In October 2002, for example, I recommended a basket of telecommunications stocks, all of which sold under $2: Lucent, Nortel, JDSU, Corning, and Qwest. With the downside factored in—thank heavens stocks can't go to negative 4—I watched as some of these stocks doubled and doubled again. Each time I took some of the investment off the table but let the rest run. I did a similar field bet in 2003 with the merchant energy companies like Dynegy and El Paso that were down on their luck and trading under $7. These kinds of field bets can serve as the speculative portion of your portfolio just as well as if you are trying to hunt for the next Amgen. Typically, in a field bet, one of the five will go to zero, another one or two will do nothing, but the others will create profit enough to make the whole thing worthwhile. I make these bets whenever a sector falls so out of favor that even if the stocks fall from where they are, the loss will not be of great magnitude. Again, you can't let the speculative portion of your portfolio exceed 20 percent of your invested capital or you are taking on too much risk. By the way, I am always making field bets in distressed areas, so stay close to what I'm up to for ActionAlerts PLUS.com, my private account where I send out e-mails to you telling you what I am going to do before I do it. I play with an open hand. For a trial simply log in at www.thestreet.com/actionalertsplus, another special URL for readers of the book only.

You have now selected five stocks from a list of diversified sectors. You can stop there or, if you have the time and inclination, you can diversify further, adding something from each of the next five items as you get more capital.

6. Rotations of the type I have described—where market players flee safety for aggressive cyclicals because the Fed is about to ease rates aggressively—often create tremendous buying opportunities in the staid and true, the Procter & Gambles, Kelloggs, the Colgates, BUDs, General Millses and Gillettes, the so-called medicine chest and fridge stocks. As you have already selected your diversified five stocks, why not wait to add the sixth, a soft-goods secular growth stock, until the market deems it out of fashion. You have a long-term time horizon; be smart and pick the stock up when nobody likes it. Use the rotation to pick it up much cheaper than you would otherwise. Use the decline to win, not lose, for once, with your portfolio. Lots of times these stocks go down hard after a particular quarter because some fund or funds get disappointed. But it is a tribute to the high quality of these branded companies that they almost always snap back. So don't be

afraid to buy the most dislocated of the companies that have big shelf space in the supermarket. That's how I gauge it—with my eyes.

7. Now, to augment that soft-goods play, I want you to buy one high-quality cyclical stock when it is clear that the economy is going to go bust and the smokestack stocks are being trashed repeatedly. My favorites: Dow, Deere, DuPont, Caterpillar, Boeing, Ingersoll-Rand, United Technologies, and 3M. These stocks, like those of the category above, *always* get slammed if you wait long enough, and the slamming will produce value for a long period of time. Again, you have to regard the rotation as your chance to pounce on the proverbial straw hat in winter or snowshoes in July. You are not affected by the "inventory" concerns that plague so many professional money managers. No one is looking over your shoulder, no one is reviewing your portfolio daily, so use that advantage to snap up the stocks that the lemmings have to get rid of to show they were "in the know." These are great American companies that, several times a year, get thrown into the discount bin or are marked down by market hysteria. You have to be ready when it happens.

8. Technology companies are risky; but not to have a technology company has proven to be a terrible risk for all but three of the last twenty years. That's why I think you have room for one after you have selected the other seven stocks. Me, I am so conservative, I like tech companies with yield. That means they are mature enough to be steady growers and you haven't necessarily sacrificed double-digit growth. If you think that I am being too stodgy, you have an easy choice: Make your tech stock your speculative stock. I have seen so many portfolios with the same old poorly performing bunch of techs that I can't bear to see you load up with too many of them. I would hate to have to buzzer you if you called me on a Wednesday when I am playing "Am I Diversified?" I know that tech can be considered the lifeblood of the economy, but so many have put tech at the first, second, and third portions of their portfolios, much to their own ruina-

tion, that I need you to deemphasize the sector. It is too dangerous to overweight until all the others have capitulated. And remember, that comes from me, an Intelaholic.

9. Add one young retailer that hasn't yet expanded to the majority of the country, and has preferably saturated only one region of the nation on a march to national status. People are always saying that the retailers are great investments, but they don't understand that it is not "the retailers" in general, but the retailers that are still expanding geographically around the nation. In fact, once the companies are everywhere they tend to be pretty poor investments, as anyone who has owned May or Federated or even Wal-Mart can attest. I like to buy retailers when they are just getting started and they have a concept that, if it works in one place, can work all over the country. That's how I discovered and owned so many great retailers, including great one-time growth stocks like the Limited, Gap, Wal-Mart, Kohl's, and even Lowes and Home Depot. Once they were everywhere, though, I sold them and never looked back. Currently I like Cabela's because it is a high-end camping and hunting store that could go for years before it saturates the landscape. Be careful, though, you must check them out firsthand.

10. Finally, buy a "hope for the future" nontech stock, perhaps a biotech company or another kind of company from the S&P 600, which is the mid cap index. Many of these companies will turn out to be the Amgens and Starbucks of tomorrow. You have to be a legit company to get into the S&P 600, and it is the proving ground for the S&P 500. It's a natural place to hunt for some good names. That's a great list to choose from; if you can't come up with something, pick a holding from the New America index of *Investor's Business Daily*. They have a phenomenal track record for selecting these kinds of medium-stage companies. Again, do your homework. *IBD* is no substitute, just another terrific starting point for ideas that you can use to find the next big stock.

Now that you have picked your stocks, you have to learn how to buy and sell for your portfolio.

I am a huge believer, as you know, in my own fallibility. I also like to make the market work for me. It puts on sales all the time. I like to use those sales to buy my stocks cheaply. That's why I have urged you to set up your portfolio to take advantage of the sales. Rotation sales are like post-Christmas sales. You know they are going to come. Unlike Christmas, you don't purchase a stock for someone else; this is for you. So wait for the sale and take advantage of it.

I also don't believe in putting too much money to work at one level. I know that the market tends to fool the most people it can. So why be faked out? Why not accept that your first buy may not be your last buy and build in the weakness? That way you are never top-ticking, something that's incredibly important if you are going to stay in the game. I know most people think that the market is rigged against them. That's because they buy a stock and it immediately goes down. Heck, if so many people complain about this—and they do on my radio show all of the time—let's do something about it.

So, let's say I want to own 200 shares of Cabela's as part of a retail bet because this retailer is only in a small part of the country and it can grow forever. It will take a decade before Cabela's has saturated anything. That means anytime it dips it could be a terrific buy.

What I like to do is buy my first 100 shares and then wait. If the stock goes down a buck or two, I will buy it; if it goes up, oh well, the worst that happens is I have made a little less money than I would like. That's how I buy everything. I like to buy weakness. Similarly, I like to sell strength. When I have decided to take something off the table I wait until a day when my stocks are running and I offer them out. I never like to exit all at once; I pare back. That's the best way; don't let your broker press you into being the big man and selling all at once.

At any given time I maintain a wish list of stocks to buy and to sell as part of my portfolio. I don't know when the sell-off is going to take place; I just presume it will happen and then I pounce. I am so religious about not buying stock all at one level that I actually sketch out the levels I will pull the trigger at, and I will widen or narrow the scale of the bids depending on how well or badly the market might be doing at the time. If I believe, for example, as I did in 2000–2002, that the market itself would serve to hinder my buys, I use a wide scale. If the market was poised to make a move because, as a whole, it seemed cheap and was ready to roll higher, I would use tighter scales. I let the market throw its sales to get my merchandise at better prices.

Of course, there will always be situations where you have been too aggressive and the market becomes brutal. There will always be situations where you simply misjudge the market. I don't care about misjudging it too conservatively: The worst that happens is you make less money. I care about being too aggressive when the timing is bad and getting your head handed to you. Again, those kinds of misjudgments come with the risky assets we are accumulating. My insurance against my own fallibility, besides the use of scales to buy on the way down, is to rank my stocks, perform a sort of battlefield triage for the moments when it seems as if the world's coming to an end and all of my stocks are getting killed. That's why I rank my stocks every Friday on a scale of 1 to 4. It helps me make judgments in a cool moment that can then hold up during the hurly-burly of the trading day. (I don't like to make these rankings during the trading day because that influences my fears more than it should. Fear is too powerful when the market's open.) My four-part scale makes the process much easier. You can easily employ the same strategy with your portfolio. A 1 is a stock that if I have capital handy—some sidelined cash or new money—I want to apply it right now, that's how good it is. A 2 is a stock that if it pulled back 5–7 percent, or a couple of points, I would buy more. A 3 is a stock that if it were to go up 5–7 percent, or a few points, I would begin to sell it. And a 4 is the mirror image of a 1, it is a stock I want to get rid of ASAP, either because it has gone up enough or because I think it could be a real bone-crusher in an ugly tape. Because I have ranked my stocks, when things get nasty I circle the wagons around my 1s and 2s and I let go of my 3s and 4s. I would be willing on the fly to whittle my positions down to my top five from ten if I felt that I was in danger of getting crushed by the market. I also know that if there are stocks that I wouldn't buy right now, then I don't have the conviction I need, I am too heavily invested, and I will panic out of my holdings when the tape turns really ugly. (If this is all foreign to you, take a trial of my ActionAlertsPLUS.com where I run my own money publicly. Lots of good ideas there, and I use this identical ranking system to make all my buy and sell decisions.)

Ranking stocks is a tremendous way to test your discipline and your conviction. If you don't want to buy more of a stock right now, right here, that says something. That says when things get tough you will jettison it in a heartbeat. What we are looking for, what ranking does, is make it so that weakness is *welcomed*. It stands the psychology on its head and turns fear into a method of buying your stocks on terms you want, instead of selling them on terms the markets dictate.

I love the flexibility, by the way, of selling a quarter or even half of my shares as a stock goes up. Selling strength is another of my trademarks. If you want to buy on a sale at a store, wouldn't you like to return some of the merchandise at a higher price if possible? When I put it like that, I'm sure you understand my "scaling out" on the way up. If the stock falls back, I can always repurchase it. If it keeps rallying, I just make a little less money than I would like. By selling partially into strength, I don't violate my bulls, bears, and pigs adage. But I also let my winners run, which is vital, particularly because I often see people sell really good stocks that are going higher where they have done a giant amount of homework, only to reinvest the money in a loser.

Ranking stocks, making sure not to defend everything because then you really are defending nothing, and waiting for broad market sell-offs that have nothing to do with the companies you are buying but are knocking down the stocks you like anyway are the disciplines necessary to maintain your portfolio in tip-top shape. They are the key to implementing a disciplined approach that allows conviction to make you money but limits the losses during the inevitable vicious markets that we have all become so fearful of. You must feel emboldened by sell-offs, not paralyzed by them. You must recognize that a sale in the market is no more frightening than a sale at Macy's. If you do that, you will prosper when others are beside themselves with pain or throwing up their hands with resignation.

You don't have the time or the inclination to build and maintain a portfolio with your discretionary savings. What can you do instead? I've got a couple of options, none of them optimal, but all of them acceptable. First, you can get your diversity and beat almost every single mutual fund manager simply by buying shares in stock index fund. Almost every major firm has them; the key is to find the lowest fees possible as these are commodities. Vanguard pioneered the S&P 500 index fund and is the cheapest and best one I can find.

Why do most managers fail to beat index funds? Because it's a lot harder to manage a lot of money than it looks. If you manage a traditional mutual fund and you do well, you will soon be inundated with money, which will cause you to change your style and, over time, unless you are incredibly good, you will begin to mirror an index fund, except you will be charging your investors higher fees.

John Bogle, the most honest money manager in the business, and the creator of the index fund, once appeared on one of my TV shows after I had run money professionally for about ten years. He said that no successful manager, over the long run, can beat an index fund. I told him that was just untrue, that I was a living, breathing example of someone who consistently beat index funds. He then asked me, "Do you limit the amount of money you take in?" I told him that not only did I limit the amount of money that I took in but that I was almost always closed to new investors.

He then asked me how much I ran. At the time I had about $200 million under management. He said that as long as I stayed under $500 million and was closed to new investors—relying only on capital appreciation for more money under management—I would be able, if I continued to be really good, to beat the market. But once I got above those levels and changed my exclusionary policy I would eventually become a glorified index fund with high fees. I never forgot that and I never went bigger than $500 million. I also never got beat. That's why.

Most mutual funds, which have a different incentive structure from a hedge fund, can't be so exclusionary. Hedge funds take a percentage of the gains—realized and unrealized. I took 20 percent. Mutual funds take a percentage of the money under management, usually about 1 percent. Given that everyone on Wall Street wants growth, the way to grow your fees is to take in more money. So the natural tendency is to get big fast, particularly after you have a hot hand. That's just the recipe for underperformance that Bogle sketched out. Nevertheless, there are some managers, individual managers, who are so good that they have been able to overcome the Bogle problem. Unfortunately, they are few and far between. Consider the game like the NBA; 99.9 percent of the basketball players aren't good enough to get in the NBA, and even when you get there, only a handful are bona fide superstars.

Before I give you the names of the great managers, let me just add that I hate giving mutual fund recommendations. As an experiment five years ago I put $2,500 into each of fifty mutual funds to see if I could keep up with who was good and discover some stars, some people worth writing about. Only three of the funds made me money, and none made enough money to get mentioned here. Bogle's right.

Still, there are some managers I recommend because they are truly world-class stock pickers. Notice, I am giving you the name of the manager, as well as the fund. *If* the managers were to leave or retire—and the industry is notorious about not telling you if they do, so you have to stay on top of it—you will have to pull your money out pronto because you only buy a manager in this business, not a fund.

The first is Will Danoff of Fidelity Contrafund. Danoff worked with my wife in the 1980s, and it always burned me up that she said he was as smart as I was. I always figured that if she weren't married to me she would be telling people that he was smarter than I am. I am a jealous guy. The only way to get even is to give the guy you think might be better than you some money, which is why I have a lot of my personal retirement money with Contra. Danoff's the real deal. He's had the fund since 1990. While his five-year performance is not a knockout at 1.69 percent, he's your index fund with a brain, as the S&P returned −2.30 percent during the same period. I like to use Danoff's Contra as a substitute index fund because it always does a little better with less risk. You can't ask for more than that from big money.

My second pick is Richie Freeman of the Smith Barney Aggressive Growth Fund. Freeman's fantastic; a stock picker *par excellence,* someone who lives and breathes stocks the way I do. He's incredibly focused and driven to beat the averages. You want him in your corner. Freeman's always good, but I particularly like to give him money after he's had a rough patch; he's so competitive that that's when he is most bankable. Richie's been in the game since 1983. In the last five years he's averaged 5.83 percent, with terrific recovery from a very tough 2002.

My third pick is the John Hancock Classic Value Fund, run by Rich Pzena. Rich got in the business about the same time I did and has always been a fantastic value guy. I'd entrust him with any amount of money because he picks stocks with the lowest risk and highest reward of anyone I know. Always has. Rich has chalked up a 13 percent annual return over the last five years. Wow!

Lawrence Auriana's been a guest numerous times on my CNBC show. He and his partner Hans Utsch have been running the Federated Kaufmann Fund for almost two decades. They are driven to find new names, great health-care and tech companies. They are wild-card players, but they play those cards more consistently than any managers I know. These two have shot the lights out over a long period of time, notching 12.5 percent annually in the last five years.

Finally, the only manager I don't know personally whom I will recommend is Clyde McGregor, who runs the Oakmark Equity and Income Fund. Unlike all of the other funds, this one has a heavy bond exposure, so consider it the most conservative of the lot. Given this fund's risk aversion, the 11.76 percent return is just plain stellar.

Remember that mutual funds are already diversified, so you don't need to own a whole bunch of them. I am always getting phone calls and e-mails from people who own ten or twenty mutual funds, which is absurd. Who can keep up with that? I would invest in the Oakmark Equity and Income Fund if you are conservative, Federated Kaufmann or Smith Barney Aggressive Growth if you want to have some risk with big reward, and the Contrafund if you are somewhere in the middle like the vast majority of folks out there. If you just had to own one fund, I would make it Contra. I don't want to overthink this process. I bet all of these managers are going to beat the index funds simply because they are better than 99 percent of the managers.

What happens if you say, Hold it, I want to be in a hedge fund, not a mutual fund. I want some of the service that Cramer gave to his partners at his firm, where he talked to his clients whenever they wanted and told them what they owned and consistently outperformed. (Mutual funds tell you nothing about what they own in real time, so you just have to trust the manager.) I have bad news for you. I have no recommendations for you. First of all, hedge funds can take only "qualified" investors, meaning rich people. Second, I don't know anyone I would like to recommend to you. I can tell you, though, that you need to interview the manager personally and be sure that he has done well in good *and* bad times. It is incredibly important that the manager give you two references whom you can call. If he can't do that, don't bother. He also has to have an outside accountant who works just for the partners. That accountant works for you, gets all of the confirmations and documents, and can tell you where you stand. Without such an arrangement, I would be scared to have my money with that fund, because hedge funds aren't regulated by the SEC in the same way that mutual funds are.

Should you be worried about shenanigans at the mutual funds, after the terrible disclosures that some made about selling the net asset value of the individuals to the hedge funds to take advantage of pricing discrepancies? Not any more. The regulators have cracked down. But far worse than the chicanery, frankly, is the poor management and the return after the fees are taken. The managers I recommend above all charge fees, but the net return of their funds after fees is still much better than the averages, and only the net matters.

If instead of giving your money to a hedge fund or a mutual fund you want to give it to an individual broker, all I can say is good luck. My experience is that no really good broker, who has made money consistently for his clients, can service you if you have less than $250,000. Of course, there will be thousands who disagree, so here's what I suggest. Find someone with your size nest egg who can recommend a broker. It is a total word-of-mouth business. The firm itself means nothing to me, only the broker, because at any firm there are hundreds of ideas and ways to make money. You need someone who can harness the best and cull the worst. Only a word-of-mouth recommendation is going to cut it for me, because, again, I have no recommendations. I don't mean that meanly, I am just saying that it is a one-to-one business, like health care, and you have to find the broker you would be most comfortable with.

If you have less than $250,000 and you want a broker, I don't think I can protect you from being treated poorly. So you either have to learn to do it yourself or you split up the money among the managers I have highlighted here.

I know I sound cynical, but just call me skeptical. Having worked as a commission broker, an investment adviser, and a hedge fund manager, and having taken and answered literally tens of thousands of calls and e-mails from investors, I know the business's limitations. I am not going to sugarcoat them. If you care about your money and you want to see it grow and you don't want it screwed up, you must take the time and develop the inclination to do the things I say here. Together we can do it; otherwise everything else is just, well, settling for less than you deserve.

Oh, one other thing: please be wary of hot funds. One time, while I was working with my wife, a decade before I talked with Bogle, I opened my fund after a fantastic quarter. I took in almost the same amount of money that I was running. What happened? Well, when I was a kid there was a game show called *Supermarket Sweep*. In the show contestants would have a couple of minutes to run through a supermarket with a cart, gathering as many expensive goods as they could. Whoever grabbed the highest-priced merchandise won the game—"Look, he's going for the hams!"

That was me. I had to put that money to work. Fast as possible. They didn't give me the money to sit on the sidelines, I rationalized. I went for the hams! Sure enough I got the market's equivalent of trichinosis. As soon as I spent the money I knew I had done the wrong thing. Within two weeks the fund had dropped 10 percent. I spent the rest of the year making up for the decline.

Why does this happen? Couple of reasons. One is that you feel the responsibility of the new money. You feel that you have to justify why you took it in. The only way to justify it is to invest it.

Second, the size that you use to buy, your deployment tactics, change when you run twice as much money. You don't know how much you should put to work at one level. You don't how you should buy things. If I used to buy 5,000 shares at a time should I now buy 25,000? I blew my head off because my usual method, 5,000 shares at a time, seemed too slow to me. I started committing capital too aggressively.

Third, what works for $20 million may not work for $50 million or $500 million or $5 billion. Maybe the secret of your first-quarter success was finding precisely the right small cap stocks. Now that you took in all of this money you feel like you have to invest, but you can't find the right small caps to meet your rigorous criteria. So you force things. That's how you make even bigger mistakes.

Eventually the stress of the money cascading through the door becomes too much for any mortal to take. The job becomes managing the input, not picking stocks, and the great stock pickers get sacrificed. The fund managers I recommend have dealt with this issue, confronted it, and have the tenure and power to tell the marketing department, "Look, I can't handle the money right now. That's why I feel so confident about them and so nervous about the new ones I don't know."

8

┌ ┐

SPOTTING BOTTOMS

in

STOCKS

└ ┘

If someone asked me what I do for a living, what's my modus operandi, I would have to tell them that I spot bottoms in stocks. That's my specialty. That's what I am best at. I'm good at buying a stock when it is down and nobody much cares for it. Most investors are momentum driven. They want to try to catch a stock while it is having a huge move. They like to buy up, pay up, find a stock that's moving like Secretariat and catch the last five furlongs. That's not for me. Not enough reward, too much risk, especially given what I know about how a company's stock can diverge substantially from the worth of the underlying company. That's why I am not a chaser; I'm a classic bottom fisher. I try to buy situations where stocks have gone down to some level that to me is just plain wrong, that is totally and unequivocally out of synch with the underlying company the stock represents. I try to buy stocks with such a limited downside that I feel they are gifts if they go any lower, not accidents waiting to happen. Given that we accept that the fundamentals and the stocks that are supposed to track these fundamentals don't act in synch, obviously the most lucrative time to buy the divergence is when the company's otherwise sound fundamentals are temporarily impaired and the stock takes a header well beyond what is warranted. That's when the company's long-term virtues are totally out of whack with the equity.

It stands to reason then that the same goes for the market as a whole. There are moments of sheer lunacy involving the S&P 500, the benchmark index that we all follow, or in the NASDAQ or even the Dow Jones averages, where these gold standards of investing go awry because of panicky sellers. They can be completely and totally wrong versus how the underlying companies or the economy is really doing. That happens at bottoms. The positive realities separate themselves from the panicked fantasies of bizarre, uneconomical, and irrational closing prices, and you have to pounce when they do.

Understand that bottom fishing is not a "technique" per se, as in "buy a stock down 10 percent from its fifty-two-week high" or "buy the market on a big dip." That's way too ephemeral for me. Nor is it a formula, as in "wait until a stock trades through its growth rate" or "don't pull the trigger until a stock trades at a 25 percent discount to the market, or at 10 times earnings." That's too hard and fast for reality. Lots of really crummy stocks of really crummy companies are going to trade down 25 percent and then go down another 75 percent. That's a fishing net that catches some salmon as well as a lot of killer orcas, murderers of your financial well-being. My bottom fishing is a collection of perceived working patterns that have held up over a substantial period of time for both individual stocks and the market as a whole. Just like the sport that I compare it to, bottom fishing requires incredible patience and a sense that just when you are about to give up is the moment that greatness strikes. You can't rush bottoms. It is no more scientific than fishing—there's a definite feel to it. The biggest mistake people make in finding bottoms is that they find too many of them and find them too often. The bottoms I am talking about are rare, rare and dramatic. True long-lasting bottoms just don't occur every day, or every month, or even every quarter. They occur just often enough to make the patient rich and to reward the out-of-favor buyer.

When selecting individual stocks, most people try to catch bottoms by looking at a chart, one of those with candles on it, or with squiggly lines that mark a two-hundred-day average of how the stock has traded. They see that a stock has gone down for a long time; perhaps it has retreated to something like its norm, as represented by the fifty-two-week moving average, and lately the stock has stopped bleeding. That's enough for many of these chartists, regardless of whether the patient has stopped bleeding because he is dead or because he's healed. To me, bottom fishing by chart is reckless. It often sends a false signal and puts you in a stock or the market way too early and without any grounding if the stock breaks down again from that level. To me a "chart bottom" doesn't make you any money and gives you an artificial and unwarranted sense of confidence. You will never spot a real stock market bottom simply by looking at a chart. Even Mrs. Cramer, who regarded herself as the quintessential chart bottom caller, was off by as much as 50 percent from the start of some of her small stock bottoms that she picked from the chart alone. That's too dangerous for me.

Nor are there successful software packages or Web sites that produce lists of surefire bottoms, even though many people pitch these products in that vernacular. Don't be taken by shameless charlatans; things aren't that easy out there. Avoid those packages that show you well-defined channels or successful entry points. They are all bogus and will cause you to double down or sell at the worst possible moments. My kind of bottom calling is also different from the unoriginal and often corrupted world of Wall Street research, where hedge funds or mutual funds lean on analysts at sell-side firms, telling them to call bottoms in some of their flagging stocks or else they will take their commission dollars elsewhere. Don't think this stuff has happened? Then you were never on the other end of the line when I berated analysts to climb out of their foxholes and make a stand to defend a Cisco or an Intel when I owned them. I used to do it all of the time; thank heavens I am out of that contest. Nor do I spot bottoms by watching and listening to the much hyped "earnings" reports during earnings season. Despite all of those "upside" and "downside" surprises, none of the bottoms I have studied were ever caused by those reports. These are almost all artificial anyway, a product of the companies' whispering to analysts what numbers to use so they can beat those lowball projections by a penny or two and take in unsuspecting new shareholders, or buyers. That was supposed to have stopped with the corporate reform—the Sarbanes-Oxley Act—but it still goes on. So you can forget about that mumbo jumbo for finding bottoms after a long slide; it doesn't compute.

Nor am I talking about capturing momentary trading bottoms, either. I am not trying to persuade you to try to scalp flow off institutional buy and sell orders, as I did at my hedge fund. You need to generate monster commissions before you will get "the call" that a seller who has mercilessly knocked a stock down while exiting has at last finished his nefarious work and the temporarily depressed stock is ready to bounce. That kind of ephemeral bottom doesn't make you big money and is completely inaccessible to you anyway. It just generates a lot of short-term profits for the hedge fund operators and a new set of commissions for the brokerage houses on top of the ones gained from working the stock down.

Not one big bottom that I have found was ever called by a Wall Street analyst with a buy recommendation, either. The "hold to buy" parlance never coincided or was predictive of the bottoms I am trying to catch. These people make you money, for the most part, by luck. Almost all of the major analysts at the large firms got hired for banking prowess—bringing in the next underwriting deals—not for stock picking. If you have to use one, be sure he doesn't do banking first, so you at least know that *you* are the client and not the investment banker down the hall. In a study of literally thousands of big bottoms in the stock market or in individual stocks I couldn't find a single big bottom that was snared by these folks. In fact, it is the opposite. I found their downgrades to be more predictive of important bottoms than their upgrades because of their inability to see the bottoms coming. So there's nothing in this chapter that relies upon my hedge fund specialty, my good calls from brokers for all the business I did, nor my close contacts with dozens of analysts from around the country. In fact, sadly, the closer you get to the vortex of information that I swirled in at my old office, the more likely that a bottom will be drowned out by the accompanying noise that often causes it.

My bottoms are what I call "megabottoms." These are the kinds of bottoms that you brag about getting for years, the kind that occur after vicious and often wildly exaggerated declines. The kind that happen when a stock seems permanently damaged even as the company underneath is suffering no more than a scant hiccup. My work on the topic is the result of examining and studying thousands of true bottoms that I have called—and some that I have missed—in both the stock market and in individual stocks. When you invest in these kinds of bottoms, you don't have to be nearly as worried about all of the other things that I caution and counsel about in this book. You can stay a bull for a while, you have a longer time to wait until you become a pig. You don't have to fear imminent overvaluation because you have caught a stock at its most severe undervaluation and the pendulum just doesn't swing that fast in this game. Your reward so outweighs your risk that you can come as close to relaxing and living off a stock as you ever will in this business. You have gigantic leeway to let your gain run. That's the best kind of gain and one that can make up for a lot of losers.

I divide the patterns into two kinds of bottoms, investment bottoms and trading bottoms. Trading bottoms don't last but are so juicy, and, in these days of low commissions and instant trading, so obtainable, that I don't want you to miss them. Investment bottoms, however, are long lasting and you can get in some fantastic prices for discretionary savings or retirement. Some coincide with overall bottoms of the stock market itself.

I love to talk about individual stocks more than anything else in the world. I would like to think I can spot a stock that is finished going down better than anyone. But with that talent comes a recognition that no matter how good you are at divining the moves of individual stocks, the vast majority of bottoms occur simultaneously with market bottoms. That's because there is so much money "indexed," or bet on the S&P 500, that if you can pick a bottom in that index, you can pick a bottom in most stocks. There are always exceptions. The gold stocks don't trade with the index; they represent an industry that tends to do well when the index does badly. Same with the oil stocks; they are a counterindex. If you can nail the index at its bottom, though, suffice it to say that you have a lot of bases covered. That's why we will review market bottoms first. At market bottoms you could have five hundred to six hundred new lows to choose from, and even the worst ones bounce if you catch the move right.

In the past twenty years we have seen four market bottoms of consequence: the 1987 crash bottom, the 1990 Iraq-Kuwait bottom, the 1998 Long-Term Capital bottom, and the 2002–2003 post-dot-com, pre-second-Iraq-war bottom. All four of those bottoms were exquisite moments to buy because if you nailed them, if you kept some cash on the sidelines for them and applied it correctly, or if you went all into equities at these moments, you beat the vast majority of managers and made fortunes for yourself or your investors. There were many other false bottoms during this study period, but none of them measured up in terms of opportunities worth committing that excess capital aggressively into the market. What mattered, in each case, was that indicators reached extremes that told you it was safe to land your capital. I chose that analogy because I like to look at the market the way a pilot examines an instrument panel when there is so much fog that he can't land on visibility alone. I like to consider the indicators as a checklist that, when enough criteria are met, signals that it is okay to bring down the airplane, or to commit capital to the market. That's why I present them in checklist form so you can use them during the periods when most market gurus and mavens are saying it is safe. You can know better.

I have studied these bottoms intensively, both as a participant and as a historian. They each had one-of-a-kind characteristics, but not enough to make the study of them useless and nonpredictive. They had so many readily observable commonalities that these bottoms are, in retrospect, discernable and investable, and, most important, worth waiting for.

Every bottom is caused by different events. In the 1987 bottom, which occurred the day after the crash of 1987, a series of mergers and acquisitions took place as corporate America recognized that the monstrous 22 percent sell-off didn't foreshadow any economic downturn and was more a matter of computerized program trading run amuck. (We haven't had a decline like that since then because of sensible moves put in by the New York Stock Exchange to control the velocity of declines.) The 1990 bottom occurred after Iraq's invasion of Kuwait, which led to a dramatic decline in the price of oil after an initial spike. The 1998 decline got staunched, ostensibly because of a cut in interest rates by the Fed. The 2002–2003 double bottom (October 2002 and February 2003) occurred with the run-up to and start of the Iraqi war.

It's because of the disparity of events and their unusual nature— the next bottom will most likely not be triggered by another Iraq war—that most people tend to think that market bottoms are too aberrational to call. That lack of history repeating itself has led to an investment philosophy that says, basically, "We don't know when a bottom is going to be reached, so you should just stay long all of the time and not worry about it." There is a certain logic to this notion: The academic work of Jeremy Siegel, the nation's foremost stock historian, shows that high-quality equities have outperformed every other asset class over a twenty-year period, so you could say, what does it matter if you spot a bottom when you already own stocks for a much larger cycle? Indeed, for retirement investment, I am in the camp that says bottom calling is not an important exercise. I routinely invest one-twelfth of my allowable retirement funds each month, accelerating that process only if we have a significant decline, one that I define as 20 percent, in the market. That staged investment, coupled with the occasional plunge during a big decline, however, has produced far above average results.

More important, though, discretionary money, money meant to augment your paycheck, should always be at hand so you can take advantage of bottoms. I almost always keep a minimum of 10 percent up to a maximum of 25 percent of my discretionary money in cash, to profit from when I see the signs of a bottom developing.

With that, let's examine what all four of these market bottoms had in common, what had to happen in each case before the stock market could stop going down. All of this information is readily accessible, by the way, through reading a combination of *USA Today,* the *New York Times, Investor's Business Daily,* and the *Wall Street Journal.* If that's too time-consuming, I constantly update this stuff during the trying periods in TheStreet.com.

1. Market sentiment. The first dashboard instrument we have to check to determine whether we have a bottom at hand is market sentiment. Sentiment's a tough thing to gauge. There are tons of anecdotal indicators and services that produce "bottom calls," but I find them dubious because they tend to be without long-term significance. We are, in the end, measuring pain, and when the pain gets to the maximum, we are going to get a bottom, which was the case in all four of our megabottoms of the last twenty years.

That said, here's my sentiment/psychology checklist of what must occur before we can be sure that a bottom might be at hand. Until you see *every* one of these indicators, you would be nuts to commit any excess capital to the market. It would be akin to running outside of a bomb shelter during the London Blitz without waiting for the sirens.

First: The pain makes the front page of the *New York Times.* This indicator, one of the absolute favorites of Mrs. Cramer, has literally never been wrong. Such a simple thing, but is worth considering why it works so well. First, the supposition here is that during the periods of incredible pain there are always people who show up in the business sections of your newspaper, in the business magazine press, and, of course, on business TV, saying that a bottom is at hand. For the most part, those who say these things are pushing an agenda. They typically have liked the market for some time and didn't get out, or they are always liking the market because it is good, at least short-term, for their business, whatever that business might be. Maybe they run a mutual fund and that fund can't short. It's therefore "always" a good time to invest in that firm. Maybe they run a brokerage business that makes its money in commissions and the worst thing that can happen is to say, "I wouldn't buy now." Given that most of the profits from equities come from writing buy tickets, chiefly of underwritings, where the sales fee is much bigger than anything that could be gotten on the sell side, the notion of trusting any of these people is simply preposterous.

Nor does it help to read in the business section of the *New York Times* or the green "Money" section of *USA Today,* the two most important papers when it comes to calling a bottom, that there is a lot of blood on the streets or that the pain is getting too great. Those are classic canards, too. In my research on bottoms I found dozens of articles about pain and losses in these sections that were written *before* some of the biggest parts of declines occurred. But all bearish bets are off when the *New York Times* or *USA Today* puts the market's pain in a prominent place on the *front* page of their papers. Amazingly, at every bottom, stories about how horrid the market is have become a staple. If the market-woes stories aren't on the front page, then simply wait; the bottom hasn't been reached yet. There hasn't been enough pain outside the little financial world to create a bottom. It is simply incredible how right this indicator always is. It's so right that every time I have come up against a terrible bear market phase, and there have been a ton of them in the last twenty-five years, I find myself arguing with my wife about the possibility of a bottom, and she will casually ask me whether the *Times* has put the markets' woes on page one. When the answer is no, stay on hold; you aren't there yet. You will miss some transient bottoms for sure, but all megabottoms meet this characteristic before rallying sharply and, largely, for good.

A **second** gauge of sentiment that has never been wrong and has snared all four of these megabottoms is the Investors Intelligence survey of money managers. Again, like the *New York Times* indicator, it is a contraindicator, a counterintuitive sign that will make sense only after you understand the dynamics of the poll.

For twenty years, Investors Intelligence, a nationwide service, has questioned newsletter writers about whether they are bullish or bearish. While you might expect that a good time to invest is when the managers are bullish, that's actually the worst time to invest. Anyone who answers the poll by saying he is bullish is admitting that he likes the market. If he likes the market, he is by definition already in and invested. It therefore stands to reason that if everybody's bullish, then everyone's spent his cash and bought his stock. Which is why the single most important sentiment indicator I follow after the front-page *New York Times* indicator is when a majority of money managers polled dislike the market. When the bull-bear ratio shows a definitive majority of bears or even a plurality of bears with less than 40 percent bulls, you are in the safety sentiment zone. Mind you, a reading alone of less than 40 percent bulls doesn't per se mean a bottom. But remember this is a checklist, and this is one of the most important indicators to hold out for to be sure you are not getting a false reading. If you jump the gun and commit your reserves because you think the market's bottomed and you aren't there yet on this ratio, you will always be wrong. That level of certainty is rarely available in any other kind of gauge. For those unfamiliar with this indicator, it can be found among all of the indicators in the *Investor's Business Daily* and is available every Thursday morning in the paper. Never buck it; doing so has cost me tens of millions of dollars. Why should you lose money after I have proven that the losses always occur when you anticipate the bull-bear percentages too soon.

It is somewhat unfortunate that so many of my sentiment indicators take advantage of the wrong-way nature of so many market participants, but remember, when you are calling bottoms you have to believe that all hope is extinguished, and so therefore everyone who has to sell has already sold. That's why I regard the **third** and one of the "meanest" indicators to be one of the best: mutual fund withdrawals. No important bottom is without these. No bottom is sustainable without mutual fund flows occurring steadily for at least two months. There can always be periods of one or two or even three weeks where you might get outflows related either to tax concerns or to unusual events that scare people. But consistent, repeated outflows of several months in duration accompany all the big bottoms. These numbers, available on Fridays through an organization call AMG, are almost always in the papers Saturday or Monday, so, again, we are not talking about esoteric hard-to-find data. If you haven't seen big outflows, again, you aren't there yet.

Perhaps the most esoteric of my sentiment indicators, and the only one that isn't readily accessible in your local paper, is the **fourth** indicator: the VIX. The VIX, or volatility index, is a measure of stress in the system. It is a compilation of worry as defined by various ratios of puts and calls (I'll explain these terms in the final chapter) that gauge either complacency or panic. Panic signals the freak-out selling that always accompanies market bottoms. A reading above 40 in the VIX— a measure of pure panic in the marketplace—indicates a market bottom. In fact, anything above 35 can trigger a possible bottom, but +40 is a requirement that all four of our significant bottoms have met. Any reading below 30 indicates that the bottom can't be trusted. One note of caution: The first reading above 35 isn't going to be the last. If you have the luxury, my work says the third week of +40 readings is the safest time to buy.

When I first heard the word "oscillator," I said to myself, Now here's some Genuine Wall Street Gibberish, some indicator that tells you whether stocks are "oversold" or not. How can some indicator that tabulates how eager people are to unload stocks by measuring how many sales occur on downticks and at distressed levels really help you identify a bottom? But as someone who daily measures the overbought-oversold condition through the columns of TheStreet.com's Helene Meisler, someone who I believe is the world's number one technician, I have come to respect this instrument to the point that I never buck it, ever, when calling a bottom. It is my **fifth** bottom indicator.

Most of the time markets are in equilibrium. Buyers buy at reasonable levels relative to the last sale and sellers sell at reasonable levels relative to the last sale. But at times market players en masse are so exuberant that they push up prices constantly with their buying. They don't wait for supply and demand to be in balance and they chase stocks up, causing higher prices.

Similarly, there are moments when sellers want out so badly that they will not wait for buyers to step up to the plate. They seek out the buyers wherever they can find them, chiefly well below prevailing levels. Oscillators measure these pressures. (There are a number of different oscillator gauges. The Standard & Poor's company updates one every night that is available for $1,000, but I prefer the one that Helene Meisler calculates herself that can be found on Realmoney.com.)

Equilibrium buying occurs when an oscillator registers in the middle, which is defined by 0 ± 2. A $+2$ reading or a -2 reading signifies nothing. Only extremes matter. At every negative extreme, defined as -5 or lower, we have gotten a terrific opportunity to buy stocks. All four of the bottoms I have researched gave us extreme readings of -7 before they bottomed. The oscillator indicator, unlike the VIX, is something that produces almost instant results. The bottom is "in" when you get that reading along with all of the others that I have described here.

If you get all of these—a -7 reading on the oscillator, a $+35$ reading or more on the VIX for three weeks, sustained mutual fund withdrawals, a reading of 40 bulls or fewer in the Investors Intelligence survey, and a front-page story in the *New York Times* or *USA Today* detailing the pain the market is causing the man in the street—you will have satisfied the sentiment indicator for a megabottom.

It sounds so simple, but in reality, using these indicators is an exercise in extreme patience. I can't tell you how many times people have called me during the last four years and said, "It's so painful, we must

be near a bottom." And I have to go over the checklist and disabuse
them about when we really are. Usually they say, "That's okay, I can
hold out," but I will let you in on a secret—nobody, not even the Trading Goddess, can take the amount of pain that has to occur in a swing
from euphoria to a swing of despair. That's why if you are feeling the
tightening around your throat or the knots in your stomach and we
are nowhere near negative on the oscillator or near superbearish on
the Investors Intelligence, I recommend that you trim your holdings
back, perhaps dramatically. That's what I usually advise people who
call in to my radio program.

2. Capitulation. The next set of indicators that we must see before
we can call an investible bottom gauge capitulation. In every one of
the megabottoms, we had what I describe as a "crescendo sell-off" before we had an "exquisite moment." In a crescendo sell-off we have
massive capitulation. Players who had been hoping to stay with the
market finally give up and can't take the pain anymore.

Spotting a crescendo bottom isn't as easy as it sounds. But there
are some overt signs that can be seen in the daily paper. A crescendo
bottom is a bottom where a great many sellers converge at once to take
stocks down to unusual levels versus the fundamentals. The accompanying detail that has marked all crescendo sell-offs is a dramatic
imbalance in the amount of new highs to new lows. At all of the bottoms that I have found to be investible, you have between four hundred and seven hundred new lows and only a handful of new highs.
That kind of capitulation is a must-have before you can be sure that
the majority of selling is over. When you have only a couple of hundred new lows, not enough damage has been done to reach a buyable
crescendo.

A second characteristic of a crescendo bottom comes from the
bizarre forced-selling method that the brokers apply at all major brokerage houses. Throughout all sell-offs, marginal players and speculators attempt to call bottoms on a repeated basis. Their meager efforts
are often a sign that we are not anywhere near the bottom. That is why

we have to monitor their selling closely to see when it comes to an end and they are washed out of the picture. Fortunately, their telltale selling comes almost entirely between 1:30 and 2:30 in the afternoon. That's because brokers everywhere are on the hook for trades done by their clients in violation of margin rules. The rules state that unless the customer borrowing from the firm puts up more equity when positions go against him to the point where his collateral no longer meets the requirements, the positions must be cashed out. The brokers badger these customers all morning, but the brokerage house finally stops fooling around and after the Federal Wire system closes at 1:00 p.m. the margin clerks swing into action and brutally sell out the common stock of overly margined players. The selling lasts until about 2:30. You will see during prolonged downturns that the selling during this margin-clerk hour is by far the most brutal of the day. If you have to buy a stock during a downturn, you would always be wisest to wait until the forced-selling period is over.

But for spotting bottoms, it is more important to recognize when the hour of trading doesn't bring further pressure on the market. If there is no strong sell-off by 2:30, then that's a sign that margin debt has shrunk to acceptable levels and speculation has been wrenched from the system. You never get a bottom before that speculation has been flushed out. You can always wait until the SEC releases the monthly margin debt numbers, but I have found that before every radical decline in margin buying has occurred, you can spot that decline simply by focusing on the 1:30 to 2:30 p.m. margin-clerk selling. Mind you, this indicator only works on down days. You need to see no selling to speak of during that hour after a series of declines, or even weeks of decline, before you know that the market has bottomed out.

Until about a decade ago, we had no one pool of capital large enough and reckless enough that its own busting could be a form of capitulation. But that changed with the 1998 bottom, when Long-Term Capital, a gigantic hedge fund, made a series of monster bets that went wrong, resulting in that company going belly-up. Its forced liquidation, which took place over the final days of September and early October, produced the only tradeable bottom that wasn't caused by widespread capitulation on the part of a multitude of speculators. I point this out only because the 1998 bottom did not produce a wave of margin selling at the retail level, just at the hedge-fund level. Fortunately, that hedge fund's decline was well chronicled and therefore could be gauged even easier than the margin selling that helped create all of the other bottoms I have studied. During big declines you will find me hard at work between 1:30 and 2:30 checking the levels of forced selling and looking for imbalances that indicate the margined folk are being led to the slaughterhouse. Once they are out of the picture for good, bottoms can be found much more easily. In 2000 there was so much margin debt that we didn't clear things up until October 2002, when the forced margin selling was so palpable that it amazed you. And then it ended. Within a few weeks, you got your bottom.

A third characteristic of a crescendo bottom is a dramatic spike in volume on the exchanges. There can be day after day of lethargic selling that produce no bottoms. You get a crescendo only when the volume is loud enough to indicate that many sellers are cleaned up.

This method of spotting a crescendo always eluded me until I became a part of one during a mini sell-off in the mid-90s. That was when *Frontline* chose to do a special about speculation and I agreed to let a film crew come in and film me at my hedge fund. Because the market had been quite terrible for almost two months and we had been buying in anticipation of a crescendo bottom, we had reached our maximum allowable buying power. During the morning when the film crew came in, the market looked colossally ugly, and we sensed still one more day of pain. Because of that we went to Goldman Sachs, one of our best brokers, and said we wanted to unload one-tenth of our merchandise, or $30 million in stock, before the market opened. We wanted the security of some cash; we were selling scared. The firm sized up our offerings and bid us down a point for each stock. We were quite relieved, and we sold them the stock. Within a half hour after the opening, Goldman came back and bid about a quarter point higher for more of the same merchandise. Volume exploded all over the Street by ten o'clock, with much higher levels of trading than we had experienced in months. We took that to mean that our own panic sale had been joined by many others. Suddenly buyers came out of the woodwork because an acceptable level had been found. The hourly volume spike made it evident that at last buyers were alive and sellers had been able to unload substantial chunks rather than dribs and drabs all the way down. Again, that cleared the decks of institutional sellers in the same way that the margin clerks clear the decks of the individual sellers. Of course, we have our bottom selling memorialized in a documentary; let it serve as a reminder to you not to sell into the big volume after a long decline. That's the time to buy, not sell. A minicrescendo had occurred, and we were part of it.

Another telltale sign of capitulation involves the flow of underwritings. Brokerage houses live by the selling of merchandise through underwritings. It is second in profitability to merger and acquisition work and the lifeblood of many of the larger sales houses. Because it is so important, firms will push these deals through the door no matter what, until there are simply no more buyers left. At that point, at last, they stop, because if they can't sell the deals, they get stuck with the merchandise. They won't bring a new set of deals until they have worked off the old merchandise. You don't commit capital until the most recent underwritings have worked. That means the excess inventory has at last been worked off in the system and the all-clear has been sounded; there's too much cash idle again at last. That's why underwritings are such perfect tests of when a bottom might be coming.

Remember the order of the stock market's underwriting cycle because it always anticipates the stock market's cycle as a whole. When you get an overheated underwriting market with wild openings (where stocks go up and up on the day they first come to market) and tons of offerings each week, that's a sign of a developing top (more on that later). So get ready to sell a lot of stock. Soon you get deals opening up unchanged, with little or no premium; that's a sign the market's getting sated and you should be in a minimum of equities. When deals just fail from the moment they come out, that's a sign of a weak market, one the underwriters will still pummel with greed. Don't be tempted to buy yet; many will be. That's a false bottom. It's only after deal after deal breaks down that the pipeline of new equity at last dries up. That's when the speculative juices are being wrung out of the market and liquidity is building up. During the period when no equity is being issued you will see a radical change in the supply and demand of equities. Well into a downturn companies will continue to buy back equity as a matter of course, but issuance dries up when the brokers get totally stung by deals. So supply and demand get way out of whack as money naturally comes into the market, through 401(k)s and other retirement accounts, and there's a continuing and natural decline in the overall numbers of shares available to buy.

You can't catch a bottom as soon as the underwriting dries up because there are still so many excess shares kicking around in marginal accounts that don't want to hold them. But one or two months after the flood of new deals ceases—never longer—you begin to see a few terrific IPOs that come public and the stocks don't go down. That's the sign that you are now past the crescendo and should be in there buying stocks. You must wait until the whole cycle plays out, though. Moving in before the new set of deals goes to a premium is suicidal. These brokers know what they are doing. They aren't taking chances at that stage; they know that the market is at last fine to operate on from the long side.

A final indicator that you might be in a crescendo bottom comes from something so odd that it is *only* seen at market bottoms. That's the "stop trading, order imbalance" sign. This signal is tricky because you need to be at a machine to see it happen. It is, in fact, the only indicator of a crescendo that cannot be spotted simply by reading the papers. It is rare, although all four megabottoms had multiple days— but not weeks—of this behavior while the capitulation was occurring.

We often get order imbalances on individual equities when we have bad news on individual companies, such as some sort of executive resignation or earnings blowup or chicanery that causes a stock to open at a deep discount to its former price. But there are moments when we get "stop trading, order imbalance" across the whole stock market, with lots of stocks opening down huge simultaneously on no news. We had precisely this kind of behavior on the day after the 1987 stock market crash—the single best buying day in the recent history of the market—and we had it again in 1990 and in September and October of 1998 and again in October of 2002. Repeated order imbalances sans news are sure signs that the capitulation has reached absurd levels and you have to make your move to buy.

I love order imbalances after big declines in stocks; they clear out all of the panicky sellers—just the people you don't want in your foxhole—all at once. That's perfect; the safest time to buy.

3. Catalyst. The ultimate goal when you spot crescendo selling and you match it with the sentiment indicators is to consider what event could occur that would trigger what I call an "exquisite moment" where you have to buy because the opportunity is so great. In 1991, at the end of a seven-month bear market, and in 2003, at the end of a three-year bear market, we got the same exact catalyst: the start of a war with Iraq. In both cases we had a pretty high degree of confidence about when the event would occur. In both cases, as is often the case with what I call the "Big Bad Event Syndrome," where a news event that so dwarfs others is about to occur, the stock market factored in all of the negatives and none of the positives.

In 1998, the catalyst that triggered the upsurge was a "surprise" federal funds cut. I write "surprise" because the Federal Reserve let some of its buddies that talk to the press have a head's-up that the rate cut was going to occur. That was the signal to jolt stocks upward.

In 1987, the catalyst was again the Fed, which when it saw all of the delayed openings in stocks, said that it would provide all the liquidity needed to make sure the markets were orderly.

Again, after each sell-off a different trigger will cause the averages to reverse. The trick is to recognize ahead of time whether enough of the precursors are in place so that you are prepared when the catalyst comes to change the direction. The trick is *not* to know or try to predict the catalyst itself; that's rarely known. But the setup for the exquisite moment can be predicted much more easily than the actual trigger that pushes the market higher. The catalysts are always different, but in each case we had priced in all the negatives and none of the positives. That's why the setups are the key and are reproducible repeatedly even though the catalyst remains something mysterious. Think of it ultimately as a forest fire waiting to happen. The sellers' inventory, the liquid that keeps the forest damp, has run dry. Then you know that the tinder is ready, and the exquisite moment is about to strike. You don't need to know when or where the spark will come from to know things are ready to ignite.

I called the exquisite moment on TV for the 2003 rally, right at the exact bottom, give or take 100 Dow points. People thought I was a genius—this was right before the war began—when in actuality all my indicators were flashing the brightest green. I am not saying it was easy; I am just saying the signs were consistent and you, too, could have spotted them if you knew what to look for. There's no magic or alchemy, just patterns readily available to all who have studied the market these last three decades.

For some people—I call them the "permabears"—these certain indicators and the exquisite moments they have begotten are still not enough to commit capital. I would point out to these permabears that the conditions are never perfect enough for us to know the exact bottom. But if we correctly identify these situations, even if we are wrong and we don't get an exquisite moment to buy, we are still not injured for trying. In every case where all these conditions occurred and we didn't get a bottom within four weeks, we still experienced no decline in capital. That's all you can ask for.

How do you know if you have missed the bottom or are too late to take advantage of it? There are dozens of subindices out there that bottom after the market as a whole has bottomed, but only one index has been coincident with or has led the market bottom in every case: the BKX, the Bank Index. If you see a 10 percent move up in the Bank

Index you are already well into the upswing, and it might pay to wait for a couple of profit-taking days to transpire before you commit capital. I always keep the BKX at the upper left hand top of my columns, right under the S&P, because of its canary-in-the-coalmine ability to detect that a big move is about to get under way. Unfortunately, a rally in the BKX has also produced several false tells, so be sure all the other indicators are working for you before you bite. The BKX predicts a lot of declines, too many to be useful, but it has always been right at confirming real bottoms as they have happened or right before them.

One other consideration: Sometimes the bottoms are so vicious and elusive that you need to test the waters first so you don't get too exposed to the market before it really bottoms and collapses again. For that, may I suggest something that has kept losses to a minimum when I am market bottom fishing? Start your buys on the morning of the bottom not with your favorites, but with some stocks that might have additional support from day traders and institutions. Buy the stocks that have been upgraded that morning. If the market does falter, the artificial buying that comes with every upgrade will at least cushion the downside for the stocks you are using to test. Don't leave it to chance or buy a stock that has no institutional support that day. You may end up in an equity that gets slammed if the market reverses down sharply, and you will be too shell-shocked to attempt the next bottom—and bottoms, real bottoms, are too precious not to try for. You can use that method to test every single bottom and never have to pay so much as a ticket for admission. It's a terrific way to feel for a bottom with minimum pain.

Believe it or not, bottoms on individual stocks are a lot harder to call than market bottoms. That's because divining the behavior of a single entity is much more difficult than trying to fathom thousands of equities that, in many ways, do trade together.

How hard is it? About fifteen years ago I was building a massive position in Control Data, now Ceridian, in an attempt to call a multi-year bottom. The stock had declined from about $150 to $15, and I thought we were nearing a bottom. So I began to build a position using what I call a "wide scale." That means that down every point I would buy another tranche of equity, and when I thought it reached absurd levels, I would make my buys even larger, pyramid style. During this period I was trading with my wife, and she used "strict" scales, meaning that she refused to deviate and try to call a bottom at a particular level in part because a bottom had eluded Control Data for more than a decade. When the stock got to 10 we had about 200,000 shares, bidding for 50,000 every point down. It then quickly dropped to 9. I got on a plane to go see the company in Minneapolis. I spent a day with management and I came back confident because the CEO at the time was truly bullish on the outlook. When I got back I wanted to double down at 8, that's how positive management had been, but Karen was convinced that we hadn't reached max pain level. Karen said we were sticking by our scale of 50,000 every point. Sure enough, the stock traded through 8, where we bought 50,000, and then through 7, where we bought another 50,000. Amazingly, the stock kept dropping. I kept calling management, they kept telling me, Chin up, not to worry; it was all going to be okay. Those were the days where we were trading out of our garden shed in Bucks County, and my wife would constantly tell me to call the company and go through the drill again and again to be sure I was right.

Then one Friday, when the market was particularly ugly and Control Data was trading at slightly above $6 and we were bidding for our usual 50,000 shares, Karen said that she saw signs of capitulation. The sellers were coming in faster and harder now and were asking for bids from the different brokerage firms. She said she was on the verge of the double down.

To me, she seemed nuts. We hadn't known each other long enough for me to acquire those German nerves of steel of hers yet. I was shaking, shaking so hard we just stood there while the sellers were out whacking everything. Shouldn't we step aside, I asked? Shouldn't we break our scale, or walk away? That's how hard the selling was.

She looked at me as though I had no idea what I was doing and then picked up the phone to our trading wire to be sure that the $6 bid was in and nobody pulled it while the sellers were busy panicking.

A few minutes later, the phone rang. Karen got it and said, "Jim, it's for you, some guy named Larry." I gulped. Could it be Larry Perlman, the CEO of Control Data, calling little old me in Bucks County, the guy who had 350,000 shares of his stock, which represented more than a quarter of my fund?

Sure enough, it was. Larry wanted to know what the heck was wrong with his stock. All was going so well, so exceptionally well, that he couldn't figure out what was causing the selling. He was at wits' end. I told him I wish I knew, that it was one tough row to hoe, and I hung up, totally rattled.

Karen asked me why I had turned so white. I said that I just got a call from a shaky CEO who wanted to know who the heck was selling his stock down and why, given how good things were. What was out there destroying the stock? I told her if he's worried, maybe I'm nuts to be so confident. I thought we should join the sellers.

Nonsense, she said, just the opposite. Only in the comic strips do lightbulbs go off over people's heads, but I swear I saw some light go on somewhere near her cranium. She picked up the phone to Jimmy, our position trader on the account, and said, "Bid six and a quarter outloud for one hundred thousand shares and keep reloading at the same price until you are filled three hundred and fifty thousand times."

She was doubling down, right then, right there.

I told her she had to be a whack job, that's how out of her mind she was. We just got a call from the CEO, I said, who has no idea what the heck's going wrong and your instinct is to double down?

Of course, she said. The definition of the bottom is when the two biggest bulls, her husband and the CEO, panic at the same time, when only the CEO knows more about the company than her husband. That's when you stand there, she said.

It got more painful initially. After we got filled on 350,000 shares at 6.25, she went "up," not down, and said bid 6.5 for another 100,000.

Filled again. Darned seller reloading. Bid again, she said. Now we had about half of our fund in Control Data.

Sure enough, we weren't filled the second time. The seller had dried up. The buyers came in. Take a look at a multiyear chart of that security. It never looked back from that moment, and we feasted off our Control Data position for many years to come.

Yes, bottoms can be called on individual stocks, but usually because the people who love the stock finally throw their hands up and the cooler heads step in and profit from the capitulation. At the bottom even the CEOs are confused. Accept the chaos!

Stock bottoms may be elusive, but like market bottoms, there are some telltale signs you can use to spot them. You just have to remember what you are looking for: the pricing in of the negatives without any of the positives being included.

One of the reasons spotting bottoms in equities is so elusive versus the averages is that the averages rarely go to zero—I can't recall even any sector indices that went to zero, and that includes the DOT, TheStreet.com's Internet index, during the worst of the dot-com bust. Given that debt causes the stocks of good businesses to go to zero, I would heavily recommend that you not try to spot many bottoms among the more heavily indebted companies out there. That said, let me give you my checklist of what to look for to detect a bottom in an individual stock.

First, a stock needs to lose most if not all of its sponsorship to form a true bottom. Even in the tough market of 2004, with just a handful of winners, it is amazing to see that in each winner's case, it didn't bottom and then begin to move up until it lost most if not all of its sponsorship. Amazon, Yahoo!, and eBay, together among the best-acting stocks in the market, each received multiple downgrades and were even the recipients of sell recommendations at the bottom. That's a classic tell, when a stock loses whatever support it has left on Wall Street. It's predictable and bankable because of the method analysts use to pick stocks. Typically they build a model of earnings, and when they can find stocks that they think are cheap on earnings relative to the growth rate, they want to pull the trigger and buy. Unfortunately, business is rarely as predictable as these analysts might have you think. When a company makes the estimates, the analysts reiterate their buys. When a company exceeds the estimates they go from hold to buy. But when a company, no matter how temporarily, misses the numbers, they by nature have to downgrade the stock. Since all of the analysts use these earnings models instead of trying to value companies for their intrinsic worth, they all tend to downgrade at the same time for the same reasons. You get a bottom when even the most patient or brain dead of those using these methods downgrades the stocks, typically because management is embarrassed that such bad stocks remain on the recommended list. After the investigations Eliot Spitzer has made, this process has become even easier because in the old days the stocks went from buys to holds. Now the analysts take them to sells because they didn't have enough sells on during the crash to please the authorities; in fact, they had almost none! At the bottom in 2002–2003, almost every great stock that had been hit by the temporary slowdown of the economy had sells on it. Broadcom, shortly before it doubled, had four sells on it! What a terrific indicator! Same with Lucent and Nortel and Corning before their giant moves.

The bad news about spotting the sells is that it might take several quarters for the turn to occur, because these analysts won't get back on the horse until it has a couple of good quarters. They've been too burned to be anything but twice shy. The good news is that when everyone has downgraded a stock, and it has a decent balance sheet, your downside is extremely limited. The most dangerous thing that can occur is that you might end up sitting out of whatever rally you might be trying to play. They can't "hurt" you with any more downgrades; they've already occurred!

A second "tell" of a bottom occurs when bad news hits and the stock ceases to go down. This indicator is a simple one, and it is common in every single bottom. That's because bottoms get formed only when all of the sellers have finished, so there is no one left who cares about the new negatives to want to dump the stocks. Again, remember, this works only with a good balance sheet, because with a bad one, the bad news could lead to some sort of impairment that removes the equity from your hands and puts it in the hands of the bond or note holders. I love situations like one that occurred in EMC in 2003 when it reported a so-so quarter, guided estimates lower, and said business is just okay. The stock went up on the news. No one was left to be shaken out. That's a classic bottom, one definitely worth waiting for. EMC had fallen 40 percent before it found its sea legs.

A third indicator is consistent, large insider buying. Insiders sell for a myriad of reasons: taxes, estate planning, divorce, prudence. They buy for only one reason: to make money. Beware here, though. The managements know that they can draw attention to their companies with token buying or with widespread but small buying by all board members. This kind of forced buying shouldn't fool you. Don't bite when you see small dollar amounts of buying by individuals at the top. They could be "painting the tape" with their buys. You need to see buys in the millions of dollars to be sure that someone isn't trying to trick you into the stock, or con some reporter. Buy only when you see multiple buys, too. There's always one board member with a lot of cash around. But multiple and repeat buyers of significant amounts shows you the insiders mean business. It's a great tell and often signals the absolute bottom in an enterprise's stock.

A fourth indicator of a bottom occurs when a stock is rumored upon negatively and nothing happens. At all times there are plenty of hedge funds that need merchandise to go lower so they can bring in their shorts, either successfully or unsuccessfully. At all times there are also unscrupulous people who are willing to say anything about a company to anybody—particularly the press—to knock the price down, knowing that it will be repeated by willing brokers who want the short sellers' business. For most of you this process seems completely insidious. You think it is outrageous that short sellers plant rumors and tell tall tales to knock stock prices down. Not for me. I am always looking for all-clear signs to beat the system. I regard it as the ultimate tell of a stock going from weak to strong hands when I hear a negative rumor about the company—broadcast widely either through a network or a national newspaper, a Web site or magazine— and the stock, which most likely would have been totaled by the rumor at a higher price, does nothing. I especially like it when a hefty dollop of puts has been purchased beforehand. That's a terrific fire to the upside just waiting to happen. There's nothing like trapping a short seller with his own lying story and getting him to feel the pain himself of a stock that won't come down so he has to come in and sell the puts, which will automatically move the stock up. Particularly because the broker who bought the puts probably told others to expect something negative, and when the negative occurs and the stock doesn't go down, these tagalongs panic and cover the target company's stock.

So, I like to keep up on the negatives of stocks that have been breaking down to figure out when all the negative news is in. That usually means some positive news is about to come down the pike or the major damage is done and you are safe to speculate on a bottom.

The final kind of bottoms I look for are bottoms based on macro considerations. These are sector-rotation bottoms, and they are the key to making unusually large profits. Let's spend some time on them, especially because these are some of the most counterintuitive bottoms out there, yet they are begging to be had if you simply stand conventional wisdom on its head. These bottoms involve decisions by big money to make moves to get out of some stocks that have been very hot and into others that have been very cold, almost entirely because of macro decisions, like Fed tightening or loosening policies. Let's stick with them because they are consistent in each cycle.

Sector bottoms, picking individual stocks as part of a big sector bet, means going back to the model of earnings and Fed tightenings and loosenings that I described earlier. There is a simple theme to these rotations. When you believe that the tightenings are beginning to have an effect, you will see a sudden rush of money over a four- or five-day period into the Kelloggs, Gillettes, Avons, Procters, and Kimberlys, the stuff that is in your kitchen and your medicine chest. I used to like to place these bets close to the midway point in the tightening portion of the cycle, but these days so many people anticipate the Fed's moves that I think you would be best to start buying right at the time of the first tightening. Usually you get the tightening after a prolonged period of inflation, which erodes the value of these key franchises. But when the Fed tightens, you get a freeze in the economy and the erosion stops. Also, when the Fed tightens, you get a fear that the cyclical companies will not make their numbers the following year, or that the future will be clouded for the companies that are heavily dependent upon the economy. That's why you have to jump into these situations in advance. One of the reasons why I was able to successfully navigate the severe downturn in tech stocks in 2000 was that I used this method to switch into a portfolio of food, soap, drug, and cosmetic companies, the type that don't slow down when the Fed ratchets rates up.

Of course, the opposite happens when the Fed does its first loosening. Traditionally you need to switch into a sector that does well with the economy, typically companies like the autos and the retailers. You rotate into the heavier cyclicals as the easings go on, until in the end you are stuck with the dirtiest of stocks out there, such as, steel, copper, and aluminum.

I point all of this out not to belabor something discussed earlier, but to point out that throughout these periods, brokers and TV pundits and mutual fund folk will be recommending the "cheap" food and drug stocks betting on a comeback, right in the middle of an economic expansion or when they have just started selling off. Think to yourself, false bottom! Same with the cyclicals. You like the cyclicals when they are most expensive, when their earnings have cratered, when they traditionally seem outrageously overvalued. But when their multiples are cheap, when you hear that Phelps Dodge trades at 6 times next year's earnings, run for the hills. It will never make that number. It might not even make half of that. That's the slowdown coming. Never be lulled into cyclical stocks when they are cheap; sell the safety stocks when they are ultra expensive. Their bottoms are both counterintuitively reached and formed by the Fed cycle, not by their intrinsic earnings power.

There are a couple of other kinds of bottoms to be aware of. Some bottoms occur when companies get so cheap as to be taken over by others, but again, I don't speculate on takeovers with bad fundamentals, unless all the risk is taken out of them and nobody likes them apropos of the bottoming process described above.

One other type of bottom is worth commenting on: the tax-loss bottom. Every year at the end of October, when most mutual funds end their fiscal year, the funds like to take their losses. There is a perception that you should wait until December to buy tax-loss names, but that's a canard because it is institutional selling that drives most stocks down, not individuals. The third and fourth weeks of October—hah, now you know why there are so many crashes during that period—represents the height of this kind of selling.

My experience is that if you are picking stocks off tax-loss selling, you should begin most of your buying in the last week of October, but leave some money for the occasional "legit" sell-off to demonstrate itself. Spend that money in the last week of November. I don't like buying stocks just because tax-loss selling is over. There are a million reasons why stocks go down, but I know enough to take advantage of the seasonal pattern that constantly manifests itself.

9

SPOTTING TOPS

Two great investment themes create the day-to-day tension in the stock market: capital appreciation and capital preservation. We have historically—and I think inaccurately—called capital appreciation by a different name: "buy and hold." I have shown that buy and hold has no place in the logical investing lexicon and that buy and homework must be the modus operandi. Buy and hold presumes, preposterously, that tops—permanent impairment of stocks after a certain attained height—don't exist. Yet dozens of tops are formed every week that could wipe out whatever capital appreciation you may have gained by buying and holding. Tops are the bane of all investing. At a top buy and hold is the enemy and capital preservation becomes king.

Yet the amount of attention paid to spotting and avoiding holding after a top in the investment canon is paltry when you consider the damage and the havoc that tops can wreak on your portfolio. If there were genuine scrutiny and rigor to how stocks originate in the first place, if there were somehow some strictures about what kind of stocks are "suitable" for investment, we wouldn't have to worry about tops. All stocks would generate solid returns, save a handful that fail. Those would be chalked up as occasional accidents that happen, nothing more than that. We would factor them in; a diversified portfolio would cushion whatever damage an occasional top might generate.

Unfortunately, we are never at a loss for bad stocks in the market. Virtually any company can issue stock without much scrutiny from the feds beyond the securities equivalent of a name, rank, and serial number. Recently, the SEC revealed the names of some thirty stocks that traded with multiple billions in capitalization that had no companies underneath them. That's right, they were made-up companies—shells—that had no earnings, revenues, or even, in some cases, headquarters or employees. These nonexistent companies traded freely for years in the hundreds of millions of shares without being flagged by any authority. The government didn't blow the whistle on the stocks until most of them had been reduced to zero, of course, not before robbing unsuspecting "investors"—if you can call this process investing—of billions of dollars in wealth. Before the government halted trading in these empty, worthless vehicles, they had been blessed, de facto, as if they were operating companies with real financials. No government entity ever came out and said, "Be careful, these aren't real companies." You can't expect the SEC or the exchanges to protect us from the fraudsters, though. And there's too much corruption out there for the SEC to be a cop on the valuation beat; it's not the government's job to examine whether a stock is worth something or nothing at all.

You can't rely on the market to sort them out correctly, either. It fails so often to do that job that you should have lost whatever faith you might have had in the screening and valuation processes of the collective wisdom of the market by now. But many of you still haven't been disabused of the market's illogic because of the buy-and-hold brainwashing that Wall Street relies upon to keep you from taking back *your* assets under *its* management. If you knew what the Street knows, you would rather be in control of the money yourself. That way your guard would be up and you could be more vigilant than Wall Streeters want to be, or, given the conflicts of interests they live under, can afford to be.

Although we are a nation that has produced stocks with phenomenal long-term returns from both dividends and stock appreciation, we are also a nation that has produced more investment fads, more short-term gimmickry, and more white-collar corruption leading to multi-billion-dollar losses than any nation other than Japan during that country's phenomenal bubble (which is still bursting). There are tons of stocks that don't deserve even to trade and a myriad of others that are topping right now and could be incredibly dangerous to your financial health.

For me, spotting a top is the equivalent of embarking on a long and winding train ride and trying to figure out if the engine's about to jump the tracks any time soon. We know nearly all trains get to their destinations, yet we accept the fact that occasional derailments do happen. This chapter's about trying to get as much mileage out of stock as possible, but not so much that you hang on while the stock jumps the track or plummets through a broken trestle. Sometimes, you've got to jump off the train to survive. It's no sin to do so and, of course, it would be pretty stupid if you knew a crash was coming and you stuck around for it. Yet, despite the common sense of it, my view is *not* the prevailing wisdom on Wall Street.

On Wall Street "sell" is a dirty word and tops don't exist; they are only temporary breakdowns that will eventually be surmounted. When I first got to Goldman Sachs I remember asking people, "When do I tell clients to sell? What's the exit plan?" The greybeards would say, "When the stock gets downgraded; that's when you sell." But downgrades, when they happen, most often come after the train has abandoned the track. The selling process is pretty alien, especially when another portion of a firm might be vying for business of the company that might be downgraded, and that business is a much larger business than whatever trading profits can be made in the stock. Even though Eliot Spitzer, the New York State attorney general, has performed yeoman's work vetting this process, it still happens as long as investment banking and research are under the same roof. You just don't get a lot of correct sell recommendations on Wall Street, and when you do, it is usually too late to sell. Indeed, there are hundreds of texts and analysts that can tell you when to buy. But selling is considered to be a sporadic, haphazard art. I contend that selling and knowing when to sell are more important than knowing when to buy. That's been the lesson during the last seven years where the S&P 500 compounded at 5 percent and many stocks lost you tons of money during that period. I have spent much of my life poring over chartbooks looking for patterns, looking for repetitive warning signs that would get you out before the top. I wanted to find a commonality, or a set of commonalities, that could be warning bells for stocks that otherwise would be too dangerous to touch, the stocks that produce short-term gains in almost parabolic style, the stocks that go up fast but fall even faster. The idea behind such reasoning is that you shouldn't deny yourself an iVillage or a Commerce One or an eBay on the way up, provided you know when to get out. You can own the sizzling stocks, take the huge gains that they provide, and then exit before the steak gets burned.

Spotting tops allows you to embrace lots more equities, including riskier ones that can be very rewarding, much more rewarding than most people think possible. If you hone your selling skills, you can take advantage of the four- and five-fold rallies that can occur in unseasoned merchandise, even if, in the end, the merchandise craters to zero—as long as it does so without you on board. This flexibility has made me fortunes even as it has created a legion of Cramer-haters who think that I have no right to hop off the griddle. This top stuff truly is like cooking. You can cook something to perfection. If you take it off before you get it there, nobody's happy, but you can always throw it back on. But once it is burned, it's finished, done, destroyed. Why stay on the griddle for that punishment when you can learn to spot the moment something's about to get fried into oblivion? This bit of cooking advice is better than anything you will ever get from most investment books. I can't tell you how many times recognizing that things have gotten too hot after a big run has allowed me to take terrific gains even as others say, "Hold it, I thought you said you liked this stock, you can't sell it now." My view? You bet I can. I am not sticking around for my meal to burn to a crisp even if I liked it a moment before. That's foolish. These are stocks; just like food, they can vaporize in an instant. They can and do go bad, all the time.

The more we are wedded to stocks, the more we ignore the changes that might be occurring in the ever-fluctuating landscape, changes that might knock our companies out if we aren't careful. Ideology's an unsteady crutch in this game; the more we have of it, the more money we will lose. This is a business of flexibility; you may have to like a stock one minute and hate it the next because the fundamentals underneath change that fast. If you think this is a business of firm, resolute stands no matter what the facts say, you are going to end up poor as a church mouse. That's no way to run money, your own or others'.

Let me give you a couple of other caveats to the top process. First, this is not a chapter on spotting *market* tops. I am focusing on when to sell individual stocks, although I reach a conclusion about the entire market and when it should be sold, more as a recognition that there have been and will be "tops" in the S&P 500 that will last long enough that they should be solidified. However, I always believe the casino will be open, and if you take it case by case, game by game, that's a lot better than saying, "That's it, I want everything out." That's worked only once, in the third week of March 2000. I don't suspect we will see such a renegade market bubble in our lifetime. If anything, I am far more concerned with some sort of biblical seven lean years after seven fat years. I don't mind mixing biblical metaphors with Vegas-style reasoning. By now you know that I think that any analogies to casinos are far-fetched; the table games have much more rigorous rules and regulations. Letting you bet on a bogus entity—something that happens with stocks all of the time—would be ruinous to the house, and the casino business just wouldn't allow it to happen. Same with illegal NFL gambling, which I regard as much more honest and less rigged than much of what passes for fair in the stock market.

Second, I am not a technician, and this is not a collection of chart patterns that lead up to tops. Chart people spot many tops; in fact, they spot many more tops than there are. That's just not valuable to me. In fact, one of the biggest mistakes I ever had in my career was to be short Genentech based on a classic top formation, which, a prominent technician told me, ninety-nine times out of hundred produced a significant decline. I got my face handed to me when, the next week, Genentech got a humongous takeover bid! I had to buy the stock back up about 70 percent. Nasty, embarrassing, and astonishingly costly. As I hung up on the technician after cussing him out for the hot tip, he was squealing, "But the chart says it should go down!" To heck with the chart! To heck with the chartists! Except Mrs. Cramer, who still manages to integrate the fundies and accepts that the chart can *never* be the final judgment, but *can* be consulted to generate ideas.

Nor am I talking about temporary fluctuations in stocks, avoiding short-term drops. If you follow my rules on portfolio management— my bulls-bears-and-pigs mantra that involves taking a little something off the table as a stock goes up—these short-term tops, false tops so to speak, take care of themselves. You quickly put the money back to work in the same equity at a lower, cooler level. Low taxes and low transaction costs now allow such moves. This kind of approach not only is important, it is prudent in a world gone buy-and-hold haywire.

The real danger of false tops is that you might be spooked out of a high-quality stock; they are hard to find and you should treasure them for as long as they last, not jettison them quickly for some lesser merchandise. Sometimes it takes months to develop really good ideas. You should depart from them only when you have serious reservations such as the kind I am about to explain to you.

No, I am addressing here the basic reasons why, unfortunately, at times, you should abandon stocks you know and love. They are reasons why you should take the money off the table and look elsewhere for opportunity because something has changed, something in the landscape either for the equity or the company itself has gone sour or is about to go sour and very few people know it. Here are the main antagonists to buy and hold, the place where tops are in sight and you can assume that the train will derail if you stay along for the ride.

1. **Competition**. The most common form of top explains why you must stay involved with the day-to-day operations of your companies, why you can't do "buy and hold" but have to do homework instead: the competitive top, when someone else comes in and destroys your company's business. You can tell when the competition is heating up only if you stay vigilant and monitor not just your company but the whole industry, one of the main reasons why I say you need to give your portfolio one hour a week per position if you are going to get it right. Seventy percent of the tops I have studied have this dominant competitive characteristic at their roots. Typically, the company itself doesn't see it coming. You may own a company with fairly decent margins on sales that is forecasting great multiyear visibility because it has terrific market share and has vanquished its competitors. Suddenly a new entrant comes in, one who can make the same product or do the same service or sell the same goods as your company, but with lower margins. The new competitor, if it means business, and they often do, will destroy your company even as your company pretends that such a thing can't happen, or doesn't even know that a competitor is lurking because it is watching only the existing players, not anyone off the radar screen.

Let's examine the greatest top I have ever seen in my life, the top involving United States Surgical. Everyone who was anybody in the market owned U.S. Surgical during the 1990s. It was a universal principle that you had to have stock in this dominator of the surgical staples, because it had sky's-the-limit growth with no competition and unlimited market potential. USS had a revolutionary proprietary technology of staples that could be used instead of stitches. USS's business was big, bigger than big. It was the only stock you just *had* to own.

In the 1990s I worked as a trustee to a fund that owned 8 percent of the stock. The position kept going up and it became a bigger and bigger portion of the fund simply because of the mammoth capital appreciation. I grew worried that we were too levered to the stock and demanded that we sell some because I thought we were being pigs. I must have asked them to take some profits for almost two years because I thought it was so rich, but no top ever developed and the stock just kept increasing in price. I ended up being kicked off the board in part because I was so negative about this wonderful stock that I felt just couldn't continue forever. It apparently could.

Just when everybody loved this stock and it was among the most widely held equities in the country, with the highest gross margins of any mass-produced product I had ever seen, Johnson & Johnson, which made Band-Aids and a lot of hospital and surgical products, decided that it had had enough of United States Surgical's domination in the operating room. Management at JNJ made up its mind that it was going to challenge USS. Management made this judgment even though everyone on Wall Street thought that USS couldn't be removed from its hammerlock on America's operating rooms. Critics of JNJ and supporters of USS thought it was reckless for JNJ even to think about taking on USS. There was one key difference between JNJ and USS. USS had high margins on its staples, JNJ had low margins on its Band-Aids and its other hospital-based commodity products. JNJ made very little money on Band-Aids; USS made huge money on its staples. If JNJ had any success at all, the company would be able to raise its margins because a new higher-margined product, staples, would be a part of its mix.

At the time JNJ announced it was moving into USS's business, USS was at $120. Every one of the USS analysts ignored the JNJ threat; most USS analysts didn't even follow the stock of JNJ. Others felt that stodgy JNJ couldn't possibly beat fleet-footed USS. I knew it didn't matter. Given that JNJ's margins would increase even if it sold its staples for half the price of USS's it was only a matter of time before USS's margins were cut to ribbons and the stock slid. I looked at the margins of the two companies and decided that USS was finished, kaput, done for. I shorted every share I could get.

As JNJ moved in with its lower-priced alternative, USS slid from $120 to $80. At that level those USS adherents who were in denial about JNJ started talking about price competition in the operating room. Heck, USS had never done anything but raise prices. Now it was cutting them?

The stock went to $30 overnight on that kind of talk as USS's margins tumbled in a price war. None of the USS acolytes even saw the JNJ train coming. If you were following only USS, you were totally blindsided. I covered the stock in the mid 20s, but I could have waited because it went still lower before ultimately, spent and confused, the company succumbed to a takeover bid.

Rule number one when you are riding a great long: Always assume that there is someone out there who could come in and make your company's product for less with lower margins. A committed competitor moving into your company's area with overall gross margins that are lower than the margins your company has signals the time to run, not hide. This kind of pattern happens over and over again in everything from tech to tampons. No one-product or two-product company with high margins can withstand a well-capitalized lower-margined competitor. Given that the competitor tends to be of the Merck or IBM or Intel or Oracle, Procter & Gamble or JNJ variety—a global behemoth with lower margins than any specialty players—you have to be totally on top of what could be a terrific momentum situation one day and a stupendously overvalued stock the next. In fact, much of the big top of the year 2000 was directly related to established, well-known, but lower-margined tech companies barging in on lots of little specialty dot-com companies that had one product and high margins. The market was littered with stocks that went from $100 or even $200 to zero almost overnight, and you would never have known to get off if you were just talking to the target companies themselves. Viant and Scient, billion-dollar consulting companies one minute, were bankrupt consulting companies the next when IBM and EDS moved in. Tampax, a fantastic single-brand company, got sideswiped when Procter and JNJ moved in with products that crushed Tampax's margins but elevated their own. None of these little companies and their acolytes on Wall Street saw the locomotive was out of control and about to jump the track. These were horrid accidents just waiting to happen. Simply put, when you hear about new competition, you must worry, whether you would like to or not. Not unimportantly, the periods of profound underperformance for Intel have come when AMD geared up with a competitive offering. Similarly, much of the underperformance for Microsoft in the 2003–2004 period before the big dividend change was related to competition from Linux provider Red Hat. Did these cause tops? We still don't know. Your takeaway should be that you must *never* underestimate the power of the competition to hurt your stock, even if it doesn't immediately hurt the company.

2. Vagueness. Whenever a management is vague about specifics, whenever a management tells you it isn't worried about the numbers, or that it doesn't want to be constrained by the projections or by the forecasts because it is talking and thinking about bigger things, sell the stock. There are no bigger things than the numbers. This is not a game of trying to make people feel better or making them more broadminded. This is not a liberal arts bull session. It's a business of hitting the numbers. When management goes vague in an interview—any interview—run for the hills. You've got a real top on your hands. Spotting this type of top can be done only if you do the homework and read about the companies that you own. You have to search for the interviews and watch them when they come on television just to see whether they are shucking and jiving or they are sticking by the hard facts.

This method, analyzing the vagueness, is how I discovered the top at Sunbeam, another one of those classic falls from grace that took a tremendous number of value and growth managers with it.

Al Dunlap, the now disgraced former CEO of Sunbeam, came into my office when the stock was riding high, in the mid 40s. He used to come on TV, notably *Squawk Box,* and be very adamant about the projections, the numbers. Adamant and positive. One time, after a TV appearance, he decided to swing by my office. Comes in with the sunglasses. Oh yeah, always distrust guys with sunglasses in a room without a lot of light like my trading room, where I hated the glare from the lights on my machines. He wanted to talk to me and my partner at the time, Jeff Berkowitz, about new products, notably some heart monitor gizmo for dogs. I kid you not. The pet market's huge, he's telling us. Berkowitz says that's super, great to hear, but how's the quarter? Dunlap looks at him with contempt and drones on about the dog heart monitor. So Jeff asks again. Dunlap ignores him and starts talking about a new gas grill that's in four parts, down from thirty. Much easier to put together, he says. I start talking about how much time it took me to put together the grill I had bought at Fortunoff a few weeks before, parts all over the place, and it still didn't work when I finished it. Berkowitz? He's listening and nodding, and then he says to Dunlap, "How's sales from grills?" Dunlap fires back that Wal-Mart and Kmart can't get enough Sunbeam products. Jeff persists, wanting to know real sales data, something that Dunlap had always provided before when asked. "Are sales good right now?" Jeff asks. That's it, Dunlap blows his top. He turns to me and asks how much more of this crap does he have to take? I wink at Jeff. Jeff steps out and sells every share.

When someone who talks up his business at every turn, who is incessantly upbeat, suddenly won't talk about the numbers and won't brag about the business, and instead wants to talk about a heart monitor for dogs, you've got a classic tell that the business has gone sour. A year later Sunbeam was bankrupt.

How else can vagueness manifest itself? A company that formerly wanted to tell you everything about its future no longer wants to give guidance, or says it can't forecast its business. That's a top because the buyers and owners of that stock most definitely owned it because they liked the predictability that the company no longer has. Another form of vagueness can be a company that won't give you breakdowns of sales when it used to, especially when it is saying it can't do this for competitive reasons. General Electric is the single most competitive company I know and it gives you all the data. Shame on those who won't.

Vagueness can also be bravado. Scott Butera, the Trump executive in charge of casinos, told us not to worry about the numbers because bankruptcy would be averted, making the $2 DJT, Trump casino stock, look like a buy. When the stock got cut to 37¢ immediately after the bankruptcy, you shouldn't have had to worry, because bravado without numbers spells a top, and you should have already sold.

Vagueness, like competition, is something that you can find out about only if you are paying attention and are benchmarking the company. If you don't listen to the conference calls and don't read the interviews or articles, how will you know about new competition and how will you know when management's gone vague? The chart sure as heck won't tell you! Only vigilance will get you out before the top strikes when management has gone opaque.

3. Overexpansion. Nothing defeats a company's dreams like over-expansion. I have written throughout this book that growth is all that matters. In the end, if you can't create growth organically you either have to buy growth or you have to use steroids to grow. Knowing when a company is overexpanding and expanding too quickly, the functional equivalent of steroids, is integral to spotting a top ahead of a train wreck.

Unfortunately, overexpansion is inherently difficult to analyze. It is tough to spot because Wall Street doesn't want you to spot it. Wall Street masks the problems of too much growth. That's because Wall Street loves acquisitions and rapid expansion, the primary ways to make quick growth happen. Acquisitions can make for instant growth, but they can also make for instant problems. Frenetic store openings or office expansions strain a young management's attention and dollars. Both are catastrophic to the core enterprise unless checked by some degree of common sense as well as the wisdom to stand up to the growth jihadists who populate mutual and hedge funds.

Often companies do acquisitions to please analysts who are working hand in glove with another department at their firm that does M&A work. An investment house makes more money doing M&A than any other activity, but the babe-in-the-woods managements that come to Wall Street don't know that. They want to please the analysts, the analysts want payback from bonuses that are controlled by the hierarchy, and the hierarchy knows nothing generates fees like M&A. The investment bankers want to do the deal, any deal, all deals! If a company cannot grow numbers fast enough on Wall Street, it has to go buy the numbers or succumb to downgrades, and those are often too much for unseasoned managements to recover from.

The integration of the takeovers, though, is something so difficult, so taxing, that even the pros screw it up. Time and time again after a company makes an acquisition, the analysts dutifully raise numbers and the stocks initially go higher. I almost always sell into that hoopla because the acquisitions don't go smoothly in most cases and the numbers come down when they don't.

What's the sell signal here if you can't pull the trigger when the numbers go higher? I will give you the code. Whenever you hear management talk about "integration problems" as in "integration problems are slowing our ability to merge these two entities," run, don't walk, to the exit. All deals have integration problems; they are a given. If they are affecting the numbers to the point that management has to acknowledge them, believe me, that's fatal.

Some companies are so desperate for growth that they do acquisitions at any cost. That's what destroyed the once-great AT&T. Michael Armstrong, the former CEO, felt his company was too stodgy and simply wasn't growing fast enough to please the Wall Street analysts who were measuring the company's growth against what we now know to have been the bogus and inflated numbers of competitor MCI-WorldCom. So Armstrong let a bunch of bankers and glad-handing analysts talk him into spending money to make acquisitions so he could grow numbers. Of course, the integration couldn't be done easily, the debt costs were unbearable, and eventually the company virtually collapsed under its own weight in borrowings. The tip-off for that collapse, the top-spotter so to speak, was the unbelievably aggressive acquisition strategy, one that happened at a pace that no management could possibly accommodate. Enron did the same; it made a flood of acquisitions and transactions designed strictly to mask the real lack of growth and the inability of management to create products or business lines itself to put points on the board. Not all companies are meant to be fast growers. Revolutionizing a slow grower into a fast grower is almost impossible; don't fall for it.

If you don't believe me, just remind yourself of what happened with AOL Time Warner. AOL made that acquisition, we now know, because business had slowed dramatically. The only way to mask that incredible slowdown was to buy another company and throw everybody, every doubter, off the scent. It was a brilliant plan. If you had sold AOL when it made that deal you'd have locked in a huge gain at a time when everyone talked about one plus one equals three. Of course a half plus one doesn't even equal one if you pay many times the worth of that half. Everyone who held still has losses and will, I believe, for many years to come. It was just that bad and desperate a combination.

Of course there will be companies that make intelligent acquisitions that don't signal the end of their growth. Procter & Gamble has made several acquisitions that have boosted its bottom line successfully; so has General Electric. But they were measured and considered and *incremental* to their core businesses, not roll-the-dice mergers done one after another to throw you off the scent. GE and P&G are established companies where mergers and acquisitions are part of the business structure. They are not anemic growers desperate to please by trying to integrate new businesses into existing product lines. P&G and GE, by the way, have never had integration problems in all the years I have been following those two great companies.

Overexpansion doesn't happen just through acquisitions. Retailers, which are under tremendous pressure to grow to please Wall Street, have often opened too many stores at once just to meet the demands of analysts who like their stocks. When you see companies put up a phenomenal number of stores all at once relative to their base, I think you have to shoot first and ask questions later. It just isn't possible for a management to maintain the quality control through that kind of expansion. It is a sign of weakness, not strength. It is also why, when a company is in extreme growth mode, I look at same-store sales, not total sales, to detect a fiasco. When retailers are growing by leaps and bounds you can't gauge a business from total sales: Adding stores overnight grows bigger numbers. So look at same-store sales, "comp store sales" as they are known, to judge how much the existing business is being hurt by the expansion.

By the way, that's one of the reasons that I would urge you, if you decide to own the stock of a retailer, to visit the stores regularly. I was able to spot a top in Restoration Hardware by a combination of visiting stores and monitoring that company's breakneck expansion to please Wall Street. When I got yelled at in the local store at the Short Hills mall, even though I had to be one of the biggest patrons of the chain, that set me to work on what ultimately turned out to be a magnificent short sale.

These companies, by the way, almost never recover when they expand at that pace, which is why I am so adamant that when you see this kind of nonmeasured expansion you have to hit the ejection button. The ultimate top is formed when a company stumbles after breakneck expansion, any company. Don't even attempt to bottom-fish; there tends to be no there, there. Particularly when the expansion is of the "roll-up" variety, where the home office keeps issuing stock to buy mom-and-pop companies. Once the earnings cool and the stock flops, there's no way to get the momentum back. No mom and pop will sacrifice its hard-earned businesses for that devalued currency. The Street is littered with bankrupt companies that didn't understand that ironclad law.

4. Government blindside. The front page of the *New York Times* spots more tops than the business page. That's because governments, both federal and state, can do more to hurt companies or permanently debilitate their earnings than any competitor. Oddly, though, the Wall Street analysts who are supposed to flag the real problems for companies to us mortals who await their verdicts don't pay much attention to government edicts. The large institutions that control the marginal shares of companies are so focused on earnings growth from internal sources that they, too, miss the big negatives that can come from any administration.

In the late 1990s, for example, the greatest stocks, the most recession-proof stocks, were the nursing home stocks. These had momentum and a thesis, the graying of America. All of the major investment houses embraced the aging theme, and everyone presumed that the government would just keep paying major portions of the nursing home bills for the elderly. Wasn't that the politically popular position? Didn't the elderly control lots of key states and vote their pocketbooks? That was the logic, certainly, of the lofty multiples these stocks sold at in the late 1990s.

Perhaps the most popular stock of the era, Genesis Health Ventures, a gigantic East Coast nursing home chain that kept issuing stock to roll up mom-and-pop nursing homes, just kept roaring and roaring higher as this thesis ascended. But President Clinton, right before the turn of the century, decided he had to rein in some health-care costs lest the country slip back into deficit spending. The feds decided, virtually out of nowhere, to change the reimbursement rate to operators of nursing homes. The companies didn't see it coming. The analysts didn't see it coming. Yet, when it happened, it was devastating news delivered from the front page of the *New York Times*. I recently looked up the First Call notes—the analysts' contemporaneous comments—and *not one* flagged the articles that were hidden in plain sight on the front page of the paper of record. They all missed it. This reimbursement change was the single most devastating piece of news ever, but the stocks just hung there as the owners and their analyst buddies ignored the guillotine that slammed down on the news pages. Once the reimbursement rates changed, every one of these companies went from great longs to great shorts, overnight. Genesis Health, the bellwether of the industry, the gold standard, would be in bankruptcy within a year. It went bankrupt while many of the buy recommendations were still intact.

How do you spot this kind of top? You have to start by reading the front pages, not just the business sections, of the *New York Times,* the *Wall Street Journal, USA Today,* and the *Washington Post.* I start my day with them, electronically, inserting my stocks' names in their indices to see where the articles come up. I never constrain myself to the business sections; that's just foolish.

During the downfall of Genesis, I spoke to a relative who had sold a company to Genesis Health. The stock had just fallen 10 points from its top and every analyst was telling me to buy it. I asked him what I should do. He had a simple answer: "Don't you read the papers? The businesses are finished." I told him that couldn't be because the companies were all saying not to worry. He said they were saying that to the analysts, urging them to keep a stiff upper lip, but in truth they were petrified. The great nursing home buy-and-hold craze was a huge top the moment that the reimbursement rates changed. It never came back.

Similarly, DoubleClick, among the most successful of the dot-coms and among the quickest to reach a multi-billion-dollar valuation, decided at what amounted to its peak that it was going to enter the business of knowing everything about its customers. It paid a couple of billion dollars for Abacus, a marketing company with a huge database of users. No sooner had the deal been completed than the government questioned whether these kinds of services invaded consumers' privacy. DoubleClick ultimately had to write off billions of dollars as it misjudged the political tremors that were evident for all to feel. As is typical, the analysts took their cue from the smug DoubleClick folks, who never knew what had hit them. Still don't for that matter.

I got hit by one of these governmental blindsides just last year when I rode Forest Labs, a drug company, all the way down from what now appears to have been a certain top. My mistake? I didn't take seriously the notion that the FDA and Congress would begin to focus on the suicide rates of young children on antidepressants, the core of the growth for Forest Lab's most important drug, Lexapro. The analysts didn't believe it, either. But it was right on the front page when the stock was in the 70s. Thirty points later, when the analysts finally started addressing the problem, it was too late for me. One of my largest losses since I left my hedge fund.

5. **Top in retail.** Retail tops are easy to spot. Some think you can spot them by measuring same-store sales, sales that are compared on an apples-to-apples basis. If sales in one store were $1 million in year one and $900,000 in year two, that's a same-store sales decline of 10 percent for that store. I like that as a measure of rapid-growing retailers, but for mature retailers, I use a different litmus test. Companies have good months and bad, and while the same-store sales are important, they inconsistently call more tops than they should. False tops are the bane of investors who own retailers, so you have to be very careful not to exit just because a company, particularly an apparel company, had a bad month.

No, the real top in retail comes when a retailer has stores in every state, when there are no new areas in which to expand. Every retailer, whether it be Gap or Wal-Mart or Kohl's or Home Depot or the Limited or Toys R Us, hits a wall when that happens. I love to own retailers early in their growth cycle when they are regional going national: lots of states ahead, and if the concept is a good one you can use every single same-store sales decline to buy more. But, and it is a huge but, once all of the locations are used up, as represented by a truly national presence, I have no desire ever to own that retailer again. It's been a terrific way to own these stocks, and I have managed to get the maximum out of every one of the majors and then leave them, never to own them again when they cracked into the last corners and crannies of American malls. Be careful. Analysts hate to get off retail horses while they are running; they will deny that this nationwide test matters. I know better; it works *every time.*

6. Fad stock tops. I can't blame anyone for playing any fad. The runs we have had in everything from Reebok to Palm to Research in Motion have been fantastic. There's always a product out there that is in short supply because it has caught the fancy of the American consumer. You can make fortunes as the stocks go higher. But as soon as the supply catches up to demand, whether it be iPods built by Apple Computer or aerobic sneakers made by Reebok, you must sell it and never look back.

How do you spot a fad top? You have to monitor the stores that sell the product. You have to listen to the conference calls. I was able to sell fads at the top in everything from Palms to Filas to Guess jeans to Keds simply by listening to the conference calls of places that sell these goods, not by the managements of the companies themselves, who never saw the tops coming. As long as the merchants said they couldn't get enough of the product, I knew I was fine and the stock would go higher. Once they said that they had enough product to be able to meet the demand, there was no price at which I wouldn't sell the supplying company's stock. It's just that simple. But if you are going to play a fad, and you don't have the time to listen to conference calls where the fad product is sold, a Best Buy or a Radio Shack for electronics, a JC Penney or Federated for a clothing line, you are going to be crushed like a bug on a windshield. Doing that extra homework, checking outside what management of your company has to say, will save you from holding the stock after a top and losing a fortune, especially because as is typical with fads, the fortune is huge but ephemeral to all but those who pay attention to the outlets where the product is sold.

7. In-the-hole secondary. One of the incredibly easy tops to spy is when a company does a "deep in the hole" secondary after a huge run. Talk about sure tops. When a company sells stock that is at a huge discount to the last sale of its equity, that's a gigantic red flag that will soon turn into the Jolly Roger to steal your gains.

At one time in the 1990s, Iomega developed a cult following. It had a Zip drive that people thought was proprietary and was always going to be in short supply. The Iomegans worshiped the stock. Me? I don't worship any stock. But I recognize that a cult following can be milked for all it's worth. Investors and friends would chastise me, saying that it was simply a piece of junk that was overly loved. I said, So what? The stock is in tight supply; the short sellers are killing themselves over it; and I am riding it until I see a secondary that is priced in the hole for it, meaning a piece of merchandise from insiders at the company that is sold by underwriters at a substantial discount to the last sale. When that happens, you sell, period, and you never look back. That's because the insiders know the jig is up. The real institutional buyers, the smart guys, have no appetite for the merchandise. Voilà, immediately after the short squeeze is alleviated, the chart goes bad, the institutions puke it up, and the stock just dies. That's exactly what happened in Iomega. The stock went from $1 to $50 and then came down to $40, where Iomega priced a secondary at $35. Okay, I didn't get out at $50, but I was able to hit that $35 bid provided by the underwriters who, foolishly, tried to support the stock. What a home run. Another few months and it would have been a strikeout.

I can't tell you how many in-the-hole secondaries were done between October 1999 and October 2000, the ultimate topping-out period for the market. Every one of the major dot-coms did these in-the-hole secondaries. It got to be like shooting fish in a barrel; you could own them until the deal came, and then you had to blow them to kingdom come. One reason why I had such a big year in 2000 was that after every one of these in-the-hole secondaries I went short the stocks that did them. You can't get a clearer top tell.

In case you still need help in understanding this one and remembering how vital it is that you sell when you see one of these secondaries that is sold deep and still doesn't hold, let me tell you the story of DIGI.

If there was a stock that embodied the more manic years of my hedge fund, it was DSC Communications, stock symbol DIGI. We owned it from $25 to $75, and it was the type of ramp that used to make our day, every day. Oh we loved DIGI. Jeff Berkowitz had just joined our firm out of the Goldman Sachs research department, where he covered tech. My wife headed the trading desk then. When we had a great stock going, my wife used to lead us in chants about it. They always chanted and played music with bongos and drums at her old shop to alleviate the pressure, and she had brought that style to our desk. Her chanting sounded like a mixture of "King of the Congo" by Kipling and a Gregorian version of the Florida State Seminole cheerleaders at the big game against the hated Gators. Every time the hope-filled stock would rise more than a dollar she would start in with "Didg-ee, Didg-ee, Didg-ee" until the stock would be up a couple of smackers. She would directly attribute the stock's levitation to the mystical powers of her chanting. Of course, it was DIGI's growth that drove it, but the stock business does have a strange karma to it at times.

In the meantime, the beat of the whole market was being set by DIGI's earnings-estimate increases, the real tonic that moved the stock higher. When estimates weren't being upped, DIGI was busy announcing contract after contract from Baby Bells and foreign companies that would eventually lead to higher earnings.

A day never seemed to go by without hot news for DIGI. This stock was telephony's gift to the Street. It had everything: fiber to the loop, home video, pay TV, you name it. It was the equivalent of Lucent, Cisco, and Nortel all rolled up into one when those stocks were revered on Wall Street.

The stock, like any hot stock of consequence, also attracted the attention of the shorts, who, every day, would die a thousand deaths as the stock would be taken and taken and taken. We would all be glued to our screens watching this marvelous animal leap through whole new handles (each new $10 level is a handle: $10, $20, $30). As the offerings lifted we would wonder aloud what short fund would be cremated today by DIGI. Short squeezes, possible takeover, earnings-estimate increases, contracts—we lapped it all up and hoped it could go on forever. We were, for all intents and purposes, the DIGI Fund.

And then one day Goldman Sachs filed a secondary for a boatload of insiders at DIGI who hadn't done any selling of late. Sometimes these big holdings get bunched and sold all at once, and that's what Goldman did with the stock of the DIGI insiders. The offering was gigantic, big enough to sate everyone's interest who wanted it. It overwhelmed the market, as these secondaries often do. The deal was big enough to allow as many short sellers who wanted to cover in on the stock that had been tight as a drum and unavailable to borrow. (Funds had sold the stock short, hoping it would go down, and then couldn't physically deliver the stock because, of course, they didn't own it, and they couldn't find any stock to borrow.) The secondary was big enough to alleviate the squeeze that had helped propel this stock so far.

Suddenly, DIGI the rock of Gibraltar became DIGI the house of cards. The day the big slug of merchandise was priced, the stock was abnormally soft. The offering got priced right through the bid, deep in the hole. It still seemed shaky, even though it was much lower than where the stock sold the day before.

The moment it was priced my wife turned to me and said, "DIGI is done-ee." I told her not to be ridiculous, that this stock had all the right moves, big orders coming, some I even knew about, and that we had to go right back in and play the DIGI game. She nodded to me, smiled, and sold every share we owned. Hundreds of thousands of shares. She just drilled the bid, the big juicy syndicate bid, and just like that DIGI was out of our lives. I was furious. I knew good things were about to occur. She just laughed.

The stock didn't hold that price. Others puked it, too. Others who knew what Karen knew, which is that deep-in-the-hole secondaries are like fire in your portfolio. The stock soon broke down and wilted. By midmorning. I felt like I had lost a limb. I didn't understand Karen's rules yet. I thought we should just buy it again. Where would I ever find as good a story as this? I demanded to get back in. She said absolutely not, that we were going to wait until the guillotine stopped falling.

The stock rolled down again the next day and the next. Then, a week later, DIGI lost a contract that I thought it should surely have won, to the manufacturing arm (later Lucent) of what was then AT&T. This was the first big order Lucent had won of the type and it virtually gave the darned thing away to get the business. (See low-margin enterprises versus high-margin enterprises and tops, above.)

DIGI's stock never recovered from that loss. The very next quarter it missed numbers. And then it blew about a half-dozen quarters until it finally got so low that Alcatel snapped it up for below where the whole move started.

If you had paid attention only to the analysts—almost all of whom loved DIGI and didn't downgrade it until shortly before the Alcatel bid—or if you had just focused on the company, or if you had fallen in love and decided that buy and hold was all that mattered, you would have given it all back and then some.

But if you followed the simple rule, Sell the deep-in-the-hole secondary, because it's being done for mystical reasons you don't know but will most certainly soon find out, you will get out with your gains intact and a smile perpetually on your face.

8. Accounting mayhem. The final top that manifests itself with frequency is the accounting shenanigans top. The main reason a company jiggers the numbers is that it can't make them. When a company can't make its estimates and resorts to these kinds of games, whether the company is Tyco or Cardinal Health or Bristol-Myers or Enron or Schering-Plough, you simply *must* sell it. There is no excuse, no justification to hold on to it. I have a sign that says "Accounting irregularities equals sell" on my quote machine. Mistakenly, in the post–Sarbanes-Oxley period, when I thought that the courts had gotten so tough that you had to be out of your mind to pull off this kind of legerdemain, I took the sign down. A week later Nortel, at $7, announced that it had found some irregularities. I was off my guard. I held instead of selling. The stock promptly went to $3. I couldn't ever recover the money invested.

Never hold on when these come up. Never. Cendant is still not back to where it was when it first served notice that its accounting was shaky. It's simply the kiss of death when these tricks surface. You must shoot first and not even bother to ask questions later. Will you end up selling some stocks too soon because of this? No doubt. But would you end up selling all of the accounting disasters higher than where they ended up? Yes, 100 percent of the time.

9. Holland Tunnel Diner top. We have whole markets that are like the griddle in that diner I described earlier (see page 147), where the market is just so darned red hot that you have to take something off the heat or get burned. Sometimes that will cause you to lose some of a good stock that keeps going higher; other times it will allow you to avoid a top or lessen exposure to a stock that has topped. Unlike the other tops, of course, it is more of a look and feel than a set measure. But when a red-hot market is coupled with an S&P oscillator reading of +5 or more and there are more than 50 percent bulls, you better believe the merchandise is going to fry. (Through its own proprietary oscillator, which I pay to consult, the McGraw-Hill Company's S&P Division keeps track of overbought and oversold markets.) Holland Tunnel Diner tops are often followed by 7–10 percent declines that the market eventually recovers from. But you would be amazed at how many stocks top for good during those viciously heated moments. Don't let your portfolio be cooked with them.

When I got out of the market in March 2000, I was heavily criticized because I had been so bullish just a few weeks before. But tops are like that. Right before you reach the summit, things are cooking to perfection and you want to be in. You have to be in to get those great gains. But one moment past and you have lethally overstayed your welcome. Don't be afraid to change your mind. This is one place where when the heat is too hot, you *must* get out of the kitchen.

10

┌   ┐

ADVANCED STRATEGIES

for

SPECULATORS

└   ┘

Most of my financial life I have worn two hats: I'm a practitioner and a real-time explainer of what I am doing to those trying to learn. I try to put the process in English, so that you aren't confused by the mathematics or the science of it. I try to make it simple because so many people in my business try to make it hard. They use Genuine Wall Street Gibberish, a form of mumbo jumbo; wittingly or unwittingly, they seem to do their best to confuse. I know when I was a salesperson, I could take advantage of those who were ignorant of the way we on Wall Street work if I wanted to be short-term greedy. Those who knew the most and had the best facility with money, though, did get the best treatment and benefited considerably versus those who just couldn't figure it out.

Most of what I had to explain would make sense to anyone who has more than a fifth-grade education: Stocks are arithmetic; the logic behind them is psychology, not quantum physics. Buying and selling a stock is no different from buying and selling a house. You are making money if it goes up after you bought it; you are losing money if it goes down. But there are two parts of what I did with securities as a practitioner that are particularly difficult to fathom and execute: options and shorting. For these there are no easy explanations, no fifth-grade analogs that make them more understandable. But they should be learned nonetheless. Why should you not be able to take advantage of all of the instruments and methods that the most advanced players use simply because they are complex and arcane? They can be incredibly valuable even to novices if used correctly. They might help you as you get started in building a winning portfolio, regardless of the environment.

Shorting is difficult to understand and potentially dangerous. It's difficult to understand because shorting involves selling something that you don't own. You can't do that in any other line of business. You can't sell a glass of lemonade you don't own, you can't sell a home you don't own, and you can't sell a car you don't own, so it's incomprehensible to many how you can sell stock you don't own. How do you deliver to the buyer shares you don't own? Where do you find someone willing to give it to you so you can sell it without owning it? How about if you first borrow it from your broker before you sell it short?

Let's go through the hypothetical. Let's say you think Intel's too high and you want to profit from the decline you expect to happen. When you sell a stock short, you say to your broker, "I want to sell one thousand shares of Intel short." The broker borrows the stock for you first, places it in your account, and then sells it for you from your account. You even get the proceeds from the sale of 1,000 Intel right into your account. If the stock goes down after you sell it, you make money, the mirror image of what happens when you buy a stock and it goes up. Of course, the opposite is true, too: If you short Intel and it goes higher, you are losing money.

When you buy the stock back that you shorted you are "covering" the short, and you should say that in the order so the broker knows exactly what you are intending. Let's say you sold 1,000 shares of Intel short at $20 and it drops to $16. You tell your broker, "I want to cover the Intel short, I want to buy back one thousand shares of Intel." If you buy back the stock at this price you make $4,000. Ah, but what if Intel went up? Then you could cover for a loss, as in, "I am covering the one thousand Intel I sold short at twenty dollars at twenty-four dollars," where you would lose $4,000. You could always continue to battle the Intel and sell more, or you could just let it run; that's up to you. But be careful, you can lose lots of money if the stock keeps going higher. The loss or the gain isn't booked until you cover the trade.

Shorting is dangerous because stocks can only go down to zero but in theory at least they can go up to infinity. That's a terribly asymmetrical risk-reward, one that could allow you to lose millions of dollars as a stock goes up and up, but make only a finite amount as the stock of even a bankrupt company stops at zero—although some stinkers I owned felt like they could go even lower.

It's tough enough when you own a stock and it goes down, but it's excruciating when you are short a stock and it goes up. It's financial suicide when you short a stock that so many other folks are short, and the brokerages can't find the stock in the vault to lend out because all shares are out already. The seller can never fail to deliver. So the brokers have to go into the open market to find stock to deliver to the buyers. Their frantic buying creates a squeeze that can produce wild gains for the longs and stupendous losses for the short sellers. That's why such moves are called short squeezes. Stocks can zoom when a large percentage of the "float," or shares that can trade freely, are sold short and new short sellers come in and fail to locate borrowed shares before they sell. That's illegal—you always have to locate stock first—but lots of bad brokers let it happen because they want the commission, and lots of stupid customers don't tell the broker up front that the sale is a short one. When the unscrupulous meet the uninformed, and execute short sales of stocks that shouldn't be shorted, it's a combustible combination. Often these squeezes happen to the phoniest of stocks, so that you could be right on the fundamentals but be betrayed by the mechanics of shorting. The shorting process entails too high a degree of difficulty and risk for the vast majority of investors because you can lose more than you have in your account if the shorted stock skyrockets. It's particularly awful to short a company many know is phony, because the real bad ones are so often targeted by multiple short sellers. That's why occasionally you see these counterintuitive 10- and 15- and 20-point jumps for stocks of companies that barely exist or are simply hype. So be very careful before you sell short. If you want to save yourself some stress and put a cap on your losses up front, you should first try to bet against the stock using put options.

Options are hard to explain. I have never met anyone who could explain these complex instruments in a simple way. So I will tell you that their degree of difficulty is beyond the average investor's ken. Options have their own language—"calls" give you the right but not the obligation to buy common stock, while "puts" give you the right but not the obligation to *sell* common stock. They also have their own rules—you need to decide to exercise or sell them when they are "in the money" at expiration. If they are misused they are extremely dangerous.

So why go into options at all? Lots of reasons. First, you are almost ready to go out on your own and nab some higher returns using the tricks of the trade I have taught you. But I don't want you going out there without knowing all of the weapons that can be in your arsenal. The main reason you bought this book is so that you could learn how to be better at handling your money, better at being a good investor or a good client. No one is going to care about your money as much as you do. Part of being a wise investor is being familiar enough with all the conventional and unconventional strategies so you can be sufficiently knowledgeable to evaluate your broker, decide if he or she is right for you. You need to retain control and not lose it to someone who might do wrong things to or for you. I have learned the hard way that bad brokers and bad managers use fear and ignorance to milk naïve clients. If you don't understand options I believe you will get ripped off by someone who recognizes your ignorance and tries to take advantage of it. Further, options are part of sophisticated but sound stock analysis. Investors need to know—at least in general terms—how everyone is betting on a stock before they buy shares in it.

I understand that options can be intimidating. I have met seasoned common stock traders, people who have traded common stock for decades, who don't understand what puts and calls are and why anyone would use them. These are complex pieces of paper (also known as "derivatives") that allow you to use a little capital to go a long way. You buy calls when you want to make a bet that a stock—or an index—is going to go higher in a short period of time. You buy puts when you think a stock or an index is about to sink quickly. You buy them like this: "I want to buy calls on Intel" or "I want to buy puts on Intel." Then the broker offers you a menu of options struck at various prices at various months out in the future. He asks you how many you want, with every option equal to 100 shares of common stock. (Don't worry, I will walk you through examples.) The puts or calls are entered into your statement in the same way that common stock is. They don't obligate you to do anything, though, and the vast majority of all puts and calls expire worthless, meaning that the owners and holders lose money on the bets. You never *have* to use either puts or calls. You can always buy common stock or a basket of common stocks if you want to profit from the upside. You can always sell a common stock or even sell all your stocks when you think that the market's going lower. My wife, for example, never understood options. She used to rail that if I really hated the market, what the heck was I doing buying insurance against my stocks in the form of puts, or contracts, that give me the right to sell the stock at the current price ("in-the-money" put) or at a lower price than it currently sold at ("out-of-the-money" put). She would tell me that stocks aren't houses; you don't have to live in them. Why insure something you don't have to live in? Just sell it. That's not bad advice.

These days, because I am limited by various media obligations, I can't use puts or calls. If I think a stock is going to go down, I just sell it; I don't buy puts on it to protect it. But I used both puts and calls to tremendous effect when I first started out as a little investor and ultimately at my multi-million-dollar hedge fund. Over the years I found that options were a fantastic way to make a little money into a lot of money. As I am a constant risk-reward hunter, I loved the idea that I could risk some money on calls to make much bigger money than I could make buying common stock. I also loved the idea that I could bet against a stock using puts without worrying about a short squeeze, where a stock rallied hard because so many others were making the same bet that brokerage houses couldn't find any more stock to borrow.

I have wrestled with this chapter more than the others because I know that the stuff I did with options in my later career may simply be too difficult and time-consuming for all but the most hard-bitten professionals. Yet I know I have to expose you to them, just so you can understand what's out there, so you can understand what to do if you ever have a hunch so good that it is worth speculating on. I've had a ton of these and I am always grateful that someone came up with options so I could take advantage of their bang for the buck. Let me walk you through how options work and how they differ from purchasing or selling common stock so you can understand their magic. Then I can present you with some advanced strategies about how to use options in a conservative way to leverage your cash and your best hunches.

As mentioned, there are two kinds of options, calls and puts. Call options are the right but not the obligation to purchase an agreed-upon amount of stock at a particular price in the future. Put options are the right but not the obligation to sell a stock at a particular price in the future. We buy calls when we have a hunch that something big is going to happen that's terrific for a stock or for the market. We buy puts when we think that a stock's going to implode and we want to be there, gaining from the collapse, rather than just being blasted out of our wealth. We can buy puts or calls on stocks or indices. Don't like the

NASDAQ? Buy a put on the QQQ, the Nasdaq 100. Like the Dow? Buy Dow Jones calls. Think the overall S&P 500 is going higher in the near term? Buy a call on it. Worried that the market's about to dive? Buy puts on the S&P 500.

You can buy a call or a put like a regular stock. The difference is that when you buy a put or a call you are buying a bet on the direction of the stock; you are not buying the stock itself. You have to be able to isolate the time frame that you want to bet on that appreciation or depreciation *before* you buy one. You can't say, "I want a put that will last forever" or "I want a call that will never end" because these are contracts with a delivery date. And you have to predict where the stock will appreciate or depreciate to, an actual level that you think it will go to. In other words, you can't just say, "I want an Intel call." You have to say, "I want a call on Intel that will allow me to capture the appreciation of the next ten points over a period of, say, eight months." If it is February and Intel is at 20, your broker or your electronic screen will give you a list of calls that would reflect that time period. He might suggest that you buy the "October 20 calls," phrased that way because it would mean that you would have until October of that year to capture the appreciation. The "20" is the "strike," the price level you are paying for all of the points Intel might make above 20 by the third week in October (all options expire on the third week of the month). Let's go through the hypothetical.

It's February and Intel's at $20. Let's buy some Intel October 20 calls. You pick up the phone and you say to your broker, "I want to buy some October 20 calls on Intel." The broker would then look up on his options monitor—they all have them and you could have one too, if you wanted to—and the broker might see that the calls are at $1.75 bid $2.00 ask, meaning that you can sell or buy an October 20 call at those prices respectively. Let's say you want 10 of them. That will cost you $2 per option. Each option allows you to buy 100 shares of common stock at $20. The arithmetic is a tad difficult to remember, because you have to multiply that $2 by 100 first. Then you have to multiply the sum of $2 times 100 by the number of calls you are buying. So, 10 calls costs $2,000 ($2 × 100 × 10 = $2,000). There are no shortcuts for understanding this process. You must know that the $2 price is the starting point to calculate the amount you are spending. If you can't follow it, work with your broker to figure it out.

Let's say Intel goes to $25 in October. Your Intel October 20 call, which you bought at $2, is now worth $5. How? You simply subtract the strike from the price of the stock to figure out what the call is worth when it expires. Congratulations, you have paid $2,000 and you have something now worth $5,000. You made $3,000 betting that Intel would go up.

But let's say you feel Intel is going down, not up, during that same period. You might want to buy the Intel October 20 puts, which would allow you to capture all of the depreciation below $20. Again, with the stock at $20 in February, the October 20 put may cost $2. You buy 10—each put allows you to sell 100 shares of Intel stock—for $2,000. If the stock drops to $15 by October, you subtract the closing price from the strike to figure out how much you have. Twenty minus fifteen is five. The $2 puts you bought for $2,000 are now worth $5,000. Congratulations. You made $3,000 betting against Intel.

Who determines the price of the puts and calls? The thousands of buyers and sellers of these instruments. Institutions sell calls and puts to bring in additional income. Individuals and hedge funds, the type of fund I used to run, for example, buy them to magnify bets, to put a little capital to work to make a lot. They determine prices for puts and calls much like stocks through the marketplace, as a function of supply and demand. You can get posted prices for small increments of puts and calls from your computer screen. Consult your broker if you want to buy more than a 10 lot, though, because the screen market may not be big enough for more than that.

Options are quite handy, and most of us have used them; we just haven't used them to buy or sell stock. When we speculate in real estate, we often ask for an option to buy something. We pay for that option even if we end up not buying the land underneath it. When we buy insurance, we are buying a put. We are putting out a little money to protect a lot. We don't want the insurance put to pay off, but if it does, we consider ourselves lucky to have had it. The insurance put and the real estate call are just like stock options in their most basic form.

Let's flesh out the real estate call so we are more comfortable with examples that look and feel a lot like options that you are familiar with. Let's say you live in a town near a heavily traveled interstate highway. You have a hunch that sometime in the next year or two, the federal government might build an off-ramp not far from where you live. You recognize that when off-ramps get built, retailers flock to these sites as natural places to erect new stores. You, yourself, are not a developer and have no desire to develop the land. You may not even be able to afford the land—far from it, in fact. But you don't want to miss this chance. It would be natural for you to call a Realtor and say that you would like an option to buy the land for the next two years, if one were available. That way, if the off-ramp is proposed, you know that you can exercise the option and sell the land, perhaps to a Target or a Wal-Mart, for a heck of a lot more than anyone thought possible. Let's put some numbers on it. Let's say the parcel of land was for sale for $300,000. You didn't have that money on hand. It is possible that you might be able to propose that for some percentage of that $300,000, whatever you think negotiable, perhaps $10,000 a year, you reserve the right to buy that property for $300,000. If you could get that option contract and the off-ramp is approved, you might be able to exercise that option and, without ever putting down the $300,000, sell it, say to Wal-Mart for $3 million. You just made an astronomical profit by exercising the option and selling it.

That's how I got started using call options. I wouldn't have the money that I needed to buy a lot of common stock, but I could put a much smaller amount of money down in order to buy the common stock some time in the future at a fixed price, and then sell the option, or exercise the option and sell the common stock afterward. Let's walk through an actual trade so you can see how I was able to use call options to make a ton of money in a legal way.

When I was a young investor at Goldman Sachs, I was always trying to figure out whether a drug company had a major new drug find that could impact the bottom line enough to make the stock worth owning. In the fall of 1986, Merck had been working on a novel cholesterol-lowering drug. The company's scientists had determined that if they could lower cholesterol through medication, they could save millions of people from having heart attacks. Today, of course, these drugs are among the most popular pills sold on earth. At the time, though, most of the analysts who covered the drug companies didn't think much of the concept of cholesterol-lowering drugs. They thought the category would be small. One of my investors, though, a cardiologist, was very excited by the results he saw in those who took the cholesterol-lowering pills. It was his hunch that these drugs could be a billion-dollar seller rather quickly for Merck. I canvassed Wall Street seeing what numbers people were using for the new medication, and no analyst thought it would amount to more than $200 million in annual sales. Once I knew that such a figure seemed absurdly low to my doctor friend, I recognized that I might have stumbled onto something that could propel Merck, a good drug company, to incredibly high levels.

At the time I was doing my canvassing, Merck traded at $80 a share. If I wanted to buy 100 shares of Merck, I would have had to pay $8,000. That's a lot of money to put to work for a limited amount of shares, especially because—as in that case of the real estate by the off-ramp—I didn't care to own the actual stock; I just wanted to own the appreciation of the stock. I just wanted the upside from $80.

How about if I could buy a right to the appreciation of Merck, *just* the appreciation of Merck, not the stock itself? What if I could get someone to give me an option on the appreciation of Merck above $80, given that I thought Merck would jump in the same way that the undeveloped parcel of land might jump? That would be a better way, especially given that I knew when the drug was going to go to market and that it would immediately impact the sales estimates, which, theoretically, would drive the company's stock higher.

That's the best example of what calls are about.

So, naturally, I asked my broker for a call on everything above $80. Here's where the fun begins. He would say, "I can offer you a contract that will allow you to get all of the appreciation above seventy-five dollars, or above eighty or above eighty-five or above ninety or even above one hundred? Which one do you want?"

You want to know how much each option costs and how much you can buy above each one. You want to figure out which has the most value, the most bang for the buck and the least likelihood that you will lose it all. Let's play it out conversationally, the way I have had to explain it to hundreds of customers.

"I would like the call that begins at eighty dollars," the first-time options customer says.

"And when do you want your contract to last to?" I, the broker, would ask.

Given the time frame of the new drug's launch, the customer says, "I need to have the option last until at least February."

I would then scroll through the menu of Merck calls that are currently being made on one of the big options exchanges and suggest as a start, "We should look at the Merck calls that last until the third week of February." Let's consider the Merck February 80s, shorthand for Merck calls struck at $80, meaning that you get all of the appreciation above $80 until the third Friday of February.

"How much will those cost?" the customer asks.

I would then tell the customer, before I mentioned the price, that each call is the right but not the obligation to buy 100 shares of stock above $80, so I would be quoting a dollar amount that would be multiplied by 100. Confusing, I know, but a call doesn't equal 1 share of stock, it equals 100 shares. So I would say, "Each call is priced at five dollars, so you would have to spend five hundred dollars per call."

Now, the customer thinks, Hold it, the call costs me $5, that's a lot of money. "If I buy this call, if I buy one call, and Merck goes to eighty-five by the third week of February, how will I have done?"

Not too well, I say. You are spending $500 for the right to buy 100 shares of Merck above $80, but that right will make it so you make no money until Merck goes above $85—the $5 you paid for the call plus $80 equals $85. You will be wagering $5 to make $5 unless it goes higher than $85.

How about the calls that allow me to get everything above $85? the customer would then ask.

"Those," I would say, "are three dollars per contract, meaning that you would get the appreciation for one hundred shares above eighty-five dollars but that would cost you three hundred dollars. Now the stock has to go to eighty-eight before you start making money." (I am approximating what the prices would be, but you get the picture.)

Most of the time you might just say at that point, Wait a second, this is too expensive. I am not going to risk all of that cash and then watch Merck go up 5 or 8 points and make nothing. I would rather take that $500 or $300 and buy the common stock. Of course, you can see the problem with that. You don't get a lot of Merck stock for $300 or even $500. You buy three shares of $80 Merck stock for $300 and it goes up 5 points, you've made $15. That's not much at all. You buy six shares for $500 and make $30.

But let's say the customer is adamant that this new drug is going to shoot the lights out, as I was. I believed that Merck could go to $100 by February. So the customer comes back and says, "I have eight thousand dollars to invest in Merck calls. You tell me what to do. I think the stock will be way above a hundred come February."

I would test the customer's confidence. If he sticks to his guns, then I would say, "Okay, you have great conviction. Let's look at the Merck calls struck at ninety dollars. They are one dollar per contract, meaning you can buy, for one hundred dollars, all the appreciation above ninety dollars for one hundred shares. You can either buy one hundred shares of Merck stock for that eight thousand dollars or you can buy up to eighty of the Merck nineties for that eight thousand dollars." (Remember, each call must be multiplied by 100 because each call represents 100 shares. So a dollar call costs $100 and with $8,000 you can buy 80 calls.) If you buy 80 of those calls, you will control the appreciation above $90 of 8,000 shares. Each call is the right to 100 shares worth of Merck.

So now let's contrast the two choices, the common stock guy who buys 100 shares of Merck for $8,000 and the options guy who buys 80 of the February 90 calls for $8,000.

If Merck does nothing, stays at $80 for the next four months, what will happen? The common stock guy's doing fine. He has his $8,000 and has probably picked up a Merck dividend along the way—the dividends go only to common stock holders, not call holders. The option holder? He's out all $8,000. Horrible trade. Just horrible. That Merck 90 call went out worthless.

How about if Merck goes to $85? The common stock guy just made $500 on his $8,000 investment. Not bad, not bad at all. Good rate of return. The options guy? He's the big loser again, out all $8,000.

How about if Merck goes to $90? The common stock buyer is now in clover for 10 points, he's up $800, he's made 10 percent on his money. Better than a sharp stick in the eye. The call holder? Still wiped out. All $8,000. How much is the right to buy a stock at $90 worth when the stock is at $90? Nothing!

So far, under every scenario, the options guy is a chump, a moron, a total loser. The common stock guy is the winner, big time.

But how about if Merck goes to $100. Then what happens?

Paydirt for the call holder.

You own the rights to all of the appreciation above $90. You just made 10 points. You have 80 calls, controlling 8,000 shares! You just made 10 points on 8,000 shares. That's $80,000! Of course you don't have to buy the common stock, you just have to exercise the call when it gets there and sell the common stock.

It goes like this. You tell me, your broker, to exercise the 80 calls in Merck. You simultaneously tell me to sell 8,000 shares of Merck, because when you exercise the calls my brokerage will deposit 8,000 shares of common stock into your account, and you don't have the $800,000 you need to own 8,000 shares of a $100 stock.

In real estate that's the same as selling the land to Wal-Mart without having to take delivery of the land. You couldn't afford to buy it, but it doesn't matter because you exercise the sale at the exact same time that you exercise your option.

You bought all of the appreciation rights for 8,000 shares of Merck between $90 and $100. That's 10 points of appreciation. Your $8,000 call turned out to be worth $80,000 (10 points times 8,000 shares because each of the 80 calls controls the appreciation of 100 shares, and 80 times 100 is 8,000).

How did the common stock shareholder do? He bought 100 shares at $80. The stock went to $100. He made 20 points; 20 times 100 is $2,000. He made $2,000 on his $8,000 investment. You plunked down $8,000 and saw it go to $80,000. You just made $72,000 on that same $8,000.

Now I've got you interested.

Let me tell you what happened to me in that example. I put about $80,000 on those calls. They went up ten times. And I had enough money to quit my job to go run a hedge fund. I know I could have been out all $80,000, but I thought the reward justified the risk.

I know I have made it sound simple, and it *is* simple when the stock explodes up. Most stocks don't. Most people get wiped out by what is known as "out of the money" calls. But if you are intrigued, I urge you to consider calls when you know something so special that it might merit such a wager.

Now, let's play the downside.

Let's say Merck's stock has gone to $100 and you get a sense that the U.S. government is going to allow people to buy Merck's Mevacor in Canada for one-quarter the price of what it sells for in the United States. That would be a disaster for Merck. You think Merck will go down 20 points when it happens. If you own the common stock, of course you would sell it. But you might be tempted to short Merck, or bet against the stock. You would call up your broker and say, "I want to bet against Merck because of a change I see coming, what do you advise me?"

I would say, "You can sell some Merck you don't own and profit from it. Let me see if I can borrow a thousand shares from someone here that you can sell short. Let's say you sold a thousand shares of Merck *short* at a hundred dollars and it went down twenty points. We could then buy back those shares you don't down twenty and make twenty thousand dollars. That's a nice trade. That's how the short side works."

But, I would quickly add, if you are wrong, you could lose your money. Worse yet, if Merck goes up, you could be out infinite amounts of money. Let's say Merck goes up 10 points. You would owe that 10 points to the guy from whom you borrowed the stock. You'd be out $10,000. And if it went to up 20, you could be out $20,000!

No customer wants that risk. So you might ask for a menu of puts, which give you the right but not the obligation to sell the stock at various prices. I would call up the menu and say that I could sell you a put that allows you to gain everything under $100, under $95, under $90, and so on, as low as you want to go.

The $100 put costs $5. The $95 put costs $3, and the $90 put costs $1. Again, we walk through the mirror image of the call arithmetic. If you buy the Merck $100 put and the stock goes down 5 points, you make nothing. The cost of the put equaled the loss in price of the stock. If you buy the $95 put and the stock goes to $90, you make a little bit of money. But if you buy the $90 put and the stock goes to $80, you could make $10 per put.

So, let's do it, let's buy the $90 put. Here's what happens. Let's keep the investment amount the same, $8,000. You buy 80 puts struck at $90 for that $8,000. Those puts give you the right to all the decline below $90 for 8,000 shares—80 puts times 100 equals 8,000 shares. If the stock goes down only to $90, you make nothing. But if it plummets to $80, you have sold the equivalent of 8,000 shares at $90 and it went to $80. You made ten points times 8,000 shares or $80,000.

Now let's compare the short seller who sells 1,000 shares of common stock at $100. He makes 20 points per share if Merck drops to $80. That's $20,000. Not bad. But he also *risks* getting crushed if the stock goes higher than $100. Twenty-thousand-dollar gain versus an infinite loss if Merck runs. Not a good risk-reward.

The put holder, though, limits his risk to his investment. He can't lose more than $8,000, and if the stock declines to $80, he makes the equivalent of 10 points on his 800 shares that he controls through the puts. He's up $80,000 versus a loss of $8,000. That's a fabulous risk-reward.

Both of these examples, the put and the call, show the true power of options when they work right. They also show that you could be out a lot of dough when you are wrong. When you know that you have something big, either way, the best way to play it is in puts or calls. But if it isn't big—and about 99 percent of the situations I hear daily aren't big—it is better to use the common stock. It's that last caveat—that 99 percent of what I see and hear should be played in common stock—that keeps me from spending more time telling you about the more tricky and dangerous ways to use calls and puts. We'll have to save that for another time.

Which stocks should be shorted? Anything you think should be going down rather than going up. I don't mean that facetiously. I like to be able to look at or argue every stock from the point of view of a long or short. When associates of mine would come to me at my hedge fund with a long, I would view it as a short seller would, and vice versa. I think it is important to be able to examine both sides and not to be dogmatic about which side to take. Given that predilection, I think what you need more than a list of which stocks should be shorted is a set of rules that exclude certain stocks from being shorted. My wife developed just such a list of basic tenets and I will share it with you. Remember it, write it down next to your monitor, whatever it takes, but don't violate it. I believe that statistically you will be doomed to lose money on a short if you do. These rules have saved me tens of millions of dollars. And as Karen is incredibly plain speaking, you won't have any trouble understanding them.

First, the *BusinessWeek* cover rule. Karen would always ask me, Do you think the company could be on the cover of *BusinessWeek* this Friday as the world's greatest company? Simple rule. Life saver. Don't go after good companies that you think are screwing up short-term. There's nothing worse, for example, than being short Merck, as I once was, and then reading a loving *BusinessWeek* cover story on Merck three days later. If your short involves a company great enough to be on the cover of *BusinessWeek,* forget it. Even if you have insight, just forget it. Great companies shouldn't be shorted.

Second, can the company be taken over? If yes, Karen would say to me, "You are on your own, just do it in puts." In my career, I've been short three companies that received takeover bids, all at a huge premium: NCR, Systemix, and Genentech. With each one I had what I thought was a great reason to be short. The first two had disastrous fundamentals, as the acquiring companies later found out. The third had traced out a perfect head-and-shoulders pattern (technical jargon for a stock that's supposed to roll over imminently), something I guess Hoffmann–La Roche didn't care about when it made its partial tender at a gigantic price above where I shorted the stock. In all three cases, I must admit, I could have guessed that a takeover could have occurred, as all three companies were in industries experiencing consolidation. I should never have shorted them. This point alone is worth millions of dollars. A possible takeover should transform a short into a put special, or you should just not play at all.

Third, never short because of valuation. Never short because you think the stock's too expensive. Expensive stocks have a way of getting more expensive. I don't care what P/E Qualcomm sells for, I don't care whether you think Yahoo! or Google is absurdly valued. It is irrelevant that some stock that trades at $50 has no earnings. You must never, ever try to call an irrational top based solely on multiples of sales earnings. There will *always* be some mutual fund out there that will keep the ball in the air and crush you with its buying. Michael Steinhardt, my wife's guru, taught this basic point to her, but repeatedly violated it himself. He lost oodles of money shorting overvalued stocks.

Is there a rational for why this method of shorting doesn't work?

Indeed, often companies that seem overvalued now turn out to be incredibly cheap when you look back at them. For instance, eBay and Yahoo! both sold at astonishingly low prices to what turned out to be the future earnings when they were in their 40s and 10s respectively. The long-side players simply ignored the near-term P/E consideration and focused on the out years. They recognized that these stocks were going to grow into their multiples eventually. Or, as Karen would say, they were smarter than those who took the other side.

Of course, there are plenty of times when the out years don't materialize, but that's not the point. You have to consider the fact that other investors might believe that they might materialize. You need a better, more rigorous answer about why a stock will come down than "it is too expensive." That doesn't cut it. You need a catalyst that you believe will turn that high-flying stock into a stock too expensive for even the hardiest of believers. You need some number, some report, some competitor that could come in and wreck the margins. Without a specific, objective reason to turn the buyers' heads around, you must remember that stocks that go up gain adherents—chartists. They will ride these winners until something fundamental happens to break the overvaluation. If you don't know what that is, don't short. You may not live long enough to collect the gains.

Fourth, please use puts when you can instead of borrowing and selling short stock. Puts don't subject you to the buy-in; they allow you to limit your losses to the value of the put, not to the potentially parabolic run of a stock. Lots of great short sellers went out of business in the 1990s because they shorted common stock, and they discovered that stocks do go to infinity, or close to it, as many of the dot-coms did before collapsing. If you are sure something is going to go down but don't know when, use deep puts going out many, many months. You will never regret paying the extra money. That way you can't be wiped out by an Energizer Bunny like a Research in Motion or eBay or Qualcomm, stocks that hung on longer than anyone thought they would. I can't tell you how many times people got caught in squeezes because they refused to pay the premium for the puts that would have at least limited their losses. You never want a short to put you out of business, but I have seen it happen dozens of times among my own friends. Don't let this be your undoing.

Fifth, never be part of what I call a gang tackle short. If you ever hear of a bunch of people shorting the same names that you are shorting, I can tell you that you are a dead man. Karen would always ask me, "Does anyone else have this call?" If the answer was yes, her answer was always no. She always wanted the information to be homegrown, not borrowed from someone else; created by my own research, not by the research of others. That's because there could be people much bigger than me shorting the stock and then covering to wreck the short when they grew impatient. Too many short sellers means too little stock to borrow means too much of an opportunity for a buy-in to occur.

Sixth, and most important: It is not cool to be short. It is not something to get a kick out of or earn your bones on. Karen sold short for a living. It is gut-wrenching, harrowing, and extremely rewarding when you are right and mind-numbingly painful when you are wrong. There's nothing gallant or suave about shorting. Hedge fund managers always like to brag about their shorts. They think that it distinguishes them as truly intense, sharp thinkers. Nah, my wife would always say. "It's the same as going long, except you can't quantify the loss."

Just in case you don't respect the power of the short squeeze, in case you don't understand how painful these can be, let me leave you with a story that happened to me early in my career and taught me to have a better case and not target takeover stocks as part of my short-selling methodology.

Before I got into the business, I remember being completely mystified by the newspaper phrase "short-covering rally." All buying seemed like "real" buying to me, so what difference did it make whether it was buying to cover a short or not? I couldn't believe that any big stock could be bid up as part of a short squeeze or, more important, a short-term imbalance that an aggressive short seller could create.

One day, after I had been trading alone for a while, I met an analyst who told me he felt that Noxell, now a subsidiary of P&G, but at the time an independent company, could be in for a disappointing quarter. As a young hedge fund operator I jumped at the chance to show my shorting colors. Weren't we supposed to be taking bold, contrary stands against companies? Noxell, an expensive NASDAQ stock, seemed ripe for a whacking. After doing my homework I started shorting Noxell gingerly, the same way I would buy a long, shorting a little at first, hoping higher prices would come so I could put out (short) more at better, more ridiculously priced levels. I sold short 10,000 shares at $50 and then said I would short my next tranche of 10,000 every half a point up. The market quickly obliged, and two days later the stock was at $54 and I was short more than 80,000 shares.

When positions would go against me like this, I would frequently go back to the analyst who turned me on to the short and grill him. In this case, the analyst was more convinced than ever that the quarter was weak. I called other analysts around the Street, including those who had a buy on Noxell, and they, too, seemed a bit concerned about how sales and margins were coming through for the cosmetics company. So I put out more stock. I kept to my scale and the stock kept climbing. At $58, now up 8 straight points from where the stock was trading when I started the process, I was short 150,000 shares. When you are running less than $100 million, which I was at that point, you begin to get pretty concerned. I became the Short Noxell Fund.

Over that weekend, of course, I stopped shaving with Noxema Medicated Comfort shaving cream. I had the familiar flush of perspiration of when I had done something wrong every time I looked at the balance sheets and saw that mammoth position. I was panicked, but I stuck with my discipline and shorted more as it kept climbing, even increasing my levels to 20,000 shares every half point because I needed to bring up my basis (the point at which I'd begin to make money). I had to believe that there was no way that profit-takers wouldn't come in to bring the stock down, allowing me to cover some of the shares that I had shorted. I trade around shorts the way I trade around longs, buying some back when a stock gets hit so I can short it again when it rebounds. That way I always feel like I have room to take advantage of the ensuing spikes. But this stock never came down, not a half point even, the whole time I was shorting it.

On Tuesday after the Noxema-free weekend, the stock jumped to $60—up 10 points from my opening short. To heck with the analysts, I said to myself, I started calling anyone, everyone in the business to ask if they had heard anything positive about what the heck was propelling Noxell. "Look, I am short the &%*%^% thing," I would say, "and I just need an explanation for what's wrong." Nobody had one. Everyone was encouraging me to put out more because it was obviously going up for no good reason.

The very next day the stock traded through $63. Now I was asking traders at the big stock houses what was happening, calling all of the honchos who made markets in Noxell asking them what they were hearing. As I was making these desperate calls I saw the stock shoot through $64 to hit $65.

Finally, I broke down and called Karen Backfisch, who would become Karen Cramer, but this was way before I thought that possible. I asked her to find out what the heck was going on with Noxell. I was too embarrassed to tell her that her boyfriend was short the darned thing. But I knew I couldn't figure it out without her. Karen tapped into her network of short sellers who do nothing but talk all the time about who is shorting what and what might be ripe for the taking. These guys knew where every short was buried; they probably even did some of the killing. The news I got chills me to this day and reminds me always how tough being short can be. She said, and I will never forget these words: "Some little joker hedge fund's been shorting the *&&^%^& out of it and now the traders are all spreading the word to anybody who will listen that Procter and Gamble is going to bid ninety dollars for the thing. He's got to capitulate and buy it back. They're going to put the little guy out of business, or force him to cover. Get on board!"

Of course little joker hedge fund guy was me.

Oh no, I thought, I am going to be put out of business. I couldn't stand the pain any longer. Not one second. I frantically called a major trading desk and told them I had 250,000 Noxell to buy. With the stock at $64, I would be willing to pay up to $69 for it all. Anything to take away the pain.

One hour later, battling a collective short squeeze of my own making, I took the biggest loss of my career. Noxell 69; Cramer zero. That's right, I paid $69 to bring the whole short position in. I was relieved, I could breathe—heck, I could shave—but the loss was simply unfathomable.

Crushed. Just crushed.

Not long after I covered, Noxell reported extremely disappointing earnings, much worse than I had expected when I put out the short. The stock plummeted to levels well below where it would be considered a terrific trade, right back to the low 50s. I had been completely and utterly had by a group of traders who fomented what amounted to a nonbuying short squeeze that snared me and only me. Such is the lot of the shorts, though, that this type of incident is all too common. I can't tell you how many times after this that I got the call about some moronic hedge fund that was short a stock that I liked and I was encouraged to walk it up in his face by a trader. Just the way I got hosed in Noxell. And I admit to doing it. The money's just that easy.

Noxell was later acquired by P&G—the rumor had gravitas, but the bid came at a price not much higher than I covered. I simply got beaten by the artificial squeeze.

You would think that the market wouldn't care about one little hedge fund that was correctly shorting a stock. You would think that somehow there would be justice or there would be more of a motivation for a stock to go higher than that a few funds were ganging up on another fund that was short. But that's not how it works. Everyone on Wall Street is out to make a buck any way possible, and if it means trying to put a short seller out of business, then so be it. The dark forces coalesce on both sides of the trade and can force victories and losses regardless of fundamental reality.

What should I have done? Simple. I should have bought deep in the money puts from a far out month that would have allowed me to preserve the trade until the time the company reported earnings. And that's just what I did whenever I shorted after the Noxell annihilation.

We've experienced a remarkable swing of the financial pendulum in the last five years. We've gone from embracing the stock market, cheering the relentlessly higher levels of the averages, to spurning equities and accepting that they are difficult to fathom, manage, or profit from. We lusted for shareholder democracy, where each person built his own portfolio and monitored and maintained stock positions, eager to take advantage of the hottest trends. Now many people believe that stocks are a crooked affair, one that only the richest and most well-connected people can possibly afford. Stocks, which regularly trumped homes in rising values for all of the 1990s, have now stayed flat while we've gotten used to 20 percent appreciation year after year for the properties we live in. We've gone from checking our portfolios daily, even hourly, to selling all our stocks and not even bothering to open the statement from our mutual funds. Firms we trusted to be fiduciaries sold our net asset values from underneath us. Research that we thought was honest turned out to be corrupt, paid for by the very companies that were being reviewed. We put faith in managements that soon will be occupying whole wings of federal prisons. We stopped funding our 401(k)s; we gave up trying to fathom which stocks went up and which ones went to zero.

My chief motivation for writing this book was to get you to understand that there are always opportunities to make money, always bull markets to find, always stocks that will go higher, even in the crummiest of markets. I think the pendulum has swung too far now, that as silly as it might have been to check our net worth by the minute on the Web, it might even be sillier—and more dangerous—to do nothing with your money today. Retirement's always around the corner. Your paycheck isn't big enough and it won't last forever. You can't sell your house without buying something else to live in, and that makes the wealth of your house impossible to tap without a dramatic change in circumstance.

That's why I know it's time for you to get back in. This time though, because you will use the principles and common sense of this book, it won't end the way it did at the turn of the last century. In fact, it won't end at all.

But let's say I am wrong about the market swinging too negatively. Let's say that the awful roller-coaster market—up and down and up and down and then finish the exact same place but with a sick-to-our-stomach feeling that makes us dread the process—continues; seven fat years, seven lean years so to speak. I think I have shown in this book that there are always needles in the haystack, groups that work, always bull markets out there somewhere. You just need these tools to know where to look for them.

By no means am I saying it is easy. I insist on buys only with homework, I insist on staying on top of your portfolio. I demand that if you are going to buy individual stocks you get involved and stay involved, and that if you don't have the time or the inclination you must hand it off to others. I know, though, without a doubt, that you have to learn to be either a better investor or a better client; there is no other choice.

Home Depot has a terrific saying: "You can do it; we can help." I think that most professionals, including those you see on television or read in print, have come to a different conclusion: "You can't do it and we can't help." As someone who has traded and made money in all sorts of terrible markets since 1979, I know you can do it, and I know

I most certainly can help. My methods, which involve hard, time-consuming work and lots of common sense, constantly generate winning ideas and cull out losers that could wipe out whatever good you might be doing. I know what you did wrong the last time around, and I know that I have offered cures, not panaceas, to that behavior.

I know I will never be willing to concede what so many folks do now, which is that you can't beat the averages, so you might as well join them. In sports, that would be the equivalent of saying that no college player can ever rise to the NBA or the NFL level so why bother to aspire. We know that some do make it, we know that in this game we don't need the God-given talents that those players have to have. We just need hard work, some rules and some discipline, and we will beat the averages.

My styles and methods aren't in the textbooks. Nobody I know divides the universe into the retirement stream and the discretionary stream and allows you to be as aggressive in the discretionary stream as you should be conservative in the retirement stream. No one I know embraces speculation, embraces the finding of lowly stocks, trying to catch the unexploited before the pack, even if the unexploited never, ultimately, amounts to anything. As long as you restrain yourself to no more than 20 percent of your discretionary funds in speculative holdings, you are not violating any rule that will come back to haunt you. And if you are still rolling the dice with 100 percent equities for retirement a few years before you need that money, you just wasted your time and money reading this book.

Will we ever return to the days when fortunes were made overnight in the market, when the closing prices flashed on billboards around baseball stadiums and every bar and health club had CNBC on round-the-clock? I don't think so. I don't want it, either, because then it is too easy, and when it is too easy, we lose the rigor, and ultimately, we lose the money that we have invested. I like it hard; I like it difficult to fathom. That makes it so there are fewer people out there to grab the great ideas. The great stocks don't get bid up so fast that we have to sell them as soon as we buy them. And sell them we must if we are going to hold on to the gains, because selling's part of the discipline of stocks that we have all forgotten.

So, go build that portfolio. Remember, even someone like me, swinging around hundreds of millions of dollars at one point, never did anything rash, never did anything all at once, never felt he had to be "big" at one level, only to see the market get cracked right after I spent all my hard-earned money. Take your time this time. Do it right, do it with caution, approach it with the same thought you would give any large dollar purchase. Live by the rules here, recognize that your rules and your discipline are your only friends in a world where the government can't protect you from the rapacious folks who we now know dominated the boardrooms of both Main Street and Wall Street.

You will make mistakes. You will lose some money. You might not become a millionaire overnight, as so many charlatans in my business claim at seminars and in books. But you will be doing it the way the real pros do, the ones who beat the markets, all markets, the ones who know that you don't have to have a bull market in all stocks to make money. I can't ask you to love stocks as much as I do, but I can ask you to take care of yourself financially, because, alas, no one will ever care as much about your money as you. Get started toward saving. Today. Unlike so many things in life, you will never regret it. And one day, I hope, you will look back and think, Holy cow, I can't believe how much money I was able to make, just when everyone else thought that stocks would never ever work again.

INDEX